VICTIMS AND SINNERS

VICTIMS AND SINNERS

Spiritual Roots of Addiction and Recovery

LINDA A. MERCADANTE

Westminster John Knox Press
Louisville, Kentucky

Scripture quotations from the New Revised Standard Version of the Bible are copyright © 1989 by the Division of Christian Education of the National Council of the Churches of Christ in the U.S.A. and are used by permission.

Book design by Jennifer K. Cox
Cover design by Vickie Arrow

First edition

Published by Westminster John Knox Press
Louisville, Kentucky

This book is printed on acid-free paper that meets the American National Standards Institute Z39.48 standard. ∞

PRINTED IN THE UNITED STATES OF AMERICA

96 97 98 99 00 01 02 03 04 05 — 10 9 8 7 6 5 4 3 2 1

Library of Congress Cataloging-in-Publication Data

Mercadante, Linda A., date.
   Victims and sinners : spiritual roots of addiction and recovery /
Linda A. Mercadante.
      p.   cm.
   Includes bibliographical references and index.
   ISBN 0-664-25508-6 (alk. paper)
   1. Recovery movement—Religious aspects—Christianity—
Controversial literature.   2. Sin.   I. Title.
BT732.45.M37   1996
261.8′3229—dc20   96-18498

For my son, David, with love

CONTENTS

PREFACE

Many people assume there are only two ways to understand the problematic behavior that our society labels as addiction; it is seen either as a failure of willpower and morality or as a disease process. But there are more options than just these two. Theology can make a contribution by offering alternative views of addiction that avoid both excessive blame and excessive victimization. First, however, the spiritual roots of the addiction-recovery movement must be understood.

Although the addiction-recovery process is often said to be "spiritual but not religious," much of it has been borrowed from religious understandings. A very distinctive understanding of sin and conversion has greatly influenced the addiction-recovery model. This may surprise many, anger some, and gratify others. The borrowing has been selective, however, for the addiction-recovery model is not just a copy but also, implicitly, a critique and a challenge to the Christian doctrine of sin. The model has played equally on resonances of and animosities toward the sin-conversion motif in contemporary culture. This helps explain the successful spread of the addiction-recovery paradigm to cover an ever-expanding range of human dysfunction.

I came to these realizations inadvertently. Nearly ten years ago I accepted a position to teach theology at a midwestern seminary. At that time I had little experience or direct knowledge of Alcoholics Anonymous (AA), or other related groups, or the addiction-recovery movement in general. But the school was unique in having a degree program in Alcohol and Drug Abuse Ministry with a significant number of students enrolled, so from the outset I found myself taking a professional interest in the topic. The ethos, terms, and stance of the addiction-recovery movement affected the classroom continually, especially as students in this program came to take the required courses in theology. Nearly all my colleagues commented on this influence.

I was intrigued and impressed by these students. Many had made profound changes in their lives, reorienting themselves after personal crises and disasters. They attributed many positive things to this movement, testifying that they had been profoundly changed by it. They made large claims for its efficacy, its spirituality, the almost "first-century church" character of its community, and its closeness to the true spirit of Christianity.

It was also evident that for many of our students—even those not in that particular degree program—the addiction-recovery model was strongly shaping their attitudes toward various aspects of Christian theology. In our dialogues, it became clear that complex theological issues were involved. They were implicitly debating and experientially testing such perennial topics as the freedom of the will, original and actual sin, and the nature of evil, yet many said theology was irrelevant in the recovery process. When I tried to raise the theological themes nascent in the addiction-recovery model, some students felt threatened. Yet I believed strongly that students could personally benefit from learning to recognize, evaluate, and compare the theological issues with views from other perspectives. Because I wanted to facilitate better communication and understanding, I decided to experience this phenomenon for myself. I began to attend various recovery meetings, have intentional conversations with its members, and extend my research into areas beyond the purely theological aspects.

All this had an unexpected personal effect. The constant exposure to the addiction-recovery ethos moved me—as it does so many—to reevaluate a personal situation. Although I did not suffer from a substance abuse problem, I began to reconsider the alcohol usage of a family member. In my opinion, addiction was not the predominant problem, since it was mixed with more long-standing and serious psychological difficulties and physical violence. Nevertheless, the addiction-recovery movement seemed to offer a helpful and accessible approach to this difficult situation, especially since many other avenues had proved unsuccessful.

I noted a degree of compassion, tolerance, and mutual aid in these meetings that often surpassed what one could find in the average contemporary church. The program and the fellowship provided its members with support, empathy, encouragement, and consistency. I noted that for many the movement functioned as an oasis in a society that remembers little about more holistic community. Persons in the grip of a compulsive behavior could learn techniques and receive the kind of support they needed to break free of the bondage. Some people went on to a deeper understanding of God or gained a receptivity to religious claims. Many were able to find hope there for the first time.

As I began to attend other meetings and study the phenomenon more closely, many of my students wanted lengthy explanations of why I was doing this. Although I did not think that class time was an appropriate place for personal revelations, I did have private conversations with some of my students. At any rate, in a small school, things do not stay hidden for long. The end result, however, was that the students realized that my personal experience improved my writing and critique.

Although all this helped the learning environment, I was unprepared for the results in my personal life. To my dismay, this experimental reframing did not improve my family situation but precipitated a crisis that had major and long-lasting consequences. As I moved through the crisis— agonizing and analyzing at the same time—I began to note more closely how in some ways the addiction-recovery ethos replicates certain important religious themes. Some members find this familiarity a comfort; others find it helpful in connecting with their past religious upbringing. Yet I knew these same themes when used in the church had not always had productive results.

During my research, I visited treatment centers, spoke with many professionals in diversely related fields, attended numerous lectures and conferences, and read widely in the relevant disciplines. Increasingly I was asked to give seminars, retreats, and lectures on the theological perpectives in the addiction discourse. Through this, I have met many laypersons, group members, pastoral counselors, and clergy who have felt either attracted and committed to the recovery discourse or puzzled and stymied by it. Many wanted resources on addiction recovery from a theological perspective.

During the years I observed, listened to stories, participated in groups, and spoke on the topic, my interest and concern emerged in stages. First, I was struck that many of the people I met at recovery meetings would be considered to have no more than the usual amount of human problems for this day and age—trouble with children, difficult marriages or divorces, failure to progress satisfactorily in their work, business reverses, vague dissatisfaction with their lives, bothersome body image, consuming more of something than they thought proper, habits they could not seem to break. Many were persons whom some psychologists call "the worried well." Second, I was impressed that these people had been willing to search themselves thoroughly to decide whether or how their particular problem might be an addiction. Third, I noticed gradual but observable changes in these persons' attitudes, cluster of relationships, and daily activities over the course of their membership. Finally, I noticed distinctive ways in which those with church involvements were affected in their faith attitudes and their religious practices and beliefs because of their membership in an addiction-recovery fellowship.

In spite of all this, I was hesitant to write on the issue. It seemed too time-specific, time-limited, eclectic, and ephemeral to warrant close theological analysis. Yet my historical work on other topics has convinced me of the usefulness of letting a particular moment in culture raise up some perennial theological issues. Theology at its best and most honest is sensitive to context, self-critical about its own rootedness in culture, and yet not so paralyzed by these realizations as to keep from making larger statements.

Therefore, this work is about both cultural reorientation and continuity in ideas of sin and evil, and conversion and change. The issues of freedom, will, personal responsibility, and bondage have been recurring themes in Christian theology. These are the very issues taken up in the addiction-recovery ethos. This book examines the changing of categories, the shifting of analyses, and the variations on and alternatives to a Christian interpretation of the human condition. It achieves this by exploring the theological roots and implications of the addiction-recovery ethos. Changes in these areas will long be with us, no matter what the future of the recovery movement. In my opinion, much of the culture is unwittingly wrestling with theological shadows. And in this match, many themes are reiterated, some dropped, and a few challenged.

This book was made possible through the generosity of several institutions and agencies, as well as the support of many colleagues and friends. The Association of Theological Schools awarded me a Younger Scholar grant that made possible the initial conception of the project during my first short sabbatical leave from The Methodist Theological School in Ohio. That work was done in the peaceful and stimulating environment of the Institute for Ecumenical and Cultural Research in Collegeville, Minnesota. Director Patrick Henry and my colleagues at the Institute including Kathleen Norris, were helpful in providing a sounding board for the early formulation of the thesis. That work was presented to the Workgroup in Constructive Theology and benefited from members' critiques. The Workgroup facilitated the publication of my initial findings. My article, "Sin, Addiction, and Freedom," in *Reconstructing Christian Theology*, edited by Rebecca Chopp and Mark Kline Taylor (Minneapolis: Fortress Press, 1994), became part of our collaborative theological efforts.

Subsequent work was funded first by a summer stipend from the Louisville Institute for the Study of Protestantism and American Culture, which enabled me to do extensive interviewing. The writing of the book was made possible through a leave of absence from The Methodist Theological

School in Ohio and funded by a subsequent grant from the Louisville Institute. It was nurtured especially by the conducive environment of the Center of Theological Inquiry in Princeton, New Jersey. A number of my colleagues there generously took the time to read large portions of the book, especially director Daniel Hardy, William Placher, Don Browning, Todd Whitmore, Daniel Schipani, and William Werpehowski. The staff at the center was also wonderful in providing their support, cheerful encouragement, and the occasional well-timed snack.

The resources and staff of the John W. Dickhaut Library at The Methodist Theological School in Ohio, Speer Library at Princeton Theological Seminary, and Firestone Library at Princeton University were invaluable. Staff members at various treatment centers in Ohio, New Jersey, Minnesota, and Kansas, including Hazelden and The Menninger Institute, also provided important insights. Special thanks go to Ernest Kurtz, who early on took an interest in this project and continued throughout the entire writing process to encourage, read closely, and provide scholarly resource suggestions in fields outside my own.

My colleagues at The Methodist Theological School in Ohio—Paul Nicely, David Carr, and Vergel Lattimore—considered various portions of the manuscript and offered helpful critiques. And my experience here at the Methodist Theological School, especially students' comments and concerns, provided the continuing impetus. Many classes listened to my ideas and were not hesitant to debate the issues with me. My editor at Westminster John Knox Press, Timothy Staveteig, provided constructive criticism throughout and was especially prompt in reading drafts and providing feedback. I also would like to thank Davis Perkins, President/ Publisher of Westminster John Knox Press, for encouraging this project as well as my earlier work on gender imagery for God. A number of close friends and family members have also endured with me through the living and the writing: I am grateful to Mary Ford of Fellowship in Prayer for insightful discussions; to Dorianne Perrucci, for listening, reading portions, and pushing me to continue clarifying my theme; to my parents for their consistent concern, even as they continue to be puzzled by why I expend so much effort on such unlucrative work; and to my son, David, to whom this book is dedicated, who provided the joy and the motivation to complete the project. Because of him, I did not simply research and write but also lived and played.

Part 1

FROM SIN TO ADDICTION

1

THEOLOGY AND ADDICTION

Many persons have received help through the addiction-recovery movement. For thousands of people *recovery* has become a program for living, a form of spirituality, an ethic, and a way to deal with many of life's problems. Addiction-recovery support groups are integral to this, offering encouragement, community, nurture, acceptance, and a clear method—the Twelve Steps.[1] Addiction-recovery themes have been extended to cover an increasingly wide range of human problems, ranging from alcohol abuse to overeating, from relationship dependencies to uncontrollable emotions. Numerous books have appeared on addiction, recovery, and related topics. Even for those not directly involved in a Twelve Step group, familiarity with the model comes through such diverse media as news programs, television talk shows, and even situation comedies and soap operas. Governmental support, through such things as drug education programs, also communicates aspects of it in schools, agencies, and institutions.

Twelve Step support groups function as an important social network for hundreds of thousands of Americans.[2] It is possible to spend significant amounts of time with people in recovery, attending not only meetings but also holiday parties, anniversaries of sobriety, retreats, seminars, and major conferences, as well as informal socializing and mutual aid. Recovery groups form a very significant percentage of the wider support group movement in America. As much as 40 percent of Americans are regular members of an organized small group, spanning the range from Bible studies to self-help. The number increases when it includes those who were once involved but no longer attend. The ancestor of the current recovery group phenomenon, Alcoholics Anonymous (AA), estimates that there are 49,943 AA groups in the United States (and 89,000 worldwide). Some 1,127,471 Americans participate in this program alone.[3] Many others participate in the numerous derivative recovery groups. It is predicted that small groups will exercise even greater influence in the coming decades, representing a genuine "cultural realignment."[4]

The recovery group phenomenon is very important in contemporary

America. It serves as an oasis in a world marked by bureaucratic anonymity, transiency, estrangement, and detraditioning. It promises what was previously provided primarily through religion and family—identification, meaning, and mutual help. It has also picked up the torch dropped by the church when the temperance movement and Prohibition failed to deal successfully with chronic alcohol abuse. In the last few decades, this movement has drawn members specifically because of its emphasis on support, community, and acceptance. Equally attractive has been its informality, wide accessibility, lack of fees, and low level of required formal commitment.

After spending considerable time participating and observing a wide range of small groups, with particular attention to those oriented to addiction recovery, I know well that these groups have attractive qualities that offer much. Often they provide a level of support that many people have not found elsewhere, including in the contemporary church. Some participants belong to two, three, or more types of recovery groups. Others at least have shopped around to find the group that best fits and describes their particular cluster of problems. The fact that people often *want* to belong and are willing to self-diagnose is noteworthy.

These support groups often benefit society by providing care and attention for people otherwise neglected. It is significant that even active church members seek them out and sometimes claim to have encountered the true church there. One factor that has facilitated this acceptance is the amazing adaptability of the movement. It has managed to appeal successfully to persons and churches along the whole liberal–conservative theological and political continuum. Thus the recovery group movement is providing some of the glue holding society together. Whether or not this movement can affect the larger societal problems related to the problem of addiction, however, is not certain.[5]

Many people who are drawn to this new construct find here a meaningful description and a method of coping with life problems. This happens for persons both with and without a religious background. Conversion is a good term to describe many persons' movement into the addiction-recovery schema, for the change is often akin to religious conversion. This can happen through joining Alcoholics Anonymous, the forerunner of the addiction-recovery ethos, or through other groups. One sociological study notes, "The process by which individuals affiliate with A.A. entails a radical transformation of personal identity in that A.A. provides the prospective affiliate not merely with a solution to problems related to drinking, but also with an overarching world view with which the 'convert' can and must reinterpret his or her past experience."[6] The person converted to an addiction-recovery ethos experiences an entire change of worldview.

The addiction-recovery perspective thus runs both wide and deep. It can affect how much and what kind of hope persons may have, as well as where it is placed. It colors what expectations people allow themselves, what goals they believe appropriate, and what efforts they expend to reach them. It influences institutions, ways of viewing problems, and ways of treating them.

THE ADDICTION-RECOVERY MODEL AND THEOLOGY

Behavior that was once called sin is often today called addiction. Many hold the impression that there are only two ways to look at this particular cluster of human problems: We view them either as a failure of willpower and morality or as disease. This limited set of options has helped spur a cultural realignment. In reaction against a doctrine of sin perceived as moralistic, judgmental and counterproductive, there has been a shift to describing more human problems as medical. The growing range and usage of the term *addiction* thus offers an interesting case study in changing cultural metaphors. It is part of a discursive shift that affects not only language but also perception, experience, and behavior.

In America the word *addiction* has become a euphemism to describe problematic, excessive, or repetitive behavior. An addiction-recovery ethos has become a component in the public understanding of the human condition: That is, it has become part of a popular theological anthropology, an available, accessible, and common way our society describes, diagnoses, and ameliorates the human predicament. As such the new model affects people's experience, choices, and vision. It functions in many ways like a theology and thus warrants theological analysis. However, such an analysis also shows that there are more than two options when considering the problem of addiction. A moralistic understanding of sin is indeed problematic and is rightly to be rejected. It does a disservice both to faith and to addiction. Instead, a carefully conceived theology can offer alternative views that avoid many of the pitfalls of both the typical moralistic understanding of sin and an unnuanced disease model of addiction.

Nevertheless, the church is not let off the hook. It must take seriously the culture's pervasive use of the addiction metaphor to describe human dysfunction, while it also considers the attractiveness of recovery groups. An analysis is especially pressing because many people believe the addiction-recovery model is an implicit rejection of traditional Christian modes, or at least a better alternative. Many see the addiction metaphor as a more apt description of the human predicament, believing the concept of addiction is a distinct and salutary counteractive to—or improvement on—the concept of sin. A slogan on the cover of one AA brochure states it well:

"Alcoholism is a disease . . . not a disgrace."[7] In the addiction-recovery ethos, the concept of sin often serves implicitly as a lightning rod, set up in the dichotomy "not sin but sickness." As such it galvanizes energy by presupposing major differences between a Twelve Step and a traditional Christian understanding of the problem of addiction.

Many scholarly and popular works have been written on addiction and recovery. Most treat the problem of addiction in general, examine specific types, or research the physiological and psychological aspects. Given that our society has chosen to call a number of problematic and disparate behaviors addiction, in many ways the category of addiction is a social construct.[8] The questions typically most debated in the addiction issue—for example, whether addiction is truly a physiological disease, whether treatment really works, and whether the movement is an alternative dependency or simply a self-help technique—are mostly inside the addiction paradigm. This limits their purview and restricts their gaze. Few works address the implicit theological roots and implications present in this ethos. Instead, many assume that *sin* and *addiction* are very different phenomena, or at least very different ways of treating a particular set of problems. Yet an examination of the historical roots of the addiction-recovery model—and an analysis of the model itself—reveal some very distinct similarities between the *sin* and *addiction* concepts. Much borrowing has gone on, of both positive and negative aspects. In both dynamics and content, there is a relationship between the terms. This helps explain the ease with which many in the church come to embrace the addiction-recovery model.

ADDICTION RECOVERY AND THE CHURCH

Many in the church are suffering from what I like to call "pew envy." This is the uneasy feeling church staff and members can get if Saturday night recovery meetings held in the church basement seem livelier and better attended than Sunday morning worship. Some in the church have looked longingly at the addiction-recovery phenomenon. They have been intrigued by its success at drawing people. They have been fascinated by its seemingly casual, nonhierarchical, and tolerant atmosphere, especially since this seems in sharp contrast with all that the culture has rejected about the church. The church, worried about declining participation and enthusiasm, may gratefully embrace a program that seems amenable to Christian interpretation. Although at first churches merely provided space for groups to meet, more churches have become interested in the process and content itself. A resonance is heard whose potential has not escaped church leaders and members.

Some two-thirds of small support groups have some connection to a church or synagogue.[9] As many as 44 percent of the various addiction-recovery groups meet there. In fact, churches have extended "perhaps the warmest encouragment" to groups that focus on addictions.[10] Although many of these groups merely use church facilities, the tie often becomes closer. A significant number of pastors and church members join standard addiction-recovery groups, such as Alcoholics Anonymous. And some churches specifically adapt recovery programs to better fit their worldview. This can be a mutually agreeable arrangement, for the new paradigm gains the sanction of traditional religion while the church feels contemporary, benevolent, and enlarged. One author notes:

> The recovery and renewal movement offers some churches a way to get people back into church. In the Chicago area a number of megachurches offer "Christianized" Twelve-Step groups. . . . Indeed the small-group movement seems to suggest that such groups can become the backbone of a congregation. The application of Twelve-Step groups is not limited to neoevangelical megachurches. In the United Church of Christ and other liberal Protestant denominations, parishes have been experimenting with self-help and support groups for years, and a few now use "Christianized" Twelve-Step groups as part of their ministries.[11]

Literature on addiction recovery is also important. Many works about addiction and recovery have been written from a generalized spiritual approach and a significant number from a self-consciously Christian perspective. These works laud recovery models, stress the spiritual component of addiction, and/or defend the Twelve Steps as congruent with Christian understandings. Some writers contend that addiction *is* the human predicament, per se, even identical with sin, especially sin understood as idolatry.[12] Some claim the addiction model is an apt replacement for the doctrine of sin and that the recovery model presents a better spirituality than traditional Christian versions.[13] Others say addiction is "the sacred disease of our time," a special type of problem, almost a "blessed fault."[14]

Like the wider culture, many within the church are concerned with the problem of addiction and sympathetic with the addiction-recovery model. Persons with substance abuse problems are routinely counseled to attend recovery groups. Few mainline pastors or pastoral counselors would have serious theological qualms about advising an identified substance abuser to attend Alcoholics Anonymous, Narcotics Anonymous (NA), or any other reputable recovery group. Spouses and family members would readily be sent to Al-Anon or Alateen. Few mainstream churchgoers would see attendance as a challenge or problem for their faith.

However, having well-attended recovery groups meeting in the church—even those few that put an intentionally Christian spin on the process—does not guarantee increased church participation. Sometimes it can have the opposite effect, siphoning off energies and loyalties. Automatically sending people off to recovery groups, with little follow-up or oversight, contributes to the drift away from church that many experience. Yet those whose primary loyalty shifts from church to recovery movement are rarely discussed in the literature. Frequently recovery groups come to function as a type of church for people. A writer notes: "On a recent plane flight a friend of mine got to talking with her seatmate about religion. When my friend asked 'Do you go to church?' the woman answered 'Oh, no, I go to Twelve Steps.' The woman went on to explain that, for her, practicing the Twelve Steps and going to meetings were her church."[15] This can happen for churched persons, as well as those with no religious background. While some persons do return to their religious roots through the recovery movement, others find their loyalty conflicted between recovery group and church. Many without religious background simply stay with the recovery group, believing because the movement claims to be "spiritual but not religious" that they have found a better alternative. It cannot be simply assumed that recovery groups will provide a back door to the church, even though many come to acknowledge the existence of God there.

The rise in addiction-oriented groups can be seen in several ways relative to the church. It may be an encouraging revitalization phenomenon, one often sponsored by and benefiting the churches themselves. Small groups have long been a part of the mission and ministry of the church, often functioning in this revitalizing way, as John Wesley's class meetings prove.[16] Yet the phenomenon may instead be serving as a bridge away from specifically religious frames to a more diffused generic "spirituality." It could be part of a "lay liberalism" or "Golden Rule" Christianity. Here persons, although somewhat favorable or neutral toward organized religion, nevertheless want to untie themselves from orthodoxy and specific religious practices, satisfied instead with making better behavior part of the good life.[17] The recovery group phenomenon would then provide a socially acceptable way station as many persons journey away from organized religion. The movement may also indicate widespread dissatisfaction with mainstream religion, emerging as a reaction to the church's failures to address contemporary problems. Finally, the rise in addiction-oriented groups may be part of the spread of the therapeutic ethos, providing a portable classroom ironically located in the church basement.

It is possible, however, that this movement may simply be a response to cultural changes, posing no particular boon or threat to the church. It may serve as a humanizing or useful adjunct to the increasing professionalization, bureaucratization, and medicalization of American life. In a mobile and destabilized America, it has become increasingly difficult for the church to offer the supportive functions it previously provided to individuals, families, and communities. Small recovery groups may merely be filling the gap.

In any case, the church must explore its contribution to the situation. In many ways the church has failed to guide people to "think theologically" about everyday life and broader cultural, political, and social issues. It has not lived out its beliefs with any kind of regularity, especially in relationship to the thorny addiction issue. Alcoholics and addicts are often not welcome in the church and are often sent to addiction-recovery groups with little subsequent oversight. Although at one time the church did take on the problem of alcohol abuse, the failure of Prohibition caused the church to drift away from this issue, as much from dejection as rejection. This has left a vacuum that addiction-recovery support groups are filling for many, including church members. This movement and the spreading addiction metaphor may also highlight the functional demise of sin in public consciousness. In some sectors, the church has begun to assume that the doctrine of sin is needlessly negative and discouraging, creation-denying, and hopelessly judgmental and exclusivist. Thus church members, too, need an alternative way of discussing human dysfunction.

THE ROOTS OF THE
ADDICTION-RECOVERY MODEL IN THE BIG BOOK

The program provided by Alcoholics Anonymous is, to many minds, the best description of addiction and a model plan of recovery. It is often understood as the most successful modality for dealing with alcoholism. In addition, Alcoholics Anonymous is the prototype, forerunner, and most viable representative of an addiction-recovery program that takes spirituality seriously. The AA version of addiction recovery is undergirded by a particular theological perspective. Even in its consciously nontheological form, this content is still evident. Elaborating the AA perspective—and especially its roots in the Oxford Group—will give a clearer picture of the theological undertones and trajectories involved.

Alcoholics Anonymous began in 1935 with a very discrete task, to help alcoholics stay sober. From its inception, members insisted that the program was not meant to take the place of religion, it must stick strictly to its defined task, and it should remain nonprofessional, grow only by attraction, and keep a low profile. This has helped protect Alcoholics Anonymous from conflict with outside perspectives. But its methods gained increasing attention. Today Alcoholics Anonymous is often recommended by physicians and clergy, sometimes mandated by the courts, and relied on in many treatment centers as a pattern for small-group meetings. AA's understandings are often referred to by practitioners and treatment personnel, and even by government, the corporate world, and the media.

Alcoholics Anonymous has been regarded as so successful—particularly considering the dearth of helpful modalities when it emerged in the 1930s—that it has been widely copied. It has had an influence far beyond what any early leaders envisioned. The AA model of the Twelve Steps has been used as a prototype for the many recovery groups that have emerged. Groups are more or less frank about their borrowing of the AA model. Overeaters Anonymous (OA), for example, says about the founders of Overeaters Anonymous in its promotional literature, "The program they followed was—and continues to be—patterned after the Alcoholics Anonymous program."[18] Members of different recovery groups are often referred to Alcoholics Anonymous and its literature as key sources. The pattern set by Alcoholics Anonymous has become for many an explanation and a recovery model for many disparate behavioral problems. This is true even though many of the emergent recovery groups are not under the AA aegis and do not strictly follow all aspects of the program.

Additionally, there is sometimes a lack of communication, even animosity, between psychotherapeutic perspectives, the medical professions, and Twelve Step movements regarding addiction recovery. Lay participants informally blend often disparate and sometimes contradictory principles from these various fields. This leads to an eclecticism that some claim as a matter of pride but that inevitably leads to practical problems for many participants. Longtime loyal AA participants have noted and complained of this.[19] Even so, AA's description of the problem of addiction is still pivotal. When one analyzes the generalized addiction-recovery model, many of the tenets from Alcoholics Anonymous remain as undergirding principles. In spite of an eclecticism in practice, the original version of the Twelve Step method still garners widespread respect, acknowledgment, and imitation. As a key source it offers the most credible and consistent version of addiction recovery.[20]

A focus on Alcoholics Anonymous is helpful as a way of laying out the addiction-recovery schema. It takes the AA influence seriously and charts a navigable course through the growing proliferation of interpretations, methods, and small groups in America that cluster around the problem of addiction. The AA model is more praised than criticized, used more often, and, at the very least, given lip service by most persons concerned with addiction issues. Additionally, this focus is relevant for the church. Alcoholics Anonymous has been for the church the most palatable and acceptable method of dealing with addictions. When positive claims are made for the addiction metaphor and recovery methods in self-consciously Christian literature, the AA analysis and the Twelve Steps—rather than, say, a purely biochemical or psychological model—is more frequently praised.

The so-called Big Book of Alcoholics Anonymous presents the clearest, fullest, and most original explication of the AA addiction-recovery model. Written in the first flush of enthusiasm over the newfound program, it is closest to the theological roots of Alcoholics Anonymous and more fully elaborates the theory behind the discipline of the Twelve Steps. Since its publication in 1939,[21] this book has routinely been given to newcomers, widely quoted, and often studied in meetings. Although it has been joined by many other works, it still holds pride of place as the foundational document.[22] Although Alcoholics Anonymous is commonly understood to be nonhierarchical, decentralized regarding meetings, and undogmatic, the Big Book has remained significant. Even though the book has gone through three editions (1939, 1955, 1976), the first half of the book has remained largely unchanged. This half—which will become the focus of this book—is the most clearly didactic section. Comprising chapters 1 through 11, it describes the alcoholic's situation and path to recovery. There are also separate chapters here to agnostics and to wives, families, and employers of alcoholics.

The second half of the book presents members' individual stories. These have undergone some change over time, as more contemporary stories were added. In many ways the retelling of sober alcoholics' stories is the emotional heart of the book. It is often what attracts first-time readers. The stories largely elaborate or illustrate the principles from the didactic section. These stories fit the genre of testimonial literature or conversion narratives. They explicate the entire change of self-perception and retranslation of one's entire life that routinely happens in and is the essence of personal conversion, based on the model taught in the book.[23]

I am not planning to make a formal distinction between book and text (such as one can find in deconstruction theory). A focus on the Big Book is not meant to set it apart as a final and codified form of the program. Alcoholics Anonymous considers freedom of interpretation crucial. In practice, selective use of the Big Book is common. In a sense, the *text* is what happens between participants, the book, discussion, and interpretation. Nevertheless, this particular writing has been formative. There is a thematic integrity in program discourse that even extends outward, in varying degrees, to offshoot recovery groups. Resonances of the Big Book schema remain in the wider recovery movement, even if modified for other behavioral problems.

A textual focus may run counter to many people's perceptions of Alcoholics Anonymous as primarily a "speech event" or "oral occasion."[24] Meeting attendance has become an essential part of addiction recovery.

Members rely strongly on one another's experience and interpretation. Certain crucial contemporary factors, such as sponsorship, are not even mentioned in the original writings. And these nonprofessional sponsors— simply fellow members with "more recovery"—often have great influence on individual members in ways that may or may not conform to Big Book themes. In the lay atmosphere of the recovery movement, there is no official oversight of these influences.

Yet there is a strong commonality and pervasive mutual influence in Alcoholics Anonymous that has a thematic integrity. Much of this grows out of the pattern set by the Big Book. In spite of efforts to avoid coercion and rigidity, there is a standard of "good recovery." Old-timers and those with long recovery influence newcomers and help to pass along this standard. Frequent meeting attendance helps spread this.[25] As in other groups, an enculturation process goes on. Much of AA socialization is formed through the narratives and themes that have been absorbed from the Big Book.

Therefore, though the process is experiential, Alcoholics Anonymous is very much an experience formed by and in interaction with a text. In this it has distinct similarities to Christianity. Certain meetings are devoted to reading from the Big Book, or sometimes from *The Twelve Steps and the Twelve Traditions,* with or without comment from attenders. Other "step" meetings focus on the individual Twelve Steps, which were first publicized in the Big Book. Even when the Big Book is not directly mentioned, resonances of its schema permeate meeting conversation. The ritual reading of the Twelve Steps at the opening of many meetings brings members back to the archetypal pattern set up by the Big Book. The reluctance of members to change, challenge, or depart from the Big Book points to its centrality in the "speech event" that Alcoholics Anonymous has become. One longtime member insisted to me vehemently, "I don't trust myself to challenge a word of this book. It saved me."[26] Although this reverence is not universal, many members hold a similar attitude.

A focus on this book is true to the original intention of the founders. It was the text, rather than the fellowship, that the early members saw as fundamental to recovery. Meeting attendance was not seen as "vital to sobriety."[27] The foreword to the Big Book's first edition simply invites "those who are getting results from this book" to communicate with the founders.[28] Ernest Kurtz explains that

> the AA Big Book contains no reference . . . to "meetings" as they developed. The early expectation was that drunks would order the book, make surrender, and as they got back to their jobs and lives would help other drunks. Once in a while, those who had new candidates might gather so the newcomers could ask questions and meet other

sober alkies. The fact that it did not work out that way was more slowly accepted by Bill [Wilson] than by most others. The fact that meetings developed as they did, I think, says more about the economy and culture of the times than about AA ideology.[29]

Some may feel that it is inappropriate to do a theological analysis of the Big Book. It implies that one is taking a stance along a spectrum inhabited by recognizable religious groups. In doing this, one inevitably agrees with some positions and opposes others. This may seem antithetical to the ethos of Alcoholics Anonymous, which is to take no partisan stand in any area outside its limited purview.[30] The Big Book insists that it represents "no particular faith or denomination" but is "dealing only with general principles common to most denominations." Ultimately, it is asserted, everyone must follow his or her own conscience, for Alcoholics Anonymous claims "no monopoly on God."[31]

All this undergirds the frequent assertion that Alcoholics Anonymous is "spiritual but not religious." However, spirituality by definition is supported or formed by conceptual and religious structure. This book attempts to trace some of these elements and will demonstrate that there are significant, if implicit, theological distinctives in this model.

THE ADDICTION MODEL AND THE DOCTRINE OF SIN

While it is instructive to trace the theological roots of the addiction-recovery paradigm, there is an additional reason for examining it. The addiction-recovery model is worth studying because it implicitly copies, critiques, and challenges the Christian doctrine of sin. It especially highlights the moralism and will orientation (Pelagianism) of the contemporary church, reintroducing an idea of human frailty that has some fascinating similarities to the idea of original sin. The Twelve Step version of the addiction model can be placed on a continuum. In relationship to contemporary culture, the addiction-recovery model—particularly as developed by Alcoholics Anonymous—stands against the culture's rejection both of moral fault and of the unavoidable human inclination to turn from God—what theology has called sin. This is both necessary and commendable. In relationship to the contemporary churches' use and abuse of the sin metaphor, in particular its Pelagianism, the addiction model stands in judgment. It unknowingly calls us back to a deeper understanding of the powerlessness of humans in the face of sin and our need for the intervention of grace. This also is a helpful critique, albeit an unintentional one.

However, I will contend that in relationship to a rich, developed doctrine of sin, the addiction model is inadequate. It can sometimes also be harmful. In relationship to a strong doctrine of grace, it offers only a limited solution and resemblance. One need not deny that the addiction-recovery movement has therapeutic power. For it does more than help persons neglected by society by providing support and nurture; it also offers, inadvertently, an overarching diagnosis for the human condition. Part of its therapeutic power, then, comes not just from its tangible help but because it touches on issues ultimately theological in character. However, the addiction-recovery motif is unable to account for the full range of human nature and divine efficacy. In spite of this, many today are desperately and thinly stretching it to function in these ways. In the absence of a viable and accessible theological alternative, people have to use what is near to hand.

In examining the theological strengths and weaknesses of the sin and addiction concepts, I propose that collaboration, rather than antipathy, is necessary. The church has had thousands of years to ponder the human condition, its potential and its difficulties. To dismiss this experience out of hand is obviously shortsighted. Likewise, those employed in the field of addiction treatment and research have spent much time working to free persons from this bondage. Those trapped in substance abuse have experienced the bondage, and sometimes the liberation, first hand. To turn one's back on this practical pedagogy is counterproductive.

CONCLUSION

Many writers, pastors, and congregations have found in the addiction-recovery movement a way to address modern problems. They are enthusiastic about a method that brings religion and culture together in a mutually helpful way. Some have found in the addiction-recovery paradigm a contemporary model for the traditional sin-salvation model. In addition, many of the Christians who find themselves caught in addictive behavior become actively involved in Alcoholics Anonymous and derivative groups. They take a personal interest in reconciling their religious faith and their recovery experience. Others have found help and hope in recovery groups but now have come up against limits and want more both spiritually and theologically.

Many professionals outside the addiction field have pondered the popularity of the recovery movement or have accepted general impressions of it. Some believe the addiction-recovery discourse is compatible with traditional theological themes, for better or worse. Many within the addiction-recovery field, having only general understandings of theological concepts such as sin, sometimes assume the addiction-recovery metaphor avoids, or effectively remedies, problems in our inherited theological schema. Others object that the addiction-recovery movement is too theological, some kind of "Calvinism in disguise."[32]

To these various readers, this book suggests instead that there is no seamless web between standard theological understandings and the addiction-recovery ethos. Yet it does point to the theological roots and trajectories of the addiction-recovery model, helping to explain its attraction. This book also suggests that the recovery model has gained an audience partly by rejecting, yet also by perpetuating, echoes of earlier theological themes. An implicit theological debate is going on. Although the metaphor of addiction is often posited as the antithesis of the concept of sin, in many ways it replicates this traditional doctrine. This book calls attention to these theological dimensions and evaluates the implicit theological dialogue undergirding the addiction-recovery ethos.

2

THE CHANGING DISCOURSE

Shortly after I came up with a working title for this book, "Victims and Sinners in an Age of Addiction," I received a letter from an acquaintance, a religious professional who helps administer an ecumenical study center. She urged me in the strongest possible terms not to use this combination of words. She wondered why I "would choose to identify addicts as sinners." Even after hearing that this was not my intention, she nevertheless insisted that "potential readers will see this title before content. I realize everyone is a sinner, but somehow, using this word in this way . . . seems to equate sinner with criminal—especially when speaking of victims. . . . I just want you to know what one prospective reader immediately thought of (and bristled at) when she heard the title."

This reaction is not unusual. *Sin* is a word that often provokes discomfort or even antipathy, particularly in connection with the word *addiction*. Many believe that *sin* and *addiction* are antithetical concepts. Although this presupposition is rarely made explicit, it is foundational for many within the addiction-recovery paradigm. It is also increasingly common for many in church and society. At the very least, there is a marked hesitancy to discuss sin and addiction in the same breath.

THE DICHOTOMY BETWEEN SIN AND ADDICTION

Newcomers to Alcoholics Anonymous and many other recovery groups learn that their problems are not moral but medical, not "badness" but sickness. This simple way of explaining the situation is both arresting and appealing. One AA member put it clearly on his first anniversary of sobriety: "I learned here that I'm not a bad person getting good, but a sick person getting well."[1] This understanding is introduced early to the heavy drinker and to family and friends, especially if they should join Al-Anon, a separate program designed for their needs. Pamphlets and other approved literature, routinely available at meetings, say, for example, "You are not a selfish, immoral monster. Indeed, you are quite the opposite. *You are a desperately ill woman.*"[2] Loved ones are told to forget everything they may have thought about the problem. They should realize that "alcoholism is not caused by weakness of will, immorality, or a desire to hurt others."[3] The cover of one regional AA meeting list insists in bold letters: ALCOHOLISM IS A DISEASE, NOT A DISGRACE.[4]

Literature on addiction for professionals and concerned laypersons replicates this theme. A commonplace opening presents the popular dichotomy between a moral or sin view and an illness view of addiction. For example, an article addressed to professional counselors begins: "Throughout history, alcoholism has been thought to be the result of poor moral fiber or lack of willpower. . . . Only recently has research begun to reveal alcoholism in its true light: a deficiency disease, often genetic in origin."[5] *The Recovery Resource Book* laments that people still look upon alcoholism as a "stigma" and erroneously "reason that alcoholics . . . are either weak people who can't control themselves or bad people who ought to know better."[6] This approach is not restricted to secular audiences. A much-used book for pastors takes a more moderate approach to the dichotomy, perhaps considering its readers' theological training. Nevertheless, the dichotomy still functions. "Alcoholism for a long time was considered a moral weakness, a sin," but the writer suggests that view is now "unproductive."[7]

This change in "language game" is often quite effective for both addicts and concerned persons. Many find the new perspective comforting, guilt-relieving, and especially helpful in coming to terms with the reality of their problem. The intent of this discursive shift is to enable the newcomer to admit she or he is powerless over alcohol and that life has become unmanageable. The newcomer is expected to feel a burden of guilt removed as the problem is defined as sickness, rather than immorality. Self-perceptions are expected to change. Rather than viewing oneself as bad, immoral, or a sinner, the newcomer now understands she or he is sick, powerless, out of control with alcohol, and a victim of a powerful disease.

Outsiders sometimes fear that the problem drinkers are giving up all responsibility for their actions. Insiders explain this is not so. Over time, it is said, members learn the disease is more than merely physical, but psychological and spiritual as well. They learn that although they may not have caused the problem, they must now take responsibility for managing it. With the crisis addressed and the drinking, one hopes, arrested, persons ideally become able through this interpretive reframing to take increasing responsibility for their actions. Many old-timers, professionals in the field, and clergy realize the sharp contrast between willful misconduct and sickness is too unnuanced. Nevertheless, they believe the strategy is efficacious and benign, and the description is apt.

Newcomers who object to being categorized as sick cannot play the new language game. However, members are often successful in dealing with this situation. They tell stories about their own refusal to admit the problem. They hint that the newcomer's attitude is evidence of the severity of the disease. They suggest it indicates "denial" or false ego and control. They may highlight the presupposed harsh or erroneous attitudes of friends or family, especially their fruitless admonishing of the problem drinker to exercise self-control. A contrast is set up. Outsiders' unenlightened attitudes of judgment and moral outrage at the drinker's behavior are compared with the program's enlightened and compassionate approach toward a sick person. Rather than finding rejection, the newcomer is led to expect compassion, tolerance, mutual empathy, and acceptance in the group. Members believe that if the person becomes willing to admit to having a disease, characterized by powerlessness over alcohol, the rest of the steps will become possible. Through all this, a sharp contrast between "badness" and sickness often functions as an important strategy.

Theological terms are rarely used. Only occasionally may the word *sin* be heard. Frequently it is dismissed as a rejected category in connection with alcoholism. Nor is overt hostility toward church or doctrine usually part of a responsible program, especially at meetings. The program is pragmatic, dealing with present realities, rather than causes or sources. Very little outright addiction theory is discussed, much less religious concepts. Nevertheless, an implicit dichotomy between sin and addiction is for many a baseline presupposition. This is revealed through the spontaneously negative reaction that erupts when the idea of sin is discussed in connection with addiction.

I had many experiences that led to this contention. In one instance, a new student took a course on addiction. She was a somewhat conservative Christian who had taken a risk to attend a liberal seminary away from home. She was from a small town and had no experience with the recovery movement. She elected to give her presentation the first week of class. On the chalkboard she drew a chart listing problem behaviors, such as drunkenness, lying, and murder. Alongside, she had a list of options, including sin, sickness, and a combination of the two. She asked class members to "place" the behaviors. She did not get far, however, before an angry outcry began. "You're not saying my mother was a sinner, are you?" demanded one student, whose mother had just died from cirrhosis. "Are you crazy?" exclaimed another. "You're saying alcoholism is a sin!" The voices grew louder as the student tried to explain herself. She said she was showing that the issues were more complex than this simple framework. After several exchanges, however, she withdrew and was silent for the rest of the term.

Sin is often identified and grouped along with immorality, willful misconduct, "badness," and perversity. It is set in opposition to a "cunning, baffling, and powerful" disease that now rules the person. This helps explain the vehement, automatic, and passionate reaction often encountered in contemporary addiction-recovery groups if the word *sin* is used. This sharp dichotomy set up between sin and addiction, however, is hard to address because it operates below the surface. Several other factors add to this. Members insist that Alcoholics Anonymous and other recovery groups are "spiritual but not religious" and that they are free to believe what they like. Alcoholics Anonymous especially works to keep free of outside entanglements, including organized religion. These factors combine to help keep the common dichotomy between sin and addiction hidden.

This dichotomy does not function for everyone in the movement. Some may conceive of problem behavior in both sin and addiction categories simultaneously, although they often make a point to delineate certain distinctions. Also, there are some writers who see the similarities between the ideas of sin and addiction. Harry Gene Levine, for instance, understands Alcoholics Anonymous to have a very definite moral code. It is derived from the Christian temperance movement, which analogized salvation from sin with recovery from drunkenness. He explained it most accessibly on a National Public Radio broadcast.

> The model of the recovered drunkard, as developed by the temperance movement, is drawn directly from the model of the saved sinner, the person who is born again. This issue of remaking yourself, the notion of the self-made man, in the 19th-century terminology, is absolutely essential to American culture, to American ideology. It has religious sources, it has secular sources, and in that way both temperance and Alcoholics Anonymous and the 12-Step Movements are quintessentially American movements.[8]

Some writers who see the similarity, however, make a value judgment about it. They may view the relationship between sin and addiction concepts as a generally negative situation. They may see it as the hidden repressive religion of a supposedly nonreligious group, or the erroneous mixing of religious and health issues. One writer calls it "a form of Christian fundamentalism which is peculiarly American."[9] In effect, they believe that bad theology is harmful. They would solve the problem by bracketing theology altogether.

Other writers see the connection between the sin and addiction ideas but consider it generally positive.[10] To many it is an encouraging link between recovery and Christian spirituality. They understand it to be good theology, albeit implicit. Even these writers, however, do not elaborate in depth on the concept *sin,* especially in connection with addiction.

The Unpopular Concept of Sin

Part of the avoidance of sin comes because sin is not a popular topic. A long-standing discomfort with, misunderstanding of, or neglect of the idea of sin has existed for decades, both inside and outside the church. Even the small recent resurgence of interest in this doctrine cannot dispel the negative overtones associated with this Christian concept.[11] The doctrine of sin is often associated with moralism, judgmentalism, and exclusivism. The popular imagination sees sin as a sour, pinched killjoy, shaking a bony finger at everything enjoyable, or as the vestige of an unenlightened, inhumane, archaic past with which we are well finished.

Many people fear that talk of sin in connection with addiction will return us to an earlier age when alcoholics were often ostracized, viewed with no compassion, and finally given up as hopeless. Professionals in the addiction field often worry that any talk of religion or sin will underestimate the physiological aspects of addiction. They also fear it will take away the gains that the disease concept of addiction has brought in making treatment accessible and acceptable. Many recovery group members insist that using any theological terms, but especially sin, evokes hurtful memories for many addicted persons. Some have experienced hurt from rigid, condemnatory attitudes and practices in the church. Some literally experienced abuse. But many both inside and outside the addiction-recovery movement simply assume this has been the case rather than having grievously experienced or perpetrated it.

Many people have an underlying and even unconscious presupposition that the doctrine of sin, and those who invoke it, will perpetuate harshness and judgmentalism. This view is prevalent within the church as well. Many church members, especially some pastors and pastoral counselors, often fear they will be considered harsh and judgmental if they discuss sin in the context of addiction. They do not want to prompt images of sinners in the hands of an angry church.[12] They, too, assume that nonchurchgoers—including or especially those drawn to recovery-type support groups—have left the church for precisely that reason, and they resolve to deal tenderly with them rather than make them feel further rejected, hurt, or condemned.[13]

Some of this difficulty comes from unclarity about the doctrine of sin. As we will see in the next chapter, sin is not first about behavior but about orientation. It is a religious category, not primarily a moral one, although these two overlap. Just as sin is not essentially about bad behavior or human willfulness, neither is it primarily about failing to realize our human potential, being alienated from self and others, lacking serenity. Although these things can be involved, sin is primarily separation from God. The doctrine of sin describes our imposed and chosen alienation from God, others, and self. The restlessness of the human soul—out of which false attachments can spring—is not sin in itself. This restlessness is a God-given goad to prevent us from shallow contentment.

Although there has been no universal Christian consensus on the particulars of this complex doctrine, many have worked to delineate the relationship of sin to the human predicament. Older understandings see human alienation and suffering growing out of our sin. In other words, sin brings suffering. More recent understandings see sin as an unfortunate response to the tragedy of the human condition, for example, our human anxiety in the face of our inevitable limitations ("finitude"). In other words, suffering promotes sin.[14]

In either case, the doctrine of sin has derivative rather than focal status in the grammar of the faith. Christianity has salvation, new life, and resurrection at its core. Sin functions largely as a description of a seemingly intractable problem to which humankind longs continually for a solution. The doctrine of sin is a derivative of the much more crucial doctrine of salvation. An accurate understanding of sin comes only through the experience of grace. Sin is not the pivot around which the Christian faith rotates. The Christian view of human nature recognizes the goodness of creation, its source in God, the glory of humans made in the divine image, the transformation that grace can effect. It can (and does) embrace a disease-healing paradigm within its framework for understanding human growth.

The doctrine of sin, in all its variety and long history, exhibits a sensitivity to the human predicament that has largely been forgotten. For inevitably the doctrine of sin raises a whole nexus of theological issues having to do with human capabilities, the nature of evil, the intentions of God, and especially salvation. Many of these are the same issues implicitly involved in discussion of addiction as a spiritual problem. A narrow understanding of sin, implied in the popular implicit dichotomy "Not sin but addiction," obscures this. It suggests that the doctrine of sin is primarily concerned with behavior, morality, will, and choice.

Nevertheless, it is inadequate simply to defend the doctrine. The contemporary antipathy does have a basis in reality. For the doctrine of sin has been used sinfully, and we have inherited a very limiting version of it. Sin has been identified with proscribed acts, bad behavior, immoderation, sexual license, failure to adhere to the norm. Whether this abuse has been perpetrated more readily on persons caught in addictions is not clear, although many believe this to be true. Surely a moralistic and judgmental use of the doctrine of sin has contributed to its rejection. In the same way, a harsher attitude toward more observable human difficulties, such as compulsive drinking, than toward more hidden ones, like jealousy, has contributed to society's rejection of the doctrine in connection with addiction.

This behavior-focused or moralistic understanding of sin can also occur when the issue of shame is considered. Some may suggest that the concept of shame is a more useful category to pursue than the issue of sin when dealing with addiction. They may focus on the popular distinction made today between guilt and shame. Shame is typically defined as rooted in who one is, a feeling that one is somehow inherently defective. Guilt, on the other hand, is said to spring from what one does, breaking one's own moral standards or that of the group. Seeing willpower as more a "sin issue," this line of thought would suggest that the recovery ethos identifies the core problem in addiction as shame, not sin. The recovery model would thus be seen as avoiding the inherited difficulties of traditional religion's focus on sin.

Undoubtedly, both guilt and shame are involved in addictive behaviors. And such distinctions can be productive in the treatment of addictions. Yet they obscure the theological roots of the addiction concept. For the connection between the sin and addiction concepts is evident when the historical and conceptual roots of the addiction-recovery model are studied. By sidestepping the connections, the addiction-recovery ethos may more replicate than repair the confusion over guilt and shame. In either case—whether we focus on sin or on shame—the addiction-recovery model can set up a sharp dichotomy between its own version of the problem and earlier understandings, particularly traditional religious understandings.

THE METAPHOR OF ADDICTION
AS A POTENTIAL REPLACEMENT

If the doctrine of sin has been abandoned or at least seriously questioned by many, something else must be used to describe human fallibility. We could not abandon the idea of sin, or some equivalent, even if we tried. All cultures need and routinely find ways of discussing human dysfunction, failure, and wrongdoing. Human beings have a gnawing feeling inside that all is not right. Religions of all kinds note the tragedy of the human condition: so ripe with possibilities, so often missing the mark, so much left undone at the end. They all make efforts to address the essential homelessness of the human soul. If the idea of sin is nonfunctional for many people, something must take its place. For many today the concept of addiction is performing that role. It has emerged to hold an increasingly important place in American culture. Although some criticize it, often trenchantly,[15] this voice is small by comparison with the volumes of praise.

The very diffuseness, generality, and adaptability of the term *addiction*—although sometimes problematic for professionals—have been its strength on the popular level. This has helped the idea increasingly gain a generic character among the public. The term *addiction* has become used to describe a broad range of human problems, everything from the widely recognized alcohol and drug dependencies to such diverse things as "excessive" caretaking, sex, eating, even religiosity. It has become, in common parlance, an acceptable way to describe immoderation, compulsion, or destructive behavior. Some, like Gerald May, take this very far, saying "all people are addicts. . . to be alive is to be addicted."[16] This suggests that a functional replacement for the concept of sin—including both its universality and its ubiquity—has emerged and is gaining broad acceptance.

Issues as pivotal as human wrongdoing, dysfunction, and disorder do not go away. No matter how submerged the theme may be, it is still alive. Mutual-help groups, especially recovery-oriented ones, still implicitly grapple with feelings of being in the wrong, of having more or less willfully committed error, and of needing resolution. They do not simply deal with bondage and victimization, although that can often be the predominant aspect. Alcoholics Anonymous, more than most other recovery groups, deliberately pushes people to grapple with their own responsibility. It helps people programmatically avoid projection, the endless search for causes, and determinist explanations. It must be given enormous credit for this, even as the task becomes harder daily as an overreliance on genetic theories, victimization themes, and other determinisms redirects or clouds the vision of recovery group members.

Many once used the doctrine of sin to understand such issues as bondage and responsibility. Today when people deal with these ultimately theological issues, the addiction metaphor is often used instead. While on the surface sin and addiction are sometimes viewed as opposites, in many ways addiction functions as a substitute concept, employing many of the same devices and dynamics. In spite of the change of scenery, there is much of the sin idea (and its distortions) in the concept of addiction. If the terms were diametrically opposed, it would be hard to effect such a rapid and sweeping cultural shift. This shift from sin to addiction contains important theological reverberations that need to be recognized and evaluated. Theological themes, in spite of modern efforts to leave them behind, have continued to echo in the collective memory.

The enthusiasm for the addiction metaphor highlights the explanatory vacuum so many feel when they try to understand human dysfunction. The addiction metaphor and movement may be tapping into something latent in society, something which secularizers have, by definition, failed to address. Many modernizers have felt that religious meaning could be discarded with aplomb. Yet they have failed to "tap the widespread but latent sense of sin that still survives underneath the surface of bureaucratically administered society. . . . [They have] ignored what is both primitive and universal in social life: the propensity to accumulate psychological forms of indebtedness." Thus it is that "the psychological sense of sin is now secularized and takes the form of a residual sense of personal indebtedness either to oneself or to the larger society."[17]

I do not want to overstate the case for this replay. Few modern persons struggle consciously or primarily over their sin and God's wrath. In earlier ages this was a crucial issue, but today there are many alternative ways to explain and thus avoid this primal problem. Consequently, there is little to spark debate over ideas of sin. The popular dismissal of the doctrine of sin and our culture's movement toward alternate views of human difficulties has many historical roots. They are too complex to be fully addressed here. However, the Enlightenment challenge to traditional Christian doctrine, the "collapse of the house of authority," left a profound vacuum. It could not long be filled solely by rationalist conceptions. Human dysfunction was too intractable to be educated away.

Over time a medical model was applied to more human difficulties. This shift has a complex history and went along with many other political and economic developments. In many ways it was, according to a sociology of knowledge perspective, a "medicalization of deviance." Increasing numbers of human problems were shifted away from the religious or criminal purview to the medical category. A deconstruction perspective, such as that of Michel Foucault, understands this as part of a major discursive shift, with distinct political and economic ramifications. Phillip Rieff speaks of "the triumph of the therapeutic."[18] The addiction-recovery ethos has taken a place within these larger shifts. Thus the shift from sin to addiction has not been a simple replacement. A different philosophical and explanatory base makes the two terms, although functionally similar, conceptually dissimilar in significant ways.

To many people the movement to a new paradigm seems attractive and practical, contemporary and humane. It makes the problem seem highly identifiable and treatable. This switch seems to move us from morals to medicine, bringing the problem within the sphere of science and rationality. Both the sin and the addiction concepts deal with the person as a whole. This gives the exchange a comparable feel. However, the idea of addiction calls up more biological and psychological images of disease and healing. It appears to leave behind moral categories of righteousness, judgment, condemnation, salvation. Thus, many hope a burden of counterproductive guilt will be lifted off needlessly stooped shoulders to permit persons to rise to their potential. The shift from sin to addiction, or the dichotomy between them, seems not only appropriate but salutary. It seems to have had pragmatic and significant benefits, especially in a culture concerned with what "works."

Inadvertently, Alcoholics Anonymous and other derivative recovery groups have greatly aided this paradigm shift. It is true that Alcoholics Anonymous has always been very careful to restrict its attention to the problem of alcohol abuse. In fact, early AA members never officially used the term "disease." Nevertheless, their first contribution was to gain a wider hearing for the idea that addiction is not simply an issue of will, morality, or crime but an illnesslike compulsion that has distinct physical characteristics. They also insisted that it is a problem with profound psychological and, especially, spiritual components. They have been attractive precisely because they have kept open the understanding of addiction. By insisting that addiction is not only physical but also psychological and spiritual, they implicitly oppose those who would adhere to a strictly univocal causal structure, such as genetics, biochemistry, or psychological conditioning. Over time, their work has made a broad understanding of addiction possible, opening the door to a spreading addiction metaphor, which can be applied to a wide panoply of human problems.

At the outset, there was a pragmatic efficacy in applying the disease model to alcohol abuse. When the model was first applied to compulsive drinking, it helped many persons admit their problems and seek help. Positive results happened where before only hopelessness existed. Medical and therapeutic approaches are even more commonplace today. A disease model still seems naturally to imply there is hope of healing. It seems to lift judgment and calls to mind possible intervention strategies. It is encouraging when the illness model actually helps persons move away from addictive patterns and resume useful lives. Over time, then, it has been extended to other areas of human dysfunction. It has seemed a logical growth and preferable to a religious view, especially when that view is perceived as judgmental and condemnatory.

Many factors influence persons to embrace a disease model to describe addiction and to expand the addiction metaphor to address increasing areas of human dysfunction. The model of addiction is both cause and effect. It is a product of a larger paradigm shift even as it also helps to fuel it. The idea of addiction as disease has moved beyond its pragmatic usage in relationship to alcoholism. Many claim that through the addiction-recovery paradigm they have found an alternative spirituality that is more perceptive about the human condition than traditional theological explanations.

The broad approach of the AA model has helped it serve as a bridge between the religious and medical views; I say this even though there are distinct differences between the AA program, the more expanded addiction-recovery movement, and the many treatment modalities that exist to address addiction. As the therapeutic mentality, the medicalization of human difficulty, and a biodeterminist tendency in public thinking increase, the distinctive AA ethos becomes harder to separate out. The new paradigm that Alcoholics Anonymous helped prompt has now spilled over its borders and conceptual framework. In many ways, there is a "clash of paradigms" going on.[19] Yet the widespread public acceptance of Alcoholics Anonymous has nevertheless been a key factor in the promulgation of the new paradigm.

CONCLUSION

The addiction-recovery metaphor has a complicated relationship to the doctrine of sin. It springs out of, replicates, replaces, and challenges it, all at the same time. Theology thus undergirds an important aspect of the addiction-recovery ethos and should not be bracketed when dealing with issues of addiction and recovery. Once the theological undertones are made clear, creative alternatives that draw on the best of theological and scientific thinking can be proposed. There are ways to understand both sin and addiction that can build on the strengths of the contemporary ethos, reclaim many benefits of the theological tradition, and reformulate where necessary. But sin must be better understood, especially in relationship to addiction.

3

THE RELATIONSHIP
OF SIN AND ADDICTION

The sin-and-salvation paradigm has ample room within it for a sickness and healing, or addiction and recovery, metaphor. Metaphors of illness and health have never been antithetical to discussions of sin and salvation. In this century, for instance, H. Richard Niebuhr explained sin in a way that would be both acceptable to many in the recovery movement and satisfactory to generations of Christians:

> In our dealing with ourselves and with our neighbors, with our societies and our neighbor societies, we deal not with morally and rationally healthy beings who may be called upon to develop ideal personalities and to build ideal commonwealths, but rather with diseased beings, who can do little or nothing that is worthwhile until they have recovered health and who, if they persist in acting as though they were healthy, succeed only in spreading abroad the infection of their own lives.[1]

This analogy is ancient and it has continued merit. Sin is holistic, affecting body, mind, and spirit, and salvation is much more about healing and newness than about retribution and punishment. Just as images of sickness and healing fit well within the theological purview, so do undertones of sin and salvation appear in the addiction-recovery paradigm. There is much overlap in the concepts. But the addiction paradigm is too narrow on its own to encompass the breadth of the sin concept. This is not always obvious, due to constricted and unclear views of sin. A broadening of the concept can overcome this difficulty and help locate addiction within a theological framework.

A focus on sin is problematic, however, without an appreciation of grace. (For this reason, some may wish to read chapter 12 at this point.) These two operate together. Sin is anticipated by, met with, and surrounded by God's grace. No one falls outside this anticipatory and sovereign love. It goes before us, stands beside us, and is an always-ready, attractive possibility, if only we recognize it. It is hard to recognize, however, if sin is misunderstood. Unless we have a better understanding of the problem, we are not likely to recognize the remedy or be able to value and credit it fully.

Much that theology says on sin is interpretive. The church as a whole has never formally adopted one definitive doctrine of sin. While there are certain defining parameters to the doctrine, it has remained controversial over the entire history of theology. Some of the confusion about sin simply comes from the variety of views about it. The early church chose to focus communal agreement on the more affirmative doctrines, concerning the nature of God and the person and work of Christ. The doctrine of sin has consequently been the aspect of theology perhaps most sensitive to cultural influence.[2] The current tendency to redefine sin in terms of addiction only illustrates this situation. While this desire to translate theology into contemporary idiom can lend relevance to the doctrine, it also contributes to its long-standing imprecision. Nevertheless, certain parameters of the doctrine can be helpful in dealing with the addiction question.

NEITHER BEHAVIOR NOR WILL DEFINES SIN

Sin is not primarily about right and wrong behavior, that is, morality. Sin is first about orientation. One's telos, direction, primary attachment—rather than beliefs or behavior—is what is most radically affected by sin. One continually has the choice to turn toward or away from God, the source of our being. There is a cumulative effect, however, in persistently turning away. Over time, it becomes harder to change. Fortunately, God constantly lures us with grace, waits lovingly for us, and comes to us from many different angles. In spite of our penchant to focus on behavior, the doctrine of sin is not primarily moralistic at its heart. The church is as much to blame as anyone for this erroneous identification. As H. Richard Niebuhr says:

> To say that man is a sinner is not equivalent to the statement that he is morally bad. Modern moralism has subordinated all other value categories to those of the morally good and the morally bad. . . . Science and art have more or less successfully resisted the tyranny of moralism but religion has accepted the yoke willingly and allowed its concept of sin to be reduced to "moral guilt" as previously it allowed its concept of God to be identified with "moral perfection."[3]

Morality or behavioral change does eventually get involved. A change in one's basic spiritual orientation will generally lead to changes in behavior; otherwise, the reality of the redirection can be seriously questioned.

Spirituality and morality are closely intertwined. But simply moving from one type of behavior to another, even if more personally and socially beneficial, is not the key point of identifying sin. Approved and disapproved behavior are culturally relative in many ways, so one cannot begin with that. A higher standard, a deeper presupposition is needed.

While behavior in itself is not the linchpin of sin, neither is will. In addiction-recovery discourse, "self-will" is sometimes made out as the culprit. The idea that self-will is the chief problem sometimes gets expressed in worry about one's "control issues." This refers to areas in which one seeks an inordinate or unrealistic level of control. The linking of evil and self-will is often too close in this discourse. Scripture (particularly the archetypal story of Adam, Eve, and the serpent), the Western religious tradition, and much contemporary theology have suggested that we find evil already present in the world.[4] Humans do not originate evil, they yield to it. In addition, the depiction of the serpent shows "that a kind of alien power comes over the man who sins, which he must obey against his better judgment because it convinces him by its assured manner and its correspondence with his own feeling." This is the "unfathomable duality which marks all sinful conduct."[5] We are tempted and overcome, and yet we also allow evil to drown out our own reservations. One needs a properly directed, motivated, and functioning will in order to resist. Thus will in itself—even self-will—is not the source of the problem. Although our wills may be drawn and yield to evil, the capacity of will in itself is not equivalent to evil. The will is distorted by sin, but it is capable of reformation through relationship with God.

It is the orientation of will—what it yields to, chooses, follows, or patterns itself after—that determines the eminence or the degradation of the person. If one does not direct the will toward God, it will be directed toward something else. Yet that something else can never bear the weight of ultimacy. What and to whom one redirects the self matters much more than the bare act of giving up. God is not a tyrant who basks in slavish submission. God is wholly for us and wholly loyal. It is we who are disloyal. In turning toward God, the point is not giving up but reorientation. We reflect the divine image in our possession of will, and spiritual maturation is a freer use of that faculty.

Sin, therefore, can never be properly understood if one begins either with sheer will or with behavior. It is a religious category, dealing with spiritual orientation and the bondage that begins when we face in the wrong direction. Our thinking takes a wrong path from the outset when we focus on either will or behavior. To start our thinking with the problem of sin is also misleading, though that has been our focus here. Phenomenologically, of course, we know sin first through our suffering in it. Yet starting at this point exacerbates the problem. If we begin with sin and continually focus on it, we find deeper and deeper levels than we ever imagined. The idea of sin only makes good sense when placed within the framework of divine grace. It does not work well the other way around. We become caught in a two-way dilemma. Either we equate our sinfulness and bondage with will deliberately and wrongly used (Pelagianism) or with our inherent finitude and weakness (Manicheanism). This does not mean that human dysfunction can only be known from a Christian perspective. All religions and many secular fields appreciate the tragedy of the human condition and our penchant for destruction. However, starting with and focusing largely on this can be devastating. Unless one starts from another premise, it is difficult to come up with a thoroughly optimistic and healing alternative rather than simply a coping strategy.

In Christianity, God is claimed to be already in the process of healing the world. Sin and evil are effectually, promisorily, defeated. This is not a completely realized eschatology but a future apocalyptic hope. We expect wrongs to be righted and justice to reign through God's actions. Christ's work has been both a preview and a beginning of this, but we still await the consummation. To many persons this may seem wildly unrealistic, naively optimistic, or simply blind. And it does leave, at least for a time, many human questions unanswered, much unexplained tragedy in place. Nevertheless, it is the message of the life and death of Christ and the ongoing work of the Holy Spirit in the world. Those who really expect this ultimate outcome develop an insatiable hunger for righteousness. They experience an unquenchable thirst for as much of this divine realm as possible now. And they gain a strong drive to establish outposts of peace and wholeness wherever they can.

Three factors need to be distinguished: the human predicament, the preconditions of sin, and actual sin itself. These factors are part of a complex issue that cannot be separated into parts. Yet the effort to discern such factors is worthwhile because persons involved in the addiction-recovery schema often seem most troubled or perplexed by this cluster. In fact, I believe that confusion over these issues, inherited from common theological misunderstandings, may be what prompts many to the addiction-recovery perspective.

THE PRECONDITIONS OF SIN

Sin is only one form of evil. Not all evil springs from or can be reduced to human sin and choice. Certain types of disease, death per se, natural disasters such as earthquakes, seem outside human causation and sometimes outside human intervention. While there is much human cooperation with, contribution to, or yielding to such nonmoral evil, one cannot always posit a human source for them. Some aspects or forms of addiction may fit into this category of nonmoral evil. Apparently biologically based addictions, for example, seem to begin almost spontaneously or with very little provocation. The percentage of such largely biological addictions seems to be small, and other factors (psychological, sociological, economic) inevitably become intertwined. Still, a genetic or inherent biological factor may contribute to various types of addiction, and there is certainly a biological habituation to long-term chemical abuse. The current popular ethos is often bent on forcing the issue, however, looking hard for genetic markers and hereditary traits in nearly every form of problematic behavior.

At this point theology makes an important—though often neglected—contribution to the discussion. For the popular ethos that focuses on genetics or biology can lead in a problematic direction. It can become a form of biological determinism, which in itself cooperates with evil. A malaise can be induced when any remaining free choice or expectation of deliverance is pushed aside. The current attractiveness of determinist explanations, and the eagerness with which people embrace them, is too often a denial of human freedom and dignity. Nevertheless, theology cannot err on the other side for fear of confirming popular misconceptions. Explanatory space must always be left for the biological factors in addiction. Human vulnerability comes in many different forms. An inordinate sensitivity to certain substances, to certain types or levels of stimulation, or to particular experiences is a real possibility. This forms part of the many aspects of tragic uncaused natural or nonmoral evil, and the particularity of human weakness and finitude. The fact that humans are physical beings means that habituation, no matter how it begins, has an inevitable biological or neurological component.

However, none of this explains why and how we so frequently choose to yield to evil rather than resist it. Theology knows this can never be answered definitively. But there is much that can be said before falling into silence. Sin can be a tragic but faulty response to our inevitable human anxiety. This anxiety or tension springs from our experience of the human predicament. Our human condition presents us with a dilemma. Humans are finite, limited, and, frankly, an ephemeral part of the world. At the same time, we are free, able to transcend our limitations, imagine greater possibilities, desire permanence and meaning, and act beyond the constraints of our own finite horizon. This tension provokes anxiety, but this anxiety is not sin. Inner turmoil can be horrible to bear, but it is not sin per se.

Many today seek a steady state of inner peace, yet ultimately this is an impossible goal in life. The anxiety prompted by our freedom and our ontological insecurity is constitutive of the human experience. It is also the source of creativity.[6]

Humans are faced with choices and possibilities, not all of which can be actualized. It is inevitable that humans feel tension, frustration, confusion, even fear. This anxiety is basic to the human condition and is the result of choice and opportunity. Although this has been a dominant interpretation, I suggest an additional angle. For a different form of anxiety is provoked when we become aware of the comparatively restricted range of choice that is ours. Many people are inordinately restricted, not just by their inherent finitude but by the deliberate repressive intervention of others. These external constraints can be especially hard to bear when compared with others less restricted. Of course, no person operates with the optimum range of choices, limited only by their human finitude. Yet in this world, some are allowed a greater range of freedom than others.

A different form of anxiety results when choices are inordinately narrowed. I call this "anguish." It is more like anguish in the face of what *should* be rather than anxiety in the face of what *could* be. This anguish is a close cousin to despair and hopelessness. Many see despair or hopelessness as ultimately a lack of faith and trust. As such, it is seen as inevitably leading to or already being a form of sin.[7] I contend, instead, that this anguish is not always and already an aspect of sin. It is instead parallel to, but opposite, anxiety in the face of wide opportunity. As such it is an inevitable, constituent part of the situated (as opposed to abstractly conceived) human predicament. In other words, there is a "legitimate" or "realistic" desperation, which I am labeling "anguish." This is prior to any sin, but springs from one's human predicament when inordinately constrained.

The reason I have made a distinction between anxiety and anguish, as pre-sin conditions, is because the response to this tension can come in many different guises. How we deal with our given inevitable situation, caught between freedom and limitation, is all important. The tension itself is neither inherently negative nor positive. It is the basis of both good and bad in human activity. From this tension springs both sin and creativity.

> It is not possible to make a simple separation between the creative and destructive elements in anxiety. . . . The same action may reveal a creative effort to transcend natural limitations, and a sinful effort to give an unconditioned value to contingent and limited factors in human existence. Man may, in the same moment, be anxious because he has not become what he ought to be; and also anxious lest he cease to be at all.[8]

PARTICULAR PRE-SIN RESPONSES
TO HUMAN VULNERABILITY

Not all reactions to human vulnerability are automatically, unequivo-cally, or primarily sin. This needs to be said, though sin is universal and all have sinned. According to Edward Farley, there are at least three other types of possible responses, "pathological injury, distractions, and bra-vado." Bravado—a "heroic" and autonomous standing in the face of ulti-mate chaos—is the rarest of the three reactions. It is less relevant to the problem of addiction, for in it the person refuses all distractions and idols and accepts tragic vulnerability. There is an evil-producing aspect to this response, however, for it can promote callous indifference to others, since it is both self-focused and inherently noncommunal. The pathological re-sponse seems very common today, or at least we are more sensitive to it. It can come from "inadequate copings with the victimizations of histori-cal existence."[9] Some aspects of genetic vulnerability, childhood abuse, and social trauma—as forms of victimization—may also prompt psy-chopathological responses. Certain reactions to these evils represent actual mental illness, sometimes involuntary and outside the realm of direct re-sponsibility.[10]

I depart from the above schema, however, in suggesting that re-sponses to victimization may not always be psychopathological. They may be closer to what I earlier called "anguish," or spring from that state. They can also be referred to as the understandable and almost inevitable reactions to victimization, identified in Korean minjung theology as *han*.[11] This is something like our Western category of "shame," although more complex. These reactions are often counterproductive and self-destructive, yet they are not always and automatically sin.[12] Overlap be-gins at this point, however. For whether they are truly psychopathological or simply "coping" responses to victimization, these reactions can never-theless set up the conditions for sin. Having been sinned against, it is al-most "natural" to want to return evil for evil. Anyone who has watched young children provoke and respond to each other has witnessed this; the retaliatory hand flails out almost automatically, with very little pause for thought.

Although *han* is the reaction of the oppressed to having been sinned against, these wounds can themselves prompt retaliation, as "the line be-tween sin and han becomes blurred in their action and reaction."[13] The same danger exists in psychopathology. One often cannot clearly distin-guish psychopathological and sinful responses. Although they represent "two dimensions of the fragile response to an insecure world, they are not sealed off from each other. . . . The pathological can serve as a discrete occasion for the expression and intensification of human evil and vice versa."[14] Nevertheless, one must distinguish sin from these pre-sin responses to ontological human vulnerability and outright victimization—whether understood as anguish, *han,* or psychopathology.

Another common reaction to our tragic vulnerability is even more closely related to what our culture understands as addiction. This response, which can be called "distraction," includes outright substance addiction and more.

> [Distractions] dull the ache of discontent [and] include chemical alterations (alcohol, nicotine, prescribed pharmaceuticals, and illegal drugs), world-views and techniques that lower self-awareness and effect indifference, and a great variety of groups (cults, religions, hobbies, therapy groups, and social action groups) whose endeavors or groups relations help absorb self-preoccupation.

These are "nonidolatrous" (I would say pre-sin) responses, but they can themselves prompt further problems.

> Even as pyschopathological defenses carry with them a new set of problems that themselves require help, so distractive responses pay a price for what they offer. We are increasingly familiar with the devastations of physio-chemical distractions. We are less self-conscious about the problematic character of distractive world-views, techniques, or group immersion.

Yet distraction can easily lead to evil and sin, since distraction cannot deliver what we ask of it. It ultimately and inevitably fails.

> Distraction in any form is never an adequate way of handling the intolerability of tragic vulnerability. . . . At its best it makes possible a round of satisfactions and disappointments. The addiction escalates; the world-view becomes ever more extreme; the group betrays. This is why failed distraction is fertile ground for the dynamics of evil; that is, the fanatical absolutizing of the world-view, the techniques, the group.[15]

Thus, these potential responses to the human predicament can birth sin. Although neither the human predicament nor the anxiety it provokes is synonymous with sin, they are the "occasions" for sin. It is a temptingly close step from anxiety, anguish, *han,* victimization, bravado, psychopathology, and distraction to sin. When we do move toward sin from these states, we are avoiding the acceptance of our human condition. A few may choose to heroically embrace their finitude and its attendant anxiety, shunning all security as illusory. Most of us simply cannot endure the anxiety. We flee from the tension, even though good might result as we deal with it. Then we seek for something on which to ground ourselves. Rather than seeking our security and permanence in God, we tend to absolutize something that is relative.

The Different Sides of Sin

There are various ways to absolutize something relative. Our sinful responses to human anxiety and ontological insecurity are not all the same. Our temptations are both more subtle and more complex than is usually realized. This needs some analysis; otherwise the vast array of behaviors labeled "addiction" will appear more univocal than they really are. There should be no rush to "place" addiction in relationship to sin, but neither can the task be avoided altogether in a rush to find grace and healing. For, using medical metaphors, the better we understand a particular case of "sin illness," the more receptive we will be to appropriate treatment. Maxims like "Let go and let God," or "Put God on the throne"—although sometimes helpful in prompting an openness to God—ultimately do a disservice to the complexity of the problem. The destructive response to human anxiety—that response we label *sin*—is no simple matter.

All sin is primarily a turning from the source of our being, God. Yet that ground is prepared by some constituent aspects of the human situation. The destructive responses to the inbuilt tension between finitude and freedom can be categorized into two main aspects: pride and sensuality. "The basic source of temptation . . . resides in the inclination of man, either to deny the contingent character of his existence (in pride and self-love) or to escape from his freedom (in sensuality)."[16] These two sides of sin can look very different from each other. However, both types are potential responses to the constituent anxiety and insecurity of the human condition.

The sin of pride can have different faces, including pride of power, intellectual pride, moral pride, and spiritual pride. In each case, a person absolutizes what is actually partial and relative. This can be one's area of control, one's knowledge, one's upright behavior, or one's identification with divinity. Pride is a denial of the inherent limitations of the human situation and a false absolutizing of the self. One attempts to deceive first oneself and then others, in the interests of security and inordinate self-love. However, a tinge of doubt always remains. "There is no level of greatness and power in which the lash of fear is not at least one strand in the whip of ambition."[17]

This way of separating the aspects of sin does have some problems. The word *pride*—although it is the traditional term—is a confusing way to describe this form of sin. For in an age that values self-esteem, calling pride sin can appear counterproductive, sadistic, or self-destructive. It also assumes that a refusal to accept finitude can be equated automatically with self-absolutization. Instead, discomfort with finitude can also be a pointer to our true source of meaning and permanence, God. When this proper orientation is not made, however, there is an absolutization of something relative instead of an orientation toward God.[18] It is therefore too simplistic to describe this sin (or all sin) as putting oneself in the place of God. Other mundane things can be falsely absolutized, and even in the pride form of sin, one never really forgets one's finitude. It is an endless running away from that reality.

Other models than pride can be used to describe this destructive impulse. For example, one may desire so much to become infinite that this impossible quest leads one further and further away from the true self, which can only know infinitude through God. Or one may resolve so much to be a self through one's own efforts that one defiantly rejects external help, even from God. This can become a "demoniac" rage, an extreme introversion, "inwardness with a jammed lock," but it is kept hidden from outside observers.[19] In these forms of sin, despair comes as the elusive self slips ever further from one's grasp. This is not really an ignorance of God so much as a resistance of God's claim. It is a refusal to find the self through the only sure reality, a perverse rejection of the true ground of the self, God.

However it is labeled, this pride form of sin has both individualist and collectivist versions. Social groupings, ranging from club to nation, claim a collective egoism that is potentially more powerful and more destructive than an individual's. "The pretensions and claims of a collective or social self exceed those of the individual ego. The group is more arrogant, hypocritical, self-centered and more ruthless in the pursuit of its ends than the individual."[20] It exerts a hard-to-resist claim over individuals, who bow to it not only or primarily out of fear but also through self-interest. This collective egoism is not limited to warmongering nations and dictatorships. It can come in many unexpected versions. For example, it can emerge as a moral self-righteousness in those who follow popular health trends by adopting various dietary restrictions, just as easily as it can come in the spiritual pride of a quasi-religious sect.

In this schema, the other side of sin is termed *sensuality*. Again, this is a flight from freedom. It is a faulty response to constitutive human anxiety, an attempted escape from the human predicament. In large part, sensuality is an immersion in the things of the world, including gluttony, drunkenness, sexual license, and material extravagance. Many non-Christian cultures have been especially harsh in their condemnation of this category of human problems. Christian culture, too, has often judged sensuality more harshly than pride. It is an easy target, for these distortions are more visible and discernible than the often well-hidden sin of pride. However, it is a mistake to totally identify this type of sin with bodily excesses. It can also manifest itself as inertia and passivity. Some cultures have ranked sensuality as the primary human fault. But a dominant strand of Christianity posits sensuality as a secondary or derivative form of sin. Inordinate pride and self-love are understood as more the consequential and essential forms of sin, with sensuality being a somewhat lesser variation.[21]

This prioritizing is problematic. The sin traditionally termed *sensuality* is as grave as that termed *pride*. Not all sin is of the "Promethean" kind, the hubris that is a "perversion of human pride." Instead, there is much in sin that is simply sluggishness, mediocrity, banality, inertia. This kind of sin can be termed *sloth*. The church has largely ignored it. "In Protestantism, and perhaps in Western Christianity generally, there is a temptation to overlook this aspect of the matter and to underestimate its importance." This is a serious mistake, because this form of sin is equally virulent and equally distances one from God. Just "because sin in its form as sloth seems to have the nature of a vacuum, a mere failure to act, this does not mean that it is a milder or weaker or less potent type of sin than it is in its active form as pride. Even as sloth, sin is plainly disobedience."[22] In other words, no matter how different the forms appear, sin is a refusal or an ignoring of the reality and claims of God.

There is another way to sin without pride, which is less recognized but typical. Rather than making the effort or taking the risk to be a true self, one shrinks from the task. In the process, the self is lost. It is lost by "being entirely finitized, by having become, instead of a self, a number, just one man more." The world hardly ever notices this loss because one is no longer a hindrance, one has "adjusted," one is "ground smooth as a pebble." One may be praised and honored for this accommodation. But we were not meant for it. Rather, each of us is meant to be a "self before God," to have a self for which one "could venture everything."[23] Equally problematic, one can reject one's true self, wish not to be a self at all, or wish to be a different self. This can come in a variety of ways. One may live largely in the moment. One may succumb passively to outside pressures. One may despair over one's own weakness. Or one may turn away from inwardness, hoping the problem of self-loss will vanish. In the end, one loses the eternal along with the self. This form of despair, this "weakness," is common in the world.[24]

Unfortunately, this sin has been stereotyped as the "womanly" variant, though elements of each form of sin are present in the other, that is, there is weakness in defiance, and defiance in weakness.[25] Sensuality has both self-idolatry and self-loss in it.[26] It may be tempting to accede to the gender categorizations of this otherwise helpful presentation. It seems to take the respective problems of men and women seriously, according distinctive types of sin to each. However, it is accompanied by numerous difficulties. A person's response to victimization, coerced self-loss, and survival-oriented coping are wrongly interpreted as outright sin. Women and oppressed groups are thus blamed for acquiescing to self-loss, when the response is actually *han*. Stereotypical sin behavior is then expected from the respective genders. This hides the fact that sin, although universal, is also complex and particular to each individual.

It is misleading to call this complex of God-avoiding behaviors "sensuality." I prefer to call this sin problem "inordinate self-loss." Calling the reverse side of pride "sensuality" is too limited a presentation of the problem.[27] The connotations are too closely tied to the physical. This makes gender stereotyping (and its linking of woman with body/materiality and man with spirit/rationality) a logical extension of the schema. In addition, it can give the impression that ascetic practices and sheer self-denial are inherently moral. Calling this sin "weakness" denies its gravity and makes genuine human weakness seem deliberately perverse. Sin as "sloth" is somewhat more useful. Our problems today often spring from interior emptiness, trivialization, and internal chaos, all due to the lack of a true center. Our problematic self-absorption comes more from this internal impoverishment than from an obstinate elevation of a grandiose self. Disabusing persons of "grandiosity," then, can work counterproductively when it does not understand this source of modern narcissism. Intensive, internal self-examination will be frustrating and fruitless without a careful guided integration of a true center in God.

Yet none of these terms is completely adequate. None depicts well how one can lose oneself in relationships. I label the anxiety that provokes this aspect of the sin of self-loss "the panic of disconnection." The fear of being unconnected can prompt acquiescence to, inordinate immersion in, or premature acceptance of inappropriate relationship, especially relationship that tends toward the disorienting, the idolatrous. Although this can happen for both sexes, it is a particularly confusing problem for women, who are socialized to value relationship and interdependence. Yet these values are both appropriate and desperately needed in our world. Therefore, it takes careful thought to discern when one is losing self inappropriately, failing to be God-oriented, and when one is rightly appreciating human interdependence. Our age is concerned with this problem. Contemporary self-help literature that deals with enmeshed or destructive relationships is especially popular. The codependency schema, for example, discusses how persons root their identities outside themselves or give themselves over to another person to avoid self-identity. However, this schema does not allow enough conceptual room for determining proper and positive interdependence.[28]

Nevertheless, these various perspectives on sin show us that sin is multi-faceted. Including the "sin of self-loss" broadens our understanding of the range of human alienation. "Self-will run riot" is by far not the only way to turn from God. In our day it may be the less common way. Identifying the core human problem as inordinate self-will or pride obscures crucial distinctions. It can reinforce and even inadvertently praise the "sin of self-loss." It can fail to identify actual coercion, *han*, and victimization. When one's core problem is truly a turning from God, a disorientation from our proper source, this can come about through inordinate self-loss as much as through inordinate self-will. Even these two generalized states are more complex, nuanced, and less easily identified than is commonly understood.

ADDICTION FROM A THEOLOGICAL PERSPECTIVE

By now we see it is difficult to fit addiction neatly into a theological framework. First, in spite of some overlap, there is a fundamental difference in the terms. Sin is primarily a religious concept, and addiction is primarily therapeutic. Groups such as Alcoholics Anonymous have tried to steer a middle course, borrowing from both the theological and the therapeutic worlds. Religiously oriented writers have tried to analogize the two terms. These efforts are often well-intentioned, but from a theological perspective they are inherently flawed. For the terms are, in the strictest sense, categorically different. This is not to say they are opposites, for that is the error of false dichotomization. Rather, they come out of different epistemological frameworks and ultimately express different worldviews. Therefore, trying to analogize sin and addiction, or using the concept of addiction to replace sin, inevitably leads to problems.

Second, the very concept of addiction is itself a construct—and a relatively recent one—used to group an increasing number of disparate problematic behaviors. This has succeeded as well as it has largely because of the "the triumph of the therapeutic" in modern thinking.[29] The therapeutic paradigm homogenizes very different categories of human problems. It also skews them toward the psychological explanation. In the end "the triumph of the therapeutic rests on a conflation of various forms or dimensions of human misery. Misery as ontological insecurity and anxiety in the face of the threatening contingencies of life, misery in the form of mental disorder or psychopathology, and misery in the form of human evil all turn out to be one thing."[30]

Addiction is a construct which, in some measure, has been made possible by this conflation. This does not totally invalidate our use of it, but it does provide a different angle on the matter. The broader perspective urges caution before either writing off the sin dimension in addiction or too quickly equating them. Third, while the modern category of addiction is untenably broad, common understandings of sin are distorted and narrow. This is another reason why persons get boxed into a corner on the topic. But now, having broadened out again the concept of sin, the problem appears even more difficult. It is not a simple matter of seeing addiction as a useful analogy for sin or seeing them as polar opposites.

How can one distinguish what is primarily biological habituation, psychopathology, or genetic factors in the problem behaviors today called addiction? How can one differentiate these from what is fundamentally a turning from God? At one level, this is not necessary. For at its most basic, sin is universal. All creation—including our bodies—are affected by corruption. All human beings are inclined to turn away from the true Absolute to false absolutizations. All of us acquiesce too easily in the banality and lure of evil. All of us sell ourselves into bondage in one form or another.

Still, if the term addiction continues to cover a wide range of compulsive or habituated destructive activity, theology must address it further. Addiction can come about for many different reasons. Knowing how one gets in is a help in getting out. Sometimes, addiction may begin relatively spontaneously, when inherent vulnerability inadvertently encounters problematic substance. Therefore, although the numbers are probably small, addiction for some persons can be quite close to natural evil or inherited corruption. It can be a biological predisposition or vulnerability that is unexplained, yet powerful.

Other cases of addiction may begin as a pre-sin response to, or attempted muting of, the human predicament. One may seek to avoid tension, to adjust one's emotions, or to mute negative stimulation in addiction. This "distraction" can develop its own dynamic, progressive character. Ultimately, it can evolve into a bondage that is biological, as well as psychological and spiritual. Addiction can also manifest itself as, or accompany, a psychopathological response to finitude, insecurity, anguish, human victimization, or abuse. The sources of such addictions are not actual sin in themselves (except as they represent one's being sinned against), but they can lead to sin.

Nevertheless, it is problematic to focus on personal sin when addressing people who have clearly been victimized, such as through domestic violence or child abuse. Great care must be taken, even if out of their victimization they have used addictive behaviors as an escape or coping device. This point, although obvious, cannot be repeated too often. Sin is still an entirely relevant and useful concept, but in such cases, a focus on being sinned against is crucial. The systemic nature of evil should be stressed, the way it both lures and traps us, especially in relation to domestic violence:

> Evil and sin, though inseparable, are to be stressed differently in varying contexts. When one is speaking of perpetrators, sin, individual responsibility, and accountability should be stressed. If, on the contrary, one stresses evil or the coresponsibility of the perpetrator, he is allowed to escape his responsibility. When one is speaking of and to victims, evil should be stressed. If one stresses sinfulness to them, they are encouraged to continue in their feelings of self-blame and over-responsibility. In neither case should the companion concept be forgotten (for it is as freeing to men to learn that they are tempted by evil structures as it is for women to learn that they are responsible in part for the direction of their lives), but it should not be primary.[31]

Therefore, though sin is universal, not every situation is one of equal responsibility. In dealing with addictive behavior, it is important to understand as many of the surrounding factors as possible. It is helpful to realize that although there is equality of sin (sin is universal), there is inequality of guilt. "Guilt is distinguished from sin in that it represents the objective and historical consequences of sin, for which the sinner must be held responsible."[32] Likewise, true victimization must be acknowledged. This religious perspective challenges a psychological systems theory that would hold all parties equally responsible. (This is perhaps a distant echo of the doctrine of universal sin.) Biblical religion clearly claims that those who have more power have more responsibility, and often more opportunity for wrongdoing.

The topic of sin can never be completely shelved, however. In the end, how one responds to one's vulnerability determines one's orientation toward or away from God. Even if the original conditions or sources of addictive behavior were outside our direct control, our responses can become a manifestation of sin. This happens when the compulsive behavior assumes the quality of ultimacy. It happens when one cooperates with it by allowing it increasingly to rule one's life, when one consents as it blocks one from the source of being, and when one acquiesces as it destructively turns one away from others rather than toward them. Thus, even if addiction originates in ways we would consider pre-sin, it can easily move into a destructive and disoriented response to the human predicament, that is, sin.

Addiction also can be more directly a sinful reaction to human anxiety. In this, it can be manifested as inordinate self-seeking, controlling, self-aggrandizement, taking power, "self-will run riot." Though addiction is bondage, it can be adopted as a false absolutization that appears to promise security, power, and control. This is what is meant in the addiction field by the "paradox of control."[33] Yet sin has a much wider range than that. Not all sin, just like not all addiction, springs from inordinate self-will. Addiction can just as easily be an inordinate giving up of the self.

> Does the drunkard or the glutton merely press self-love to the limit and lose all control over himself by his effort to gratify a particular physical desire so unreservedly that its gratification comes in conflict with other desires? Or is lack of moderation an effort to escape from the self? . . . Is sensuality, in other words, a form of idolatry which makes the self god; or is it an alternative idolatry in which the self, conscious of the inadequacy of its self-worship, seeks escape by finding some other god?[34]

Still, this form of sin need not be always an immersion in the sensual factors of life. It can instead be a giving up in the face of life itself. Refusal to be a self under and oriented to God can manifest itself as a compulsive or habituated "giving over." This can be as much to a person, group, or ideology as to a substance. It is a serious temptation. Becoming a self under God can put one uncomfortably at odds with the world's wishes. Even when self-loss is coerced or survival oriented, one eventually must acknowledge some measure of choice in mental and spiritual assent.

Addiction can be sin when it springs from these false orientations. It can be sin when it is primarily a refusal to orient self and will to God. It can be sin when it is disloyalty to the source of one's being, acquiescing to rather than resisting one's own destruction, or simply wasting life in trivial pursuits. Even when addiction eventually takes on a biological life of its own, it may well have begun in a turning from God. It can come when we run from the constitutive anxiety of existence. It can come when we refuse to become a self, just as much as when we annex others in order to posit ourself, rather than God, as the source of meaning, power, or good. All sin is ultimately ignoring or turning away from God, a disinclination to be centered in the only Absolute. It is a false absolutization or idolatry of something that cannot bear this weight. Or it is a "giving up" to something that does not deserve this gift. To the extent that addiction begins from this state, leads to it, or contributes to it, it overlaps with sin. Yet, from the start, we are all conditioned into this state. We often have less choice than we would like to have. And so many of our choices, from early on, become part of our being. The more we sin, the more we turn away from grace, the easier and more "natural" it becomes.

In the end, trying to decide where addiction belongs is little different from trying to decide where other problematic human behaviors fit theologically. It cannot be known definitively whether the root of any particular human problem is more in original or actual sin. That is, whether the problem is more a result of inherited corruption and the influence of evil or more from individual inclination and disorientation. In fact, things invariably get mixed up. One may see freedom where there is really bondage, and bondage where there is really freedom. It is helpful to contemplate this when pondering both sin and addiction. For "there is . . . less freedom in the actual sin and more responsibility for the bias toward sin (original sin) than moralistic interpretations can understand." [35] The hidden danger in the addiction-recovery schema is similar to the more overt danger in religion. Both can turn moralistic.

In the end, it is not possible to classify all the forms of and reasons for addiction into discrete theological categories. One cannot decide whether any particular addiction is primarily pre- or post-sin, primarily original or actual sin, primarily physical corruption or disordered will. It can be affirmed, however, that addiction can be linked with the theological categories of evil (including "natural," nonmoral, and radical evil) and sin. These categories encompass much more than the compulsive behavior we label addiction, and all problems within them do not always resemble addiction. Nevertheless, addiction is not a condition that is outside these areas. Whether the problem behavior generically called addiction begins biologically, psychologically, or pathologically, inadvertently or willfully, it is a state that increasingly works to separate us from our true source, God. It may in fact represent many different conditions with a variety of sources, but none of them are benign or value-neutral. Determining whether, or to what extent, addiction is sin will always be a difficult task. It will be particular to each case, ultimately determined within one's own heart, before God and with the help of others.

It is enough of a starting place to know that sin is disorder, disorientation, disinclination. It is enough to know that God intends integrity, order, and right orientation for us. And it is crucial to know that God fully appreciates our situation and has already taken all the steps necessary to return us to wholeness and divine companionship. In the end, this quandary—deciding whether addiction is sin—comes primarily from confusion over, distortions of, and increasing ignorance of sin. It comes also from confusion over and misuse of the term *addiction*. A vacuum has been left by the functional demise of theological categories. As a result, the term *addiction* has been used too widely, too loosely, too easily. It cannot perform this impossible task.

A disservice has been done to human complexity and to the resourcefulness and intricacy of God's grace. Experientially, we may have been awakened by the problem. Intellectually, too, the problem of sin often needs to be analyzed thoroughly in order to arouse and recognize a thirst for grace. But from a theological perspective, beginning with the problem is starting at the wrong end of the equation. A prolonged focus on the problem, whether addiction or sin, causes the solution to be slighted. Additionally, too much anxiety is provoked, for we tend to believe we must find the solution ourselves. But God's grace is a seeking thing. It finds us.

THE SIN-VERSUS-ADDICTION DICHOTOMY

The relationship between sin and addiction is complex. They are neither synonymous, sharply different, nor totally unrelated. In my experience, the greatest handicap to discussing this complexity is the frequent dichotomizing of the sin and addiction concepts. Some perspective to this entrenched dichotomy is needed. When the dichotomy operates, the terms *sin* and *addiction* are stereotyped. On the surface, this seems convenient, for common images are often useful and readily understood. These images promise an efficient way to categorize problem behavior. They promise to help in determining whether a particular behavior is deliberate (stereotyped as "badness"), or out-of-control (stereotyped as "sickness"). They suggest we can then decide whether compassion, correction, or censure is the best approach.

Yet these shorthand images in many ways are deeply counterproductive for both sides. In the dichotomy between sin and addiction, sin is falsely represented in a narrow, distorted, moralistic, and thoroughly voluntarist mode. Willpower and choice become its essence. It is truly a "brittle and emaciated" view of sin.[36] Addiction is not treated much better. It is narrowly presented as a purely physiological, uncaused, and determinist condition. Victimization and lack of responsibility prevail. Even though the sin-versus-addiction dichotomy today helps attract persons to the recovery movement, these stereotypes of sin and addiction do a serious disservice to *both* positions. Fortunately, however, "we are saved from our own folly only by our inconsistency."[37] In other words, the addiction construct is allowed to be more nuanced and less dichotomous than popular slogans imply. Unfortunately, relevant theological constructs do not always receive the same opportunity to show their range and depth.

Problematic Understandings of Sin

Four current understandings of sin work against the elaboration of the concept's depth. It is useful to summarize them here, although they have been broached earlier.

First, sin is often viewed largely from a voluntarist perspective. Here the freedom with which sin begins is heightened and expanded to undue proportions. This is a misfocus on the formal capacity of will. This impasse frequently diverts conversation as people try to determine the extent of their powerlessness, or lack of free choice, in particular cases. The problem is, we do not begin in pristine freedom. And our choices over time have a cumulative, formative, and hardening effect. We become, eventually, thoroughly conditioned by the sum total of our choices, actions, and reactions.

Second, it is problematic to understand sin primarily as a moral rather than a religious category. When taken as a moral category, virtue is made the key to our relationship with God rather than faith. This leaves us with a distorted understanding of salvation, for sin is then defined moralistically, as wrong behavior, rather than as a disorientation and a turning away from God. Behavior considered good or moral may be an indication of a God-ward orientation, but it can also deceive. God looks at the heart— faith and trust are harder to observe but more indicative of orientation.

Third, there is a widespread but erroneous impression that sin is limited to self-aggrandizement, overweening pride, god-playing. Instead, sin is a much more complex, nuanced, and hard-to-discern condition. It is worked out in ways particular to a given individual, though certain defining characteristics can be suggested. Sin can be as much about inordinate self-loss as about inordinate self-will.

Fourth, and finally, a distorted understanding of sin leaves us in a quandary over issues of weakness, radical evil, and victimization. We sometimes too easily interpret them as personal sin but other times excuse wrongdoing because of them. Without guidance in these areas, almost anything that tangentially touches on or promises to deal with these conditions will gain an eager, needy audience. The church, in its lack of confidence and silence, often leaves a vacuum here. The recovery movement is to be praised for facing the issues, and this helps account for its popularity. Yet a deeper understanding of available theological resources is needed to clarify these difficult issues in productive ways.

Other Issues Behind the Dichotomy

Stereotypes of sin and addiction also tap into other long-discussed dichotomies that predate the recovery movement. These include sin versus sickness, mind versus body, and free will versus determinism. Tendrils from each of these dichotomies reach down into the sin-versus-addiction debate. These complicated issues get confused and conflated in contemporary discussion. Sin versus addiction is immediately ancillary to a larger sin-versus-sickness dichotomy. The terms of this either/or construct encourage people to evaluate a given problem based on whether it is willfully self-caused or physically rooted. Sin again is set on the side of will, and disease on the side of physiology. This connects to another popular distinction, that between mind and body. This distinction continues to be made even though increasingly we learn how interwoven these aspects of humanness are. These three related dichotomies play on a similar theme.

> The assumption is made that problems are caused either by the body or the mind, and certain connotations follow. Problems caused by the body are considered "real" and beyond the control of the individual. Something is to be done *to* the body so the person can be made more comfortable. On the other hand, problems caused by the mind tend to be seen as "imaginary" and as under the control of the individual. This being the case, continued difficulty is deemed the consequence of moral failure or weakness, and the individual is often regarded as blameworthy.[38]

The sin-versus-sickness dichotomy has larger repercussions than the limited purview of the recovery movement. It has often hampered pastoral care as pastors and counselors fear appearing judgmental or harsh if they use the terms *sin* and *repentance*. The resulting silence hampers pastoral work since these basic terms are as integral to Christian theological discourse as salvation and healing. It has also made secular psychotherapy less useful for religious clients. Many such clients need to talk about specific moral values and religious standards, even if some pathology has rendered their judgment personally harmful. Their legitimate faith issues can become seriously hindered, rendered silent, or categorized according to pathology. When the sickness theory focuses on mental states, it poses difficult problems for the above fields. It is also troublesome for the legal system, requiring us to decide if persons are "mad or bad."[39]

These dichotomies in some ways stand for and shorthandedly recapitulate a version of two older arguments. The first examines the interplay between free will and determinism. How much do human beings willingly and consciously direct their choices? How much is predetermined by previous causes, whether natural or social?[40] This ancient argument is itself a variation on a theological argument between free will and determination by God. How can human freedom to choose for or against God coexist alongside a God who is all-powerful, all-knowing, with a divine plan for electing individuals to salvation? Both arguments pivot around the issue of choice. The addiction debate repeats the same problem in its insistence that addicts have *no* free choice in relation to their problem substance or process. The argument claims that addicts are powerless to resist the psychological lure, related environmental cues, their own cravings, and internal physiological mechanisms that impel repeated usage.

This conceptual echoing of the older arguments is done unconsciously and unclearly. Some needed perspective is gained by realizing that the powerful influence of the long-pondered prior arguments reaches forward into the current sin-versus-addiction debate. Here is another example of a religious tune continuing to echo in the collective memory. As long as the tune remains as background music, it cannot be wisely evaluated. Without recognition of its structure, roots, or import, its richness cannot inform current understandings and practices. A few relevant points from the older arguments will illuminate a discussion of sin and grace as they relate to addiction.

One way to resolve the dilemma over free will and determinism suggests that freedom exists primarily on the spiritual plane, outside the reach of the determinist laws of nature that operate on the body. Alcoholics Anonymous and related groups echo a similar settlement by insisting that someone may forever be subject to the vulnerability of addictive disease, yet free to turn his or her life and will over to God. This solution has problems, for it falls short of a holistic approach to humanness. Although "body, mind, and spirit" are convenient categorizations, they are artificial separations of an interwoven unity.

The complicated theological argument behind this positing of two different levels of freedom moves well beyond the purview of the addiction-recovery issue. Particularly in its predestination version, it deals primarily with issues of eternal salvation and only secondarily with problems in living such as addiction. The spiritual freedom to respond to God's grace, conform oneself to God's plan, or choose for God may activate the freedom to cope with problems in living. But it can neither be equated with that nor done primarily for that reason. Otherwise, our proper orientation is reversed, and God is largely made an adjunct to our own needs or goals. In any case, history itself has shown over centuries of debate that these issues can never be resolved if perennially fixed as either/or propositions. Yet this is exactly the impasse in which the sin-versus-addiction dichotomy leaves us.[41]

This impasse reveals a misunderstanding of the theological meaning of "freedom." The concept of sin cannot simply be equated with the "free will" (or "mind") side in any of the above dichotomies. It is true that Christianity emphasizes the freedom of human beings. In their freedom, human beings both image God and are also allowed to relate to God freely. There is no divine compulsion in our choice for or against God. But freedom in Christian theology is not about formal or arbitrary freedom of choice. On the mundane level, freedom to act, make decisions, and choose remains, whether one is trapped in sin or increasingly lured by grace. Freedom is not about the formal freedom of choice but about one's ability to conform more closely to a divine standard for well-being. As Edward Farley states:

> In the classical tradition freedom is a comprehensive symbol for the telos of human beings and for their capacity to move toward that telos. Freedom is the power by which agents are able to actualize themselves toward their well-being. If that well-being is defined by such idealities as honesty, knowledge, and love, freedom means the power to realize these things. Its absence is the absence of that power. Thus, freedom is not the formal capacity of choosing but that about the agent that shapes desire and sets its direction.[42]

This is more an ontological issue than one of choice. It has everything to do with our orientation toward God, and God's reaching out to us with grace. The gift comes first. However, our orientation and status changes when we acknowledge and receive this gift. A process of spiritual growth begins. Spiritual maturation does bring greater freedom, but it is experienced as a greater ability to choose the good. One becomes both better able and more willing to conform to the divine pattern for human life, pictured most fully in the life and mission of Jesus Christ. Although Christianity maintains that sin is at some level freely chosen, this choice is often presented as a kind of "voluntary necessity." That is, although the agent cannot, without grace, resist the lure of evil, he or she also willingly goes after it. Sin begins in a kind of freedom, but ultimately sin destroys freedom rather than epitomizing it. Therefore, the doctrine of sin, in all its variations, has presented a subtle argument that contains elements of both free will and a sort of determinism. To pose the human dilemma as sin versus addiction overlooks this nuanced position.

Part 2

FROM THE ALCOHOLIC TO THE HUMAN PREDICAMENT

4

THE THEOLOGICAL ROOTS
OF ALCOHOLICS ANONYMOUS
IN THE OXFORD GROUP

The Oxford Group was an independent evangelistic religious movement that arose in the early 1900s, flourished for several decades, and then
declined. Although it achieved considerable popularity for a time, it was a
minority voice in American society, reviving an older approach to sin and
conversion. In part, the Oxford Group was a reaction against the social
gospel and other liberal emphases in mainline churches. Echoing the late
nineteenth century, it privatized morality, seeing private behavior, rather
than the public good, as the proper focus for revival efforts. Sights were
narrowed by focusing on personal rather than societal concerns. In this, it
functioned for many people as a temporary refuge from the overwhelming
social, political, and economic problems of the day. Many also found it to
be spiritually invigorating, but the Oxford Group made little permanent
mark on society. Unlike more liberal Christians who considered systemic
social issues, this group located the entire problem of human existence in
personal sinfulness, the entire solution in individual conviction, confession, and surrender.

The Oxford Group was founded by Frank Buchman, an ordained
Lutheran minister. Unimpressive-looking but possessing a powerful, mag-
netic personality, Buchman was raised in central Pennsylvania and given a
conservative German Lutheran upbringing and schooling. After a formative conversion experience at a Keswick convention in England, he minis-
tered in various ways—running a residential settlement house in Philadelphia, YMCA collegiate evangelist at Penn State, and sometime lecturer in
evangelism at Hartford Seminary. Eventually, he struck out on his own in
a ministry of personal evangelism and gathered a group of young people
around him. First called the First Century Christian Fellowship, it soon became known as the Oxford Group because of the considerable time spent
ministering at that university.[1]

Buchman stressed theological simplicity and showed little interest
in the intellectual life. He summed up the group's philosophy in just a
few central concepts: All people are sinners, all sinners can be changed,

confession is prerequisite to change, the changed can access God directly, miracles are again possible, and the changed must change others. Groupers, as they were called, said this was just basic Christianity; the difference, they claimed, was that they were putting it into practice. AA's roots in the evangelistic Oxford Group thus had a distinct theological perspective. Both practices and principles from this evangelistic conversion-oriented group undergird the AA approach. Especially at the level of spirituality, the Oxford Group contributed much to early Alcoholics Anonymous.

Both founders of Alcoholics Anonymous were Oxford Group members. Bill Wilson was active for several years, having sustained, pivotal, and formative contact. His first exposure came when he was approached by former drinking buddy Ebby T., who had become sober through the group. Wilson subsequently responded to an altar call at Calvary Episcopal Church and Mission in New York, headquarters of the American branch of the Oxford Group. Calvary Church was led by an American Oxford Group leader and Episcopal priest, Samuel M. Shoemaker. Wilson was in many ways formed by this experience. Even after leaving the group he remained in contact with Shoemaker for years, and at AA's twentieth anniversary, he invited the priest to give a major address.

AA co-founder Dr. Robert Smith was an active Grouper well before meeting Wilson. Just months after Wilson's experience at the group-influenced Calvary Mission, Wilson was on a business trip to Ohio. Tempted to enter the hotel bar, he desperately phoned clergy, hoping they could locate an alcoholic for him to talk with, since he knew helping someone else would keep him sober. One pastor put Wilson into contact with Henrietta Seiberling. This wealthy and prominent woman introduced him to fellow Groupers Anne and Robert Smith. Although Bob Smith had been a member of the Oxford Group for some years, his struggles with alcohol had continued. But Wilson and Smith found that talking together helped them both, and he was invited for a lengthy stay. Through this partnership, Alcoholics Anonymous eventually emerged. From Bob and Anne Smith and his own membership, Wilson absorbed much of the group's philosophy.

It is not necessary to document the full extent of the Oxford Group's influence on Alcoholics Anonymous, or to prove AA's implicit theological orthodoxy.[2] The two movements do not need to be exhaustively compared, nor does one need to claim a rigid lineage from the Oxford Group to Alcoholics Anonymous. However, some striking commonalities between the two emerge when an impressionistic drawing of the Oxford Group is given. It becomes clear that, in both method and concept, there is a strong linkage.

THE NEGLECT OF THE OXFORD GROUP CONNECTION

In spite of its significant influence on Alcoholics Anonymous, the Oxford Group connection is frequently downplayed. In most studies of Alcoholics Anonymous, the topic is passed over quickly. Even less are the theological connections between Alcoholics Anonymous and the Oxford Group seriously discussed. AA literature occasionally mentions the Oxford Group, and studies of the Oxford Group sometimes briefly refer to Alcoholics Anonymous. But few studies compare the two groups in a detailed way. Those who do see connections stress the common practical methods rather than the common theological principles. Not many current AA members are aware of the theological contribution of the Oxford Group, and even among those aware of its early history there is a marked hesitancy to claim much from the Oxford Group connection.[3]

Yet "to leave out the Oxford Group is like saying that the Ford Motor Company began in 1927 with the Model A," one man who attended Oxford Group meetings with Bill Wilson insists.

> The two people who really gave Wilson and Smith their tools were Frank Buchman, the founder of the Oxford Group [O.G.] . . . and . . . Samuel Shoemaker. The latter was Bill Wilson's spiritual mentor, and Bill always referred to him as his chief source. It was from the O.G. that Wilson and Smith discovered the life-changing mechanisms they brilliantly codified into the Twelve Steps and marketed for the benefit of millions.[4]

There are many reasons for the routine popular and scholarly minimization of AA's Oxford Group roots. For one thing, even in its heyday the Oxford Group was a throwback to an earlier time. Although they achieved substantial popularity in the early twentieth century, Groupers were well aware that they were swimming against the tide, especially in their focus on sin. By echoing a previous century's focus on individual sin and conversion,[5] the Oxford Group was dealing with an unpopular issue. One Group writer noted in 1933 that to many people "the very word [sin] is out of date; it smacks of street-corner salvation meetings; they think only people who are behind the times believe in Sin these days. In their conversations it is seldom used, except, perhaps, to raise a laugh."[6]

Additionally, the church was always ambivalent about the Oxford Group. Some church leaders contended that the group was beneficial, even within its admittedly limited range, since it revitalized dormant religious and moral impulses. Some suggested it was simply a new form of American revivalism and could be used either disastrously or productively by the churches. But criticism was also implicit and grew over time. Some church leaders insisted the Oxford Group was naive and simplistic, a head-in-the-sand, bourgeois, individualist approach to monumental problems that needed more extensive and social solutions.[7] By the 1930s—the time Alcoholics Anonymous split away—the group's evangelistic thrust had fallen into public disfavor, associated in the public mind with a revivalist Protestantism that many mainstream Protestants and most Roman Catholics rejected. The Oxford Group began to be ridiculed in popular plays and books.[8]

With the onset of World War II, important figures like Reinhold Niebuhr protested the Oxford Group vehemently, especially when founder Frank Buchman was reported in a New York paper as having personally endorsed Adolf Hitler.[9] Protest grew after the Oxford Group underwent a name change in 1938, becoming Moral Re-Armament, and its style became less religious and more political.[10] AA's departure was only one part of the public distancing as the group fell from favor and lost respect. This negative view of the Oxford Group has remained, even though recent scholarship credits Moral Re-Armament with helping promote international dialogue after World War II, especially its little-known contribution to Franco-German reconciliation.[11]

As the years between the Oxford Group and Alcoholics Anonymous grew, Wilson himself—in a move followed by many proponents today—began to place more emphasis on the reasons for splitting from the Oxford Group and less on what had been gained. Wilson did note his indebtedness to the group when, in looking back on AA's history, he said that many key principles of early Alcoholics Anonymous came "straight from the Oxford Groups."[12] Yet when he summed up the connections, he largely detailed the group's elements that had not worked well for compulsive drinkers, rather than more positive borrowings.

There are also some less apparent reasons for a contemporary distancing from the Oxford Group. It appears there was long an informal division between the New York and Ohio strains of Alcoholics Anonymous. The New York Alcoholics Anonymous officially disassociated itself from the Oxford Group (1937) before the Akron members did (1939). Unofficially, the Akron group maintained their loyalty to the Oxford Group a little longer. This difference proved a problem for years. Fear of raising old internal controversies may still cause some members to hesitate to discuss the group's roots.[13]

There are also some contemporary reasons why the Oxford Group connection is played down. Many AA supporters like to stress its wide appeal. Highlighting the evangelistic Oxford Group roots would detract from AA's self-conscious tolerance of divergent religious and nonreligious views. Admitting a strong connection with the religious Oxford Group would challenge the more scientific mien of present-day Alcoholics

Anonymous. Even when AA's spirituality is highlighted, it seems politic to minimize the clearly evangelical Protestant Oxford Group. Stress instead is placed on more "generic" spiritual influences and impulses.[14] Roman Catholic roots are sometimes mentioned.[15] These are the more acceptable routes, since these influences are not associated with an evangelism popularly considered outdated, oppressive, and narrow.

Recognized or not, the Oxford Group influence lives on. An Oxford Group understanding of the human condition—including a strong view of sin—is evident in Wilson's formulation of the alcoholic's dilemma and program of recovery. While many disparate elements have gotten mixed into the addiction-recovery ethos along with the Oxford Group roots, nevertheless its ideas still provide a theological base from which to formulate a generic version of the human predicament. And the influence of the Oxford Group's methods of evangelism can still be detected in certain key practices of Alcoholics Anonymous and related recovery groups.

METHODS AND PRACTICES:
SOME COMPARISONS

Although the key concepts held by the Oxford Group were traditional, the methods and the language were deliberately contemporary. Groupers refrained from heavily theological language, used small groups instead of tent meetings, "interviews" instead of altar calls, elaborate entertainments rather than frontier frugalities. In the previous century, frontier revivalists had moved out into remote areas, hastily setting up temporary tent communities to which farmers traveled sometimes great distances; the Oxford Group brought its message to the cities, hosting "house parties" in the homes of the wealthy or in hotels and resorts. Frontier revivalists, including the Dwight Moody and Billy Sunday versions, used dramatic sermons and altar calls to make converts; the Oxford Group worked instead through small-group sharing and personal confession. Unlike other forms of evangelism, the Oxford Group appealed specifically to the wealthy and the powerful, using personal referral, the targeting of specific individuals, and publicity about prominent converts. This caused it to be caricatured as a "Salvation Army for snobs."[16] Yet both the nineteenth-century revivalists and the Oxford Group were interested in awakening a sense of sin. They wanted to prompt a desire for conversion and get listeners to turn their lives over to God.

At the group house parties, to which many came by personal invitation, the emphasis was put on committed participants sharing stories of "being changed." Intimate concern for and knowledge of newcomers were fostered. Intense conversations were held about personal issues, the need to confess and redress sins. People were exhorted to allow God to fully direct their lives. Increasingly they began to produce showy plays and musical productions that drove home their points. Some observers said they were never left alone, either during "house parties" or at their various headquarters, and complained that the hearty goodwill and positive attitude could be overwhelming. Others found it persuasive and uplifting, making them want what the others clearly had. Large and appealing claims were made. As one scholar remarks, " 'It Works!' was a phrase most frequently heard in the testimonials and endorsements of the Group program and practices." Once a person was changed, it was expected that "problems of every sort must melt away and disappear."[17] For Groupers a joyful "glowing face" was seen as evidence of change, for they now knew "the secret of real happiness on earth. . . . In fact, they have become sane."[18]

Some of AA's practices are similar. Meetings, which take place in clubs or borrowed rooms, are marked by informality, friendliness, and ease of movement. Although courts sometimes mandate AA attendance today, membership historically has grown through personal invitation and attraction. Intense personal conversations before and after meetings, intimate concern, and the willingness to tackle any issue is something newcomers often find attractive. The group tells members, "Keep coming back. It works." Members look for the "AA twinkle" in the eye as evidence of a restoration to sanity.

A key method of the Oxford Group movement was to intrigue the imagination before appealing to the will. To that end nearly every gathering featured the personal stories of individuals, formerly beset by intractable sins, who had become "changed" through submitting to Christ. Buchman took the power of personal relationship very seriously. He and his leaders would sometimes strategically arrange seating at dinners. A Grouper who had overcome a problem such as drunkenness would sit alongside a newcomer known to have the same difficulty. At other times, Groupers would be sent out to confront, through the sharing of stories, a notorious troublemaker at a school or university. Personal narratives of changed lives, rather than didactic or theological reflection, made up a significant part of influential group lore and literature.[19]

Early Alcoholics Anonymous, too, practiced this method extensively, and many people witness to the continued importance of this aspect. Today members sometimes lament at meetings that treatment centers, interventions—planned and staged surprise confrontations of a presumed addict by a group of significant people (spouse, employer, therapist, family members, friends) in his or her life—and other professional methods have greatly reduced the opportunity for this essential "Twelfth Step work." In this, alcoholics are actively sought and told about the program if they show any willingness to listen. Ideally, recovering alcoholics do this work themselves. Narratives of personal change are persuasive today too, forming a foundational component of Alcoholics Anonymous and other addiction-recovery groups. The Big Book is more than half narrative, and at the frequent "lead meetings" a designated member will share his or her personal journey to sobriety. At other types of recovery meetings, personal stories are often the most acceptable form of comment.

Both groups also have focused attention on alcohol abuse. Although the Oxford Group looked at a panoply of problem behavior, compulsive drinking was an issue they tackled frequently. Penn State was a rough heavy-drinking school when Buchman arrived as a YMCA collegiate evangelist. One of Buchman's first and most notorious converts was campus bootlegger and heavy drinker Bill Pickle (Galliland). He became a staunch supporter of Buchman throughout his life, even forming a successful Saturday night worship meeting for other former bootleggers, with Buchman presiding.[20] Heavy drinking was a central part of campus life in both America and Britain. Thus the Oxford Group had many other opportunities to see if their method worked with that problem. Sources indicate that many compulsive drinkers did reform, and the Oxford Group soon adopted a policy of no alcohol or smoking at many functions and sites. Indeed, the story of the reformed drunkard was one standard in the repertoire of highly publicized Oxford Group conversion narratives.[21] This background is intriguing. It raises some questions about traditional AA lore that founder Bill Wilson left the Oxford Group partly because the group decried Wilson's focus on alcoholics as a largely fruitless or inefficient effort.[22] Given the sweeping claims and perfectionistic expectations of the Oxford Group, it is hard to imagine them giving up on any type of problem. Indeed, this would have called into question their whole premise that God could change virtually anyone who was willing to admit defeat and surrender self-will.

The Oxford Group prided itself on being available at any time to help the troubled. Group literature assured readers that no one had ever sunk too far for their efforts. They insisted that only a simple wish to change was necessary for the work to begin:

> Witnesses will go anywhere at any time to help any one whose life has become a burden of Sin, and will stand by until that person has been set free from trouble and brought to a true understanding of Christ and life. No soul has sunk too far, no case for spiritual cure can go beyond their scope. The knowledge that we are in need and have a need for change in our lives is all that is necessary for these life changes to work on.[23]

That will sound familiar to those who know Alcoholics Anonymous, for the Big Book says, "No one is too discredited or has sunk too low to be welcomed cordially—if he means business."[24] Additionally, for the Oxford Group the motivation to continue this work was not simply out of concern for others. Buchman said, "The best way to keep an experience of Christ is to pass it on."[25] Similarly, AA members are convinced that helping others is essential to maintain their own sobriety.

Those who became "changed" by Oxford Group efforts were incorporated into small local groups. These would meet frequently for prayer, for quiet times in which God's guidance was solicited, and for further evangelistic activity. Still, the organization of the group was loose: no rolls were kept, no creed formulated, and no financial pledges requested; there were no formal regulations, and no clergy/lay distinctions. This lack of formal organization, so unlike the mainstream church, was a matter of pride for Groupers. An insider wrote, "They are not an organization. None can tell their number. For in their own words, 'You can't join; you can't resign; you are either in or out by the quality of the life you live.' "[26] Individuals could participate as they liked, admitting as much or as little group influence as they chose.[27] Alcoholics Anonymous, too, incorporates individuals through small local meetings. It prides itself on noncoercive organization, studious refusal to keep rolls, lack of dues or fees, and its only creed, "Take what you like and leave the rest."

The Oxford Group presented itself as a movement continually sensitive to the prompting of the Holy Spirit. Most workers volunteered, giving up jobs and leaving family to devote their lives to Buchman's vision. Although money was rarely overtly solicited, donations were often considerable. The group possessed various international headquarters, sent large teams and stage productions all over the world, and supported hundreds of workers. Small-group intimacy, openness, and expectation of forgiveness and tolerance was key to the success of the Oxford Group. Still, members insisted this was not an easy life. Striving to live by the "Four Absolutes" (honesty, purity, unselfishness, love), they said, was a lifelong moment-by-moment endeavor, requiring much discipline and self-sacrifice. Individuals frequently felt led to make confessions of sin to a small-group or larger public gathering. The emphasis would be on the change that had taken place or was expected as a result. The group assumed that restitution would be made where possible. Even so, families could be fractured when the enthusiasm was not shared by all.

Similarly, small-group intimacy is the pride of the AA recovery movement. Members take daily problems to the group, where a sympathetic and accepting audience is assumed. Nevertheless, AA members insist that truly "working the program" is a demanding task. Slips and faults are confessed and day-to-day guidance sought through the group spirit. Amends are expected where possible, yet relatives and friends report that families can be divided when one member becomes devoted to the program and others are not similarly enthusiastic.

Oxford Group workers had to be ready to shoulder huge tasks and travel at a moment's notice. Buchman was a demanding leader, willing to point to areas of weakness in his workers when he thought it necessary. Although he never claimed to be perfect, his followers seemed to trust that his God-listening skills were more acute than theirs. While he did delegate monumental tasks to his close subordinates, he kept a firm hand on the work and was deferred to on most issues, including matters personal to workers' lives. All this made for a rigorous and self-sacrificial lifestyle. Yet apparently it was also frequently a pleasant one. The tasks were clearly defined and geared to ability. Pains were taken to make each person feel valued. Many young men learned leadership skills. The women, however, seemingly by design, were "cumbered with much serving." This was a considerable burden, considering the size of the groups hosted and the high quality of meals and accommodations.[28] For all, though, there was frequent edifying entertainment, lavish meals, beautiful surroundings, committed companions, and interesting and important guests.

Through his long ministry, Buchman traveled extensively and sent out large teams throughout the world. In addition, at various times he had headquarters in Caux, Switzerland; London; New York; and Mackinac Island, Michigan. Because of this, he was personally aware of international difficulties through the turbulent 1930s, 1940s and 1950s. Nevertheless, he was consistent in his focus on individual sin. In spite of world conditions, the Oxford Group's focus of morality remained privatized. The group continued largely to direct its efforts to the "up and outers," the elites of society. Over time, it had increasing contact with governmental and union leaders around the world, but it did not directly challenge their political views or institutional financial practices. Instead, it focused on their personal morality.

Buchman believed that all change happens from the individual outward. The fact that his message thus did not directly challenge the status quo probably increased its popularity with the wealthy and the well-to-do. Although in the early days the group did not consciously intend to be reactionary, this was the inevitable effect of their methods and underlying theological presuppositions. Even their claim to eschew theology added to this effect. When the Oxford Group became, in the late 1930s, Moral Re-Armament, this tendency became overt and solidified. This was especially so as the group became identified with a simplistic anticommunism during the Cold War.

Alcoholics Anonymous, too, has become a worldwide institution, facilitated by keeping its focus on alcohol problems and personal issues. In the present-day Alcoholics Anonymous, one hears strong support for the individualist approach. One student insisted in class, "All change must start from inside me." At a conference, a member had a typical reply when I asked why Alcoholics Anonymous does not specifically work to change the conditions that contribute to addiction: "There are some two million people in recovery. Don't tell me that all those happy marriages, intact families, and sober individuals don't have an effect on society."[29] Alcoholics Anonymous has gained an amazing amount of acceptance in society by narrowing its focus to one behavioral area. Its principles are often used in treatment centers, in drug education programs for public schools, and in many support groups. Its message can be heard from sports heroes and talk show guests. The corporate world does not hesitate to refer troubled employees or even require them to join the program. An AA-style ethos finds replication in recovery groups spanning the liberal-conservative church spectrum. It is often a matter of pride that this influence is not limited to any one social stratum.

OXFORD GROUP BELIEFS
RELEVANT TO ALCOHOLICS ANONYMOUS

Sin and Conversion

Theologically, there was nothing especially novel about Buchman's message. Although some of his speeches were eventually collected, Buchman never wrote for publication.[30] His influence was spread largely through personal contact, word of mouth, and group practices. Buchman was largely uninterested in theology, even suspicious of it, seeing it as another potential roadblock to the "changed" life. Intellectual doubts were considered sins. Groupers refrained from theological argument with prospects and professed to be uninterested in the person's religious beliefs.[31]

Walter Houston Clark notes several main roots of the Oxford Group's ideas: conservative Lutheran pietism, the Keswick movement, and American collegiate evangelism. Lutheran pietism contributed a lay character, with its focus on the priesthood of all believers, a pragmatism that shifted focus to conduct, feelings, and will at the expense of intellect, and a shunning of religious controversy. This form of pietism also promoted a moral perfectionism and an ascetic revulsion against worldliness. It focused on awakening one's recognition of individual sin to the point of despair, a process which was believed to open the way to regeneration. The relevant influence of Keswick was its strong focus on the abandonment of sin, surrender to God, and appropriation of God's power to live the transformed life. American collegiate evangelism was influential especially at the level of method, with its religious meetings, personal evangelism, and personalized approach.[32] Some of these elements carried over to Alcoholics Anonymous, particularly the lay character, pragmatism, and the asceticism of total abstinence.

While the Oxford Group attitude toward theology made it easier for persons of differing beliefs to participate together, it was also an indication of the group's anti-intellectual bent. Far from opposing specific doctrines of the church, members often considered theology a "waste of time for a 'changed' person."[33] A similar tendency can often be found today in various recovery groups, when questioning and debating are dismissed as "intellectualizing." Nevertheless, the group did consistently maintain a few key ideas, especially the insistence that individual sin was the key problem. They claimed to be "modern" and did not want to alienate "pagans" with revivalist language. Therefore, prospects were often referred to as "patients" rather than as sinners.[34] Other medical terminology was used as well, such as "soul surgery" for rooting out sin and the goal of making a "spiritual diagnosis."[35] Though sin was frequently likened to disease, the underlying focus was not biology but morality. Although Alcoholics Anonymous gained an early warrant for disease language from the Oxford Group, it broadened the diagnosis. For early Alcoholics Anonymous, alcoholism was understood to be a spiritual illness and a psychological one, but also very much a physical one as well.

The Oxford Group taught and practiced a form of ethical and religious perfectionism that could be reduced to a call for renewed morality. There was nothing more here, Buchman said, than what you had learned "at your mother's knee." Nevertheless, the perfectionist impulse was not entirely human-based, for submission to God was understood to give a power that undergirded subsequent and successful human effort. Groupers were directed to live in absolute honesty, absolute purity, absolute unselfishness, and absolute love. The four requirements for attaining these absolutes were sharing (including confession and witness), surrendering to God, making restitution, and following divine guidance. Guidance was to be obtained each morning, optimally during a "quiet time" in which the Grouper waited, pencil ready, to record God's directives. Buchman read from the Bible, quoted it, and exhorted others to do likewise. But direct guidance from God held revelatory importance. To listen and to follow required a complete surrender of the will to Christ. Only sin prevented this.

Sin, according to Buchman, was anything that stood between the individual and God. Sin was deadly because it frustrated God's plan for oneself and for others. Selfishness or self-centeredness was key, but also included were such things as greed, hate, fear, and personal shortcomings. In a style typical to the movement, a writer explains, "In the 'I' in the word Sin . . . lies the secret of Sin's power. The 'I', or the ego, is more important to sinners than spiritual health; all we do contrary to Christ's teaching is traceable to it. If we can surrender that 'I' to God, Sin goes with it; when we live without that 'I' in our lives we are without Sin."[36] In effect, however, sin was not primarily offense against God, sin was primarily against the self. Sin was misguided behavior with consequences that kept one from operating optimally, to the fulfillment of one's God-directed potential. The Oxford Group believed that individuals knew their sins; the challenge was getting them to admit them and to realize that sin was the cause of every difficulty.[37]

Alcoholics Anonymous—and, derivatively, the modern addiction-recovery movement—is similar. It understands addiction as primarily a violation of the self. It insists that addicts struggle with "denial," although that term was not used in the Big Book. In this and other respects, Alcoholics Anonymous adopts, in a generic way, the Oxford Group sin concept. This is key to understanding its program and the metaphor of addiction. But AA's particular stress on powerlessness is a distinctive change of focus from the Oxford Group. Alcoholics Anonymous began by scaling back the group view; it did not see the will as powerless over sin in general but powerless primarily over alcohol. Bill Wilson learned from a doctor that "in alcoholics the will is amazingly weakened when it comes to combating liquor, though it often remains strong in other respects."[38]

Over time, however, this theme expanded with the growth of the addiction-recovery movement. It began to be used to encompass more problem behavior and more aspects of a person's life, moving back closer to an Oxford Group understanding. However, the bondage of addictive disease is understood as something that cannot be cured, only controlled. This is a major departure from the Oxford Group, which stressed the possibility of complete victory over sin. They expected much from God and from themselves. The Oxford Group did not take sin's power and bondage so seriously that some problems could be considered intractable. In the group, more weight was given to human capacity, either to deliberately block God's intentions or to submit and let God rule. If the latter course was followed, complete change would take place in the person's life.

The strong focus on individual sin made the Oxford Group quite apolitical at its outset. This apolitical stance changed only when it became Moral Re-Armament in 1938. Nevertheless, the key theme remained throughout the group's history. Groupers continued to hold that even the largest societal problems did not ultimately lie in socioeconomic conditions or institutions, much less in some form of systemic or radical evil. As one writer insisted, "Individual self-interest is the causation of world sin,"[39] and Buchman contended in a 1936 transatlantic broadcast from London that social "collapse is simply the selfishness of all of us together."[40] Groupers believed that to criticize social institutions was futile, " if not a way of dodging one's prime social responsibility, which was to surrender oneself to God."[41] Individuals had to be changed one by one. All problems were ultimately rooted in individual sin, or a fault in the human nature, and individuals were taught to hold themselves personally accountable. For the Oxford Group, the solution came as individuals cooperated with the Holy Spirit to rectify the fault.

The Oxford Group's general principle that individual sin is the font of all evil had conceptual and practical limitations. Nevertheless, it came to life through the charisma of Buchman and his trained leaders. Especially as the group turned more political after the late 1930s, their "modus operandi in conflict resolution was . . . to engender a heightened spiritual sensitivity in both parties and to thereby induce them to enter into a genuine and deep dialog marked by a reciprocal sense of moral obligation."[42] On its own, however—divorced from the personal abilities of Buchman, the carefully crafted and extremely conducive environment, and the dedication of large blocks of resources and time—the principle was ineffective in its extreme privatization of morality in a way that largely left the public realm untouched.

From the start, Alcoholics Anonymous also has studiously avoided political connections or opinions on outside issues, remaining focused on the particular illness it wishes to treat. I have heard members staunchly claim that the only person one can change is oneself, and that even if one desires wider change it must start from changed individuals. During the Gulf War, one member of Al-Anon, an offshoot group for families and friends of alcoholics, lamented how depressed her friend was over the political situation. "It's a shame that he's so upset about it. He can't change a thing. This is something he's powerless over. He can only change himself."[43]

For the Oxford Group, the conversion process was expected to happen in stages. There is disagreement whether the "five 'Cs' of the Oxford Group—confidence, conviction, confession, conversion, and continuance—were subsequently enlarged upon by Wilson to become the famous Twelve Steps."[44] However, both groups take a processive approach to spirituality. For the Oxford Group, it was more a self-initiated and group-aided process of submission than a reliance on the already accomplished work of Christ.

The group conversion process was often spurred by specific pressure on prospects. They were prompted to locate and repent of their personal failings, even if this should lead to a condition of extreme anxiety and guilt consciousness. This trauma was expected to dissipate when the individual turned his or her life over to God. But the pressure continued. Changed individuals were to practice recurring submittals of the will to God. Groupers pursued "God control" as the chief and ultimate goal. Only this would make the attainment of the four absolutes possible. Mutual and sometimes public confession aided in this. However, the sins confessed tended not to be of the cataclysmic variety but more relational, family-based, or about petty crimes. Alcoholics Anonymous and some related recovery groups practice a similar spiritual dynamic. In Alcoholics Anonymous, problems may be more or less serious but all are believed to respond to the same spiritual approach. No matter what the issue, individuals are often urged to admit powerlessness, to "let go" of problems, to "detach," and to give themselves or their difficulties up to God.

Unlike the Oxford Group, Wilson was very careful to warn against pressure of any kind, since he had found that alcoholics could not take it. However, contemporary modifications and uses of Twelve Step methods are sometimes more directive. Here Alcoholics Anonymous is appropriated in ways contrary to its original intentions. Courts can mandate attendance and require attendees to receive a signature after the meeting, testifying to the court that they have been present. In the therapeutic field, "interventions" can be planned by families and professionals to impel troubled persons to get help. Treatment centers often include meetings as a required part of residency. And, as one Hazelden addiction-treatment counselor admitted to me, many clients enter residential treatment "with a foot in their back."[45] Although this is not in the original spirit of AA, members are gained today through these methods.

The Oxford Group did not have an explicit position on gender relations. Sin was considered a universal condition, not subject to specific distinctions based on gender, race, or class. Nevertheless, Buchman's approach to women reveals that, in concert with the times, traditional attitudes toward gender predominated. Males functioned as core leaders, though occasionally an especially prominent, talented, or wealthy woman would assume a central role; additionally, women often provided material resources. Although Buchman never married, many marital difficulties came to his attention as he worked with guests and helpers. In keeping with movement objectives, he and other trained leaders would help marriage partners discover and confess their particular sins. Anecdotes show that he ascribed to women such stereotypical "sins" as domination, excessive talking, and frivolity. Again, individual sin, evidenced in her as selfishness and self-centeredness, was considered the cause.[46] Nevertheless, at least one source indicates that mutual submission to God was offered as the solution to both husbands and wives. Although each was treated as equally a sinner, neither was expected to "submerge" their personality for the other.[47]

Early Alcoholics Anonymous, too, was a male-dominated movement. Some writers now claim this is an inherent conceptual deficiency.[48] Recent AA publications and other recovery literature have considered the particular issues that addicted women face. Nevertheless, the reigning perspective is that the phenomenon of addiction is univocal. Even a feminist perspective does not often question the dominant metaphor of addiction. As one writer says, a feminist perspective "in no way negates the disease model, nor is it in opposition to a 12-step recovery approach."[49] This is similar to the Oxford Group's understanding of sin as universal.

Yet, as with the Oxford Group, this does not prevent men and women in Alcoholics Anonymous from often being treated according to gendered social roles. It is noteworthy that the cluster of AA-related groups was originally structured as a family system. Alcoholics Anonymous functioned largely as a place for alcoholic men, Al-Anon for their wives, and Alateen for older children. This has become more complex today, with more women in Alcoholics Anonymous, some men in Al-Anon, and meetings of ACOA—adult children of alcoholics—for both genders.[50] Nevertheless, lingering gender stereotypes can be found. In one church where I attended meetings regularly, Alcoholics Anonymous and Al-Anon shared the facility, meeting simultaneously on different floors. Child care was provided for all members, but it proved a perennial source of conflict. Many AA men, often either divorced without custody, single, or married without child-care duties, balked at sharing the responsibility for the babysitting service. Many Al-Anon members who were mothers could not come unless there was child care. They would take turns working in the center. However, they felt it was unfair that this general service for both meetings was not equally staffed by AA members. Eventually the situation stalemated, child care was ended, and many mothers had to discontinue their Al-Anon attendance.

God, Christ, Church

Views regarding God, Christ, and church were implicit in Oxford Group teachings. Inevitably, they also were communicated, however roughly sketched they might be. For the Oxford Group, God communicates primarily with and through individuals. This God is intent on explicitly guiding the minutest of human activity and, although loving, is frustrated by human shortcomings and autonomy. Christ, closely linked with God and Spirit in a rudimentary trinity, is the one to whom a believer submits the will totally. He serves as key role model and is always near. Christ's atonement is a central reality and is efficacious. It cannot be understood, writers insist, but it does break the bondage of sin.[51] Nevertheless, individual submission of the will is more important than reliance on the accomplished work of Christ. Increasingly, Buchman was prepared to sidestep or bracket Christology if he felt his hearers would be attracted by a more generic spirituality.[52]

AA spirituality begins where Buchman increasingly moved. It is generic, with no mention of Christ. Yet AA's hope that human bondage can be broken or controlled is derived from the Oxford Group version, with its earlier explicit faith in Christ's work. If Wilson maintained a place for Christ's work in his own religious understanding, he did not consider it useful to carry this over to the AA program. AA spirituality, several steps removed from its Oxford Group roots, retains the conversion dynamic and hope without its foundation.

The Oxford Group understanding of the church was undeveloped and has to be largely inferred from group practices. Members may have sometimes been encouraged—or at least not discouraged—to participate in their respective religious traditions. In this, the group could be seen as a complement to the church, "a bridge between the religious organizations and a secularizing society."[53] Buchman consciously addressed pastors and sometimes sought the approval of the wider church. However, though he was an ordained minister, he apparently did not participate in denominational activities or submit himself to its authority. Apparently he did not attend or officiate in a local church on any kind of regular basis. Samuel Shoemaker, in breaking with the Oxford Group, claimed that group members only attended church when it would make the desired impression.[54]

Underneath this nominal relationship was a negative judgmental attitude toward the institutional church, similar to many sectarian approaches. The Oxford Group saw the church as moribund compared with itself. It was not unusual for younger members to "decry the Church, because, while, as they said, they had been brought up to attend church, the Church had done nothing for them."[55] Clark finds a "contempt, poorly concealed, for the more conventional type of religion practiced in the churches," noting that, although Buchman contended he only sought to revive the churches, "an implicit hostility" was often present in the movement.[56]

The Oxford Group did not model the "church universal," that is, the communal, historical, and connectional aspect of Christianity. Mutual accountability was maintained only within its own ranks. Their concern for the mission and integrity of the church at large seems to have been limited to changing individuals according to group standards. They desired to appeal to a wide variety of people and, later, to work with persons outside Christianity.[57] The group's shunning of much religious terminology and theological reflection was explained as a way to make them more effective with "pagans." Their implicit judgment of the church was combined with the sense of persecution that out-groups often adopt. One writer, for example, noted that the Oxford Group would always be "reviled and persecuted [by] material anti-Christs and intellectual Pharisees."[58] This attitude probably contributed to their isolation from other church bodies. In the end, their neglect of an explicit understanding of and responsibility toward the wider church left them in a weakened position; they had no inherent connection with or built-in support from any outside groups. This worsened as Buchman aged and he became less able to function as the center of the movement.

Similarly, AA and recovery-group members often exhibit an ambivalent attitude toward religion. This is not officially pronounced, and it can vary with the geographical, social, and ethnic context. But as with the Oxford Group, the potential is structurally built in. AA's careful shunning of outside organizational ties, and the assertion that those outside "the rooms" cannot help alcoholics nearly as well, can foster this. Early Alcoholics Anonymous sought to remain on cordial terms with the church, yet it also distanced itself. Although members are still sometimes counseled to return to their religious traditions when a deeper spirituality is needed, the opposite can also happen. As with the Oxford Group, persons can become more deeply attached to their support group. Unlike the Oxford Group, however, Alcoholics Anonymous makes no claim to revive the churches. Members explain that Alcoholics Anonymous is "spiritual but not religious" and Wilson claimed that it was only a "spiritual kindergarten."[59] Yet many Christian writers and church leaders have looked to Alcoholics Anonymous for spiritual revitalization. This is ironic when members often claim to have found their "true church" or religious home in the recovery group.

Many Oxford Group members had come from religious backgrounds. They often used the group experience as an ethical and spiritual vitalization. The lack of theological depth was thus buffered by the fact that many persons came with a storehouse of knowledge that only needed to be put into action. Active participation in the group was often short-lived. The most successful cases, and often the best leaders, were those who had come from religious homes. Many of them left the group to take up teaching, religious, or other altruistic work. Some churchgoers were inspired by group practices yet felt "something more" was needed. These people sometimes turned back to the devotional and sacramental aspects of church life, which eventually led them to reject certain group principles.

Nevertheless, some rejoiced that through the group's efforts they had experienced a "real season of recovery and renewal," which fitted them better for Christian service.[60] Theologian Emil Brunner, who had some group experience, claimed he knew many who had "only found their way back to the Church through the Group."[61]

The contemporary support-group phenomenon is different. Far fewer members today come with religious backgrounds, much less with theological knowledge. Without past affiliation, or with only loose connections to organized religion, these people understandably find that the recovery group comes to assume great significance. Additionally, the implicit judgment on the church and the sin-versus-addiction dichotomy work to further distance people from religious affiliation or theological inquiry. In spite of this, some persons who begin a spiritual journey through recovery groups are drawn into local churches to deepen their awakened spirituality. As with the Oxford Group experience, much depends on the receptivity and astuteness of church leaders and their ability to offer the "something more" needed.

THE CONTRIBUTION OF SAMUEL SHOEMAKER

Episcopal priest Samuel Shoemaker was for nearly two decades (mid-1920s to 1941) the main American spokesman for the Oxford Group. He had direct and sustained contact with AA founder Bill Wilson.[62] Having met and been converted through Buchman while in China (1918), Shoemaker became one of Buchman's rising young men. Although he did travel with Buchman from time to time,[63] Shoemaker worked largely from Calvary Episcopal Church and Mission in New York. The priest's busy parish house functioned as the Oxford Group's American headquarters. Much of Shoemaker's theology remained solidly influenced by the group's principles for his entire career.

It was at Calvary and with local groups that AA founder Bill Wilson experienced the Oxford Group. It is unclear how close Shoemaker and Wilson were during his time in New York. However, they remained in contact through the years, even after Wilson's "alcoholic squadron" split off. They strengthened their relationship in the 1940s and 1950s when Shoemaker was called on to lend a religious sanction to the organization.[64] At AA's twentieth anniversary celebration, Shoemaker was invited to share the platform. There Wilson explicitly credited Shoemaker, calling him "one of the great channels, one of the prime sources of influence" for Alcoholics Anonymous.[65]

Unlike Buchman, Shoemaker wrote prolifically, giving explicit attention to theological issues. This was not a professional brand of theological work (in fact, Shoemaker had no seminary degree) but more an "apologetic" or motivational task. Shoemaker was making a deliberate effort to link Oxford Group practices and principles with traditional Christianity. As an evangelical Episcopalian, Shoemaker was solidly committed to the church. Evangelism was his primary focus. In this task, however, he did reflect some of Buchman's anti-intellectualism. Echoing the Oxford Group slogan, "Read men, not books," Shoemaker wrote, "I know how much easier it is to dig at a book than . . . to change a man."[66]

Shoemaker focused on spiritual experience, especially conversion. Like Buchman, he specialized in conducting lengthy private "interviews" on personal spiritual matters. Shoemaker took following God's guidance seriously, as Groupers were taught to do. He preferred small-group work (as he did in his new ministry of Faith at Work, after breaking with the Oxford Group). This close work with individuals, which the group practiced so successfully, was carried over to Alcoholics Anonymous. The idea that each individual should have the opportunity to share feelings and thoughts was to become an essential part of addiction-recovery work.

Similar to Buchman's arrangements with his teams, many of the Calvary church staff members resided in the parish house built during Shoemaker's tenure there. They met together frequently and practiced group guidance. The residence was large enough also to allow long-term visitors for the specific purpose of training. Close contact and sharing were important parts of spiritual formation. The atmosphere was of an "informal permanent conference."[67] Like the Oxford Group, and then Alcoholics Anonymous, Shoemaker emphasized close attention to specific needs and a focus on experience. Similarly, he prompted people to admit their faults and completely surrender self-will to a God of their understanding. The process began and ended with the individual in a circular dynamic that revolved continually around personal difficulties, victories, and personal but "guided" assignments. Addiction-recovery work is similar, whether done through residential treatment, outpatient care, or frequent meeting attendance. It focuses on personal difficulties and programmatically stresses close contact, sharing, and a situation of deliberate but temporary intimacy.

Sin was a primary focus of Shoemaker's thought. True both to Christian tradition and to his Oxford Group roots, he stressed the universality of sin, no matter what one's status or background.[68] Deep fellowship came "from a mutual recognition that sin is sin and Christ is the only Cure, whether one comes from Park Avenue or a park bench, 'whether he's in jail or in Yale.'"[69] Shoemaker understood sin both as inherited condition and as willful choice to turn against God. Like the Oxford Group, he believed sin was anything that separates us from God, but he put additional stress on God's activity. Sin was a "rejection of God's repeated invitations."[70] Shoemaker located almost the entire problem of sin in pride, saying that, although sin was more than pride, this was its core. However, he did not simply equate pride with selfishness. The focus was more God-oriented than Buchman's, with sin as rebellion against the claim of God.[71] Shoemaker stressed conversion as surrender. He prompted people to throw themselves on the mercy of God. Without this, conversion could not happen. This action was expected to elicit God's response. But one's pride must be humbled through confession and restitution.

Alcoholics Anonymous does not use the words *sin* or *conversion*. It does not see the problem of alcoholism as universal but as restricted to a particular group of people. The Big Book hints, however, that this is simply one form of the generic spiritual disease of self-centeredness. The process it advocates is very similar to Shoemaker's. One learns to identify oneself as an alcoholic, take a "searching and fearless" moral inventory, confess one's shortcomings and character defects, and make amends. The humbling of pride is an important part of the process. Additionally, the commonality and social leveling within the limited confines of the recovery group echoes Shoemaker's view that deep fellowship springs from a mutual recognition of sin.

Like the Oxford Group, Shoemaker used colloquial rather than theological language and sometimes relied on medical metaphors and disease language in his treatment of sin. The focus was on morality, not biology, with sin a "moral sickness." Yet for Shoemaker, disease was not something causing total paralysis, helplessness, or bondage.[72] Instead (in an "Arminian" fashion, focusing on human effort), he expected that a self-directed movement of the will was not only possible but necessary in spurring the conversion experience. The human part was to surrender. Only if that were done could God do the rest. "God will do His part in His time if we fulfill ours."[73] The results were great because, true to the Oxford Group, Shoemaker believed a complete break with sin was possible.

Shoemaker and Oxford Group influence on Alcoholics Anonymous is especially evident here. In a modified and delimited form, Alcoholics Anonymous adapted a number of these key themes. Theological language is eschewed when addressing alcoholics, even though alcoholics are said to have a spiritual disease. Surrender is pivotal to the recovery process. The person's willingness is considered essential to start the process. But early Alcoholics Anonymous modified the claim that one could break with sin entirely. Instead, this claim was reduced to a lifetime break with alcohol. Alcoholics Anonymous expects that complete abstinence is not only possible—even if it takes repeated slips to learn the lesson—but essential to survival. Yet it is not a "once-for-all" experience, as with salvation. For Alcoholics Anonymous, the only expectation is that one can maintain sobriety "one day at a time." Some teach that if alcoholism progresses unchecked, there are only two places to end up, the mental institution or the grave. The theme of death can still be heard in many recovery meetings. In "leads" or testimonies and general conversation, members mourn those who slipped away from the program and died, or those who never heard the message in the first place. It would be farfetched to consider this a distant echo of a traditional conversion-prompting theme, "The wages of sin are death," if not for the Oxford Group background of Alcoholics Anonymous.

Shoemaker, like Buchman, was willing to be somewhat unspecific about God. In truly American fashion, he did this for pragmatic reasons, as an apologetic device. The prospective member, particularly one with little religious grounding or profound doubts, would be encouraged to trust as much of God as he could understand. This device was used so that the person could be won experientially first, rather than being put off by dogmatic requirements or complicated theology. Still Shoemaker, more than Buchman, expected content to be added as the person matured in faith. He expected this would have a christological base. Alcoholics Anonymous is similar. It asks only that people start from whatever of God they can accept. It has long been willing to adapt its presentation of God to gain maximum effectiveness with a diversity of people. Whatever Wilson may have believed privately or learned from the Oxford Group, for the purposes of Alcoholics Anonymous he did not follow Shoemaker's christological emphasis. Later, when Shoemaker identified himself as an AA friend, he held less tightly to this doctrinal expectation.[74]

Shoemaker knew that the Oxford Group was criticized for its privatist and quietist attitude toward social problems. Nevertheless, like the Oxford Group, he was suspicious of the social gospel and espoused conservative economics.[75] His early focus on Christ, however, made him believe that the tension was more apparent than real for those in the church. "I do not see how any Christian with a 'social conscience' intends to do without Christ; and I do not see how any disciple of His can fail to want the full blaze of His light to shine in every corner of our corporate life."[76] Shoemaker was sensitive to the mission aspect of Christianity. He was aware of the narrow impression that a singular focus on personal change could give. Nevertheless, he continued the privatization of morality he learned from Buchman, and he did not hesitate to criticize social reformers.

> There is a familiar picture in the minds of social-minded people, of comfortable evangelicals, hugging personal salvation to themselves, living off the sweat of underpaid labour, blind to their own guilt for

social injustice, and fattening their souls for heaven: and that is a terrible picture. But there is another quite as bad, and in this day quite as common: it is the picture of the social liberal or radical, the basis for whose desire to reform society and the world is an inner frustration and maladjustment which can only forget its own sick soul by tinkering with the affairs of people at a distance.[77]

Alcoholics Anonymous, too, focuses on the immediate identified issue of compulsive drinking. It staunchly refuses to be moved into other arenas. From this perspective, it and the recovery movement appear similarly apolitical and privatistic.

In some significant ways, Shoemaker veered from group understandings. His commitment to the church was deeper, and he focused more specifically on Christ. Shoemaker also was bothered by Buchman's increasing authoritarianism, the Oxford Group's political turn, and its diminishing Christology.[78] Shoemaker had a more theologically informed and institutionally connected approach than Buchman. The concept of sin was set within a broader theological base. Although fairly privatist, it was not reduced simply to moralism or focused solely on the individual. Neither was Shoemaker as authoritarian and socially disconnected as the Oxford Group became. When the group began to turn decidedly political in 1941, Shoemaker broke away. Nevertheless, he maintained many group themes and practices throughout his ministry. He was indebted to Buchman and the group for energizing his faith. Shoemaker's version of Oxford Group principles strongly influenced Bill Wilson. And Wilson's worry over excess authority in Alcoholics Anonymous may have been significantly influenced by this concern of Shoemaker's. An examination of the AA description of the alcoholic predicament shows how many theological emphases remain, even if in more generic form.

5

THE BREAK
WITH THE OXFORD GROUP

The temperance movement had struggled for decades to achieve the goal of legal restriction on the production and sale of alcohol. Its culmination in 1920 in the Eighteenth Amendment was a major triumph for American Protestantism. This victory blended the rural and nativist impulses of small-town Protestants with the optimism of the social gospel. From a certain perspective, Prohibition represented a constructive approach to social problems.[1] Since alcohol was considered inevitably addictive, it made sense to remove the temptation. It was recognized that inebriates were already in bondage to alcohol. This could be ameliorated, and further cases prevented, it was thought, if liquor was unavailable. In some ways, the religious attitude was most stern toward moderate drinkers, for they could still choose to avoid temptation. It was sometimes more compassionate toward compulsive drinkers, who were seen as already trapped. Within a short time, however, it became clear that this major social experiment was a failure.

Alcoholics Anonymous began less than two years after the repeal of Prohibition, in 1934, with passage of the Twenty-first Amendment. Though it was formed in the wake of repeal, the early history of the group does not show that it emerged as a specific rejection of the churches' efforts. Neither is there indication that it emerged as a determined flight from religious harshness or the doctrine of sin. It is true that key founder Bill Wilson, never a regular churchgoer, had an eclectic, even aversive, approach to religion.[2] This helps explain why his initial reaction was extremely negative when former drinking buddy Ebby T., amazingly sober, insisted it was religion—through the Oxford Group—that had finally helped him. Although spirituality had never seemed a dominant concern of Wilson's, eventually his compulsive drinking and exhaustion of other resources forced him to seek a similar spiritual awakening. The conceptual underpinnings of this were laid through the message of the evangelistic and moralistic Oxford Group. Since this group had helped Ebby T., he directed Wilson to it. Wilson's experience with the Oxford Group was formative; it was much more than just a helpful way station in his quest for sobriety. His spiritual awakening was to prove long-lasting and pivotal, providing a dominant ethos for his subsequent approach to alcoholism.[3]

Yet Wilson's and the other early AA members'[4] tenure with the Oxford Group lasted only a few years. In 1937 the "alcoholic squadron" officially broke with the Oxford Group, and Alcoholics Anonymous was on its own. Since today many make a sharp opposition between sin and addiction, one might surmise the early AAs—although helped at first by the group—eventually left because of the Groupers' focus on sin or its application to alcohol abuse. Investigation of the break does not confirm this assumption. In fact, the thematic of sin and conversion—in modified form—became a major part of the AA method of helping alcoholics.

An examination of the Big Book narratives gives little indication that early Alcoholics Anonymous saw itself as a rejection of religion per se, of the church's approach to alcoholism, or of the doctrine of sin. If this theme had been determinative, something of it would have emerged in the early testimonies of AA members. Given that they had all lived through the Prohibition period, they could not have avoided encountering the temperance ethos and its religious underpinnings. Yet a blanket rejection of this ethos is not evident. Instead, some of the early narratives in the Big Book suggest Prohibition had actually been welcomed at first by some problem drinkers, who hoped it would put an end to their difficulties. Others found ironically that they had become heavy drinkers during this period.[5]

Although the early testimonies were probably carefully chosen and edited—and an effort made not to give offense to potential friends in the churches—there is nevertheless not much hint of members joining Alcoholics Anonymous to protest the current religious approach to alcoholism. No doubt some or many had experienced direct rejection and hostility from the church on account of their drinking. Yet the Big Book does not present this as a key motivation. Although early members were helped by understanding their problem as an illness, no sharp contrast between sin and addiction is set up.

The main claim is that these compulsive drinkers had appealed to doctors, psychiatrists, and sometimes to clergypersons but were disappointed to receive no substantive help with their intractable problem. Of course, this presentation was both politic and circumspect. It presented Alcoholics Anonymous as a unique organization for problem drinkers, without specifically setting it in opposition to the churches or to the medical establishment. Organized religion was very influential at the time. The fledgling group had to worry about such things as Roman Catholic rejection, Protestant-Catholic tensions, and being seen to encroach on sacrosanct domains. They were gathering persons whose problem had previously received concern and solicitude but was now neglected in the wake of Prohibition's failure. They needed allies, not enemies, especially from the historically dominant church and the increasingly important medical profession.

Their attitude toward the church was more than simply politic. Many had had some religious training, but others doubted that organized religion could help.[6] Either way, these early members found their cause championed by some church leaders. First the Oxford Group and Shoemaker and then other clergy and laypersons expressed interest in helping these alcoholics. As historian John Woolverton says, "When medicine and psychiatry fell short of providing immediate, sufficient and large-scale direction to those suffering from alcoholism, Wilson and other AA founders turned to the Christian community for help." For almost a decade, Alcoholics Anonymous was actively undergirded by, and cooperated with, several segments of the church to deal with a common goal—picking up the torch dropped by the failure of Prohibition to deal with alcoholism.[7]

THE BREAK FROM THE OXFORD GROUP

Looking back some twenty years later, Wilson cited several main reasons why early AA members split from the Oxford Group. Alcoholics could not take pressure, he said, particularly "aggressive evangelism." They found "team guidance" too "authoritarian." Also, he said, most alcoholics were not at first interested in personal growth but simply in sobriety. The Oxford Group behavioral absolutes were "too much for the drunks." The idea of absolutes was also rejected because it was publicly identified with the Oxford Group, and early AA members wanted to avoid the connection. In clear contradiction to the Oxford Group, which publicized its conversions, early AA members remained anonymous. This was not just because of the stigma of alcoholism but because the new organization's reputation must be preserved. It seems that Alcoholics Anonymous expected slips and "erratic" behavior from its members.[8]

Nevertheless, many similarities with the Oxford Group process and principles remained. The underlying dynamic that fueled the new language of alcoholism and recovery was remarkably like the ethos of sin and conversion learned from the Oxford Group. Far from protesting this emphasis on sin, conversion, and surrender, early Alcoholics Anonymous carried through these themes in an adapted but consistent manner. Bill Wilson himself explicitly used the word "sin."[9] He and other Oxford Group–trained members of early Alcoholics Anonymous continued their focus on the spiritual aspect in alcoholism. Still, a minority voice had significant influence regarding the use of theological terms. The dynamic remained, but it was stripped of its theological language and underpinnings.

According to AA lore, a few early members wanted no overtones of religion. They struggled both with those who wanted a straight Christian orientation and with the more equivocal Wilson. During his writing of the Big Book of Alcoholics Anonymous, Wilson listened to both sides. He had been deeply affected by the strong spiritual orientation of co-founder Bob Smith, also a Grouper. Nevertheless, Wilson let the minority's caution exert an important influence. Toning down the religious language of the Oxford Group seemed sensible to him, given the goal of reaching as many potential members as possible, whether they were agnostic or, more likely, Roman Catholic. In effect, this toning down extended the process begun by the Oxford Group and carried on by Shoemaker. Although Wilson's conversion and group experience had been pivotal, he was not focused on keeping intact the full theological message inherited from the Oxford Group.

The extent of Wilson's commitment to the Oxford Group message can be debated, as some writers try to claim or disavow the connection between Alcoholics Anonymous and traditional Christianity.[10] But determining the extent of Wilson's conversion is beside the point. No matter what the faith orientation of Wilson or other early AA members, Wilson's actions set a definite direction for the group. From the start, his overriding concern was with reaching people who were alcoholics like himself. Although this drive was supported by Shoemaker, other Groupers decried it. They were determined to deal with the wider range of problems that kept people from God. The narrow focus on alcoholism fell short of their evangelistic goals.

Although much had been borrowed from the Oxford Group, as time went on the debt was increasingly forgotten or minimized. It was no longer politic to identify with the Oxford Group. By AA's twentieth anniversary in 1955, acknowledgment of the Oxford Group connection was greatly reduced, mentioned in just one paragraph of a forty-eight-page essay by Wilson, published in 1957 to commemorate the event. Items borrowed were now limited to "self-examination, acknowledgment of character defects, restitution for harm done, and working with others." Connections with more mainstream religion were instead acknowledged, such as gratitude toward religious-based hospitals and claims that the Twelve Steps were similar to St. Ignatius of Loyola's Spiritual Exercises. Since it was estimated that nearly a third of the members were Roman Catholics by then, the latter was an especially helpful suggestion from AA friend and Jesuit father Ed Dowling.[11]

Several decades later it was to become even less useful for Alcoholics Anonymous and the recovery movement to identify too closely with the

Oxford Group or even with Christianity, as both secularization and religious pluralism progressed in society. The implicit sin and conversion thematic was now widely understood as generically "spiritual but not religious." Wilson had set the tone for this conceptual distancing, saying that the principles brought over from the Oxford Group "were ancient and universal ones, the common property of mankind."[12]

The split and the widening gulf between the Oxford Group and Alcoholics Anonymous reveal both commonalities and differences. The Oxford Group had been quite communal for the sake of its mission. Members supported and admonished one another and listened for divine guidance together. This team guidance or "checking" obviously made an impression on Wilson and the other alcoholics. A similar approach was used in the writing of the Big Book and in other organizational matters, and today recovery groups still pride themselves on their mutuality. However, the "alcoholic squadron" did not accept communal involvement when it conflicted with their own more focused mission. They wanted to be free from the wider evangelistic goals of the Oxford Group in order to focus on reaching individuals with the same drinking problem. Although they rejected team guidance here, they were nevertheless modeling an Oxford Group method. The early group had practiced a similar effort at identification between members and prospects. Thus, early Alcoholics Anonymous retained the "old" or "personal" style of the Oxford Group rather than embrace its new stress on a more political or broader form of evangelism.[13] Bob Smith spoke highly of the fact that fellow Groupers had come forward to share their own sins with him in an effort to identify with his particular compulsivity. This had made him receptive to Wilson's approach.

The Oxford Group's objection to early AA's single-minded focus was directly linked to the group's evangelistic goals.[14] From that perspective, early AA members were reducing their sights to a particular kind of problem and a more limited solution. This was tacitly suggested by Wilson. In reflecting back, he admitted later that he was driven both by ego and concern and that he directly disavowed the evangelism.[15] No doubt the Oxford Group's version of evangelism was in many ways naively optimistic, narrowly conceived, and perfectionistically interpreted. Given AA's successful use of the more focused approach, many have since praised its single-minded emphasis and its genius in working on one particular problem. Nevertheless, the Oxford Group conceived of itself as an outward-facing group, committed to exemplary behavior to create a disciplined team focused on world evangelism. AA and later recovery groups were more content to act as mutual-help programs with limited and more inward goals.

FOCUSING THE THEOLOGICAL LENS

The break is illuminated when viewed more closely from a theological lens. Early AA members did not break away from the Oxford Group because of its sin emphasis. Indeed, the opposite is more accurate. Early Alcoholics Anonymous was actually more focused on sin's hold than the Oxford Group, for the Group emphasized the human potential to break out of sin's bondage. Wilson had found that alcoholism was more intransigent than many realized. He knew that only a spiritual experience could get and keep him sober and that this was only a day-to-day reprieve. It appears that early AA members strongly disagreed with the Oxford Group's optimistic assessment of the potential of the human condition once under God's control. In effect, they also disagreed with the rate at which change could occur, at least regarding alcoholics. True, from the first the Big Book contained stories of transformed lives and offered the hope of great renewal and joyful life if the program was followed, but the illness itself could not be eradicated. The evil that alcohol represented to the vulnerable person could never be completely overcome, even by God. It could only be avoided, scrupulously, one day at a time, with the threat of death or insanity waiting for those who succumbed.

It is possible that earlier in Alcoholics Anonymous—closer in time to its religious roots and living in an era more comfortable with faith talk—members did expect more from recovery than contemporary ones do. Some original sections of the Big Book speak with confidence of members who have the temptation taken away (although this does not allow controlled drinking).[16] Today, however, many current members speak of addiction as a lifelong disability. There is less expectation that recovery is a "maturing out" of alcoholism. One ten-year-sober member told me at a meeting that although he has kept sober for a decade, he still attends regularly. He did not trust himself to challenge a word of the Big Book, he said vehemently, nor did he trust any possible objections from his peers there. He explained, "Everyone in this room is crazy. We're alcoholics." A teenage member echoed, "I have learned here how very sick I really am."[17]

A theological reading of the split between Oxford Group and early Alcoholics Anonymous reveals that sin was not the aspect rejected. It suggests instead that the high expectation for postconversion behavior—rather than the low view of the initial human condition—was what early AA members left behind. In splitting, Alcoholics Anonymous departed from a certain broad, optimistic, and global vision of regeneration and mission. In many ways this fit well with a growing contemporary awareness of intractable human imperfection and a resulting reduction of expectations.

There is a very frank recognition in early AA writings of the fallibility, imperfection, and powerlessness of human abilities in the face of alcohol. Later this pessimism was to be expanded, as addiction came to be seen by some outside Alcoholics Anonymous as a more widespread or even universal human condition than originally recognized.

The Oxford Group, on the contrary, expected that after conviction, conversion, and submission to God, the potential for human regeneration was great—so great, in fact, that they could speak of attaining the four absolutes of honesty, purity, unselfishness, and love. If this was an admittedly difficult goal, at least members felt warranted in aiming for it. Some Oxford Group members rested their optimism squarely on God's initiative. Others, just as likely, focused more on their own abilities as empowered by their God-ward submission. In either case, it was a mind-set that expected miracles and exemplary behavior. The addiction-recovery phenomenon takes a more pessimistic view of human nature. The AA slogan of "progress, not perfection" echoes this divergence from the Oxford Group vision.

Early AA members departed from this optimism because of their view of alcoholics. In a pivotal way, alcoholics were understood to be distinctive. They were believed largely unreachable by medicine, psychiatry, or standard religious methods. Alcoholics were seen as constitutionally unreceptive to the group's forceful conversion techniques, high expectations, and pressure. Although the difference appears simply methodological, it represents a significant theological adjustment. Early AA members did believe that the alcoholic's problem was probably an exacerbation of the human problem, self-centeredness. Also, like the Oxford Group, they aimed for some character "perfection," though they were more guarded in this. (Step Six speaks of being "entirely ready to have God remove all these defects of character.")

Yet their success in treating alcoholics differently suggests an implicit theological adjustment. Where the Oxford Group, like much traditional Christianity, understood all human nature to be distorted by sin, early AA members edged away from this. They did this by separating out one group of individuals because of their alcoholic condition. As a practical strategy, this was successful. However, it has expanded well beyond AA's efforts and intentions. Distinguishing groups of individuals based primarily on a particular vulnerability or status as victim has taken root in the culture. It has eventually become a touchstone for the many derivative recovery groups that began to emerge some forty years later.

This has theological implications that both work against and are indebted to the AA strategy. In an ironic twist, the spreading of the addiction metaphor is bringing back a type of universal explanation for human dysfunction. Today an ever-expanding array of human difficulties is being categorized as forms of addictive disease.[18] Inordinate behavior of any kind is liable to be labeled an addiction. This works against the initial AA understanding. If anything can become an addiction, why should alcoholics see themselves as distinctive? Yet Alcoholics Anonymous has also contributed to the return of a unitary explanation for dysfunction by continuing to see alcoholism as, in some ways, an extreme example of self-centeredness. Outside AA bounds, this has been expanded. Some search for specific addictions in particularly vulnerable persons. Addiction itself is posited as the paradigm of the human predicament. The concept of addiction then assumes metaphorical qualities. It becomes, for many, a functional replacement for the concept of sin. Although both these moves are beyond AA oversight, they have been helped by the AA strategy and its theological implications.

Samuel Shoemaker had actually hoped for something like this. He approved of the AA strategy to restrict its work to alcoholics, but he hoped for more someday. In reflecting back on AA history at its twentieth anniversary, he said, "I think A.A. has been wise to confine its organized activity to alcoholics, but I hope and I believe that we may yet see a wide effect of A.A. on medicine, on psychiatry, on correction, on education, on the ever-present problem of human nature and what we shall do about it, and not least of all on the church itself."[19]

In a way Shoemaker predicted the expansion of an addiction-recovery ethos, although he was not specific about the kind of influence he hoped Alcoholics Anonymous would eventually have. He believed strongly that "AA has derived its inspiration and impetus directly from the insights and beliefs of the church." But he hoped that now the church would learn from Alcoholics Anonymous. "Perhaps the time has come for the church to be reawakened and revitalized by the insights and practices found in A.A. I don't know any fields of human endeavor in which the Twelve Steps are not applicable and helpful." Shoemaker expected the wider influence of Alcoholics Anonymous, even beyond the church. "I believe A.A. may yet have a much wider effect upon the world of our day than it has already had and may contribute greatly to the spiritual awakening which is on the way but which has come none too soon."[20]

This hopefulness on Shoemaker's part should not hide two important factors. First, Shoemaker himself modified his message when it came time to address Alcoholics Anonymous. He moved closer to Alcoholics Anonymous by toning down his specificity about God and by moderating his Christology. But second and more important, there were subtle but significant (although implicit) theological differences between the Oxford Group and Alcoholics Anonymous. This did not come by a rejection of the concept of sin but through a heightening of it. Alcoholics Anonymous was more serious and resigned to the hold of sin, even in its semisecularized form. This cooperated with the AA tendency to delineate a distinct group of individuals as constitutionally different. Alcoholics Anonymous and the Oxford Group strongly disagreed about the human condition and its potentialities. The rupture of early Alcoholics Anonymous from the group suggests this. In the end, AA's implicit view of sin is harsher and more determinative than that held by the Oxford Group and Shoemaker.

This is the case, even though both the Oxford Group and early AA members believed in a transcendent active God, in group support, and in the value of experience over theory. Neither flinched from identifying particular human weaknesses, failings, and sins, and both promoted confession and restitution. Most significant, both agreed that human self-centeredness or self-reliance was the heart of the problem. But instead of the Oxford Group confidence that conversion and regeneration could open the way for God to work miracles, early Alcoholics Anonymous focused more attention on limits. From the human angle, high standards motivated Groupers but drove alcoholics to despair. From the perspective of divine agency, Groupers daily expected God to work miracles. Early AA members desperately wanted change and saw evidence of it, but they had more limited expectations, even from God.

Alcoholics Anonymous was always ready to offer help if a person truly wanted it. Almost everyone was worth the effort (although there was doubt about those "constitutionally incapable of being honest with themselves"[21]). In this, it was similar to the Oxford Group. Yet, for AAs, there would always be certain constraints: on one level the vulnerability to alcohol, but on the broader level the fact of being "not-God." Being "not-God" means one is limited and imperfect.[22] Although an accurate insight, such a focus produces a spirituality that puts a strong emphasis on human finitude and sin. This also can lead to a problematic perceptual merging of finitude *with* sin. This is different from the Oxford Group, which focused more on human potential when infused by grace. Groupers took sin very seriously, but they took grace even more seriously. The difference may seem subtle, but it has important practical implications. For one's dominant focus—whether on potentiality or disability—significantly affects one's outlook, energy, activity, expectations, and goals.

There was another theological factor inherited from the Oxford Group. It was carried further by early Alcoholics Anonymous and has become significant for contemporary practice. The Oxford Group did not found its community life on a vision of the Holy Spirit working historically through the church. It saw itself as set apart, not beholden nor responsible to religious structures. Neither the Oxford Group or, later, Alcoholics Anonymous

> sought firm grounding for community life in classical Christian doc-
> trine or for that matter in scripture itself. "Primitive Christianity" or
> the "First Century Christian Fellowship" remained an idea simply
> stated not closely pursued. . . . Shoemaker, though well-read himself,
> remained consistently anti-intellectual. . . . Buchman for his part needs
> little comment: The fact that he could throw over Christian faith en-
> tirely in the later 30s proves sufficiently the Oxford Group's lack of
> grounding in any vital theological current.

Because of this lack, Alcoholics Anonymous was not given a firm grounding for its own community life, beyond shared vulnerability, mutual
strength, and a vaguely defined hope in God. That this last factor could
emerge at all, however, was a triumph. For Alcoholics Anonymous

> never had a chance to develop a resonant theology because it was
> never offered one. That it did not wholly lose a sense of the *tran-
> scendent* power of God or fold it entirely into an Immanence which
> would become simply the communal mind of the group is to its credit.
> Indeed something of a miracle.[23]

This success story has become influential today. It has brought certain
theological elements full circle. Sin, the universal explanation for the human predicament—as expounded by the Oxford Group and then narrowed by Alcoholics Anonymous—has come back through the expanding
of the addiction diagnosis. Some go so far as to posit that addiction is a
metaphor for the human predicament, that "to be alive is to be addicted,"[24] or that "the phenomenon of alcoholism replicates the essence
of the human condition."[25]

6

HOW THE BIG BOOK
SEES THE ALCOHOLIC PREDICAMENT

The Big Book has been used by hundreds of thousands of people since its publication in 1939. It is usually the first literature a newcomer is given. As the oldest and most foundational description of the AA way, it is the conceptual bedrock of the movement. The importance of the Big Book may seem qualified by certain factors. Freedom of interpretation is considered pivotal in Alcoholics Anonymous. Certain aspects of the Big Book are more influential than others (for instance, the "How it Works" section). Members are told they can be as selective as they want in appropriating AA themes ("Take what you like and leave the rest") and pride themselves on their independence of mind. All of this may make a book, no matter how prototypical, seem optional or tangential.

Yet this apparent lack of normativity is deceptive. For the AA program has distinct themes, easily traceable to the Big Book, that echo continually in meetings and conversations. There is a standard of "good recovery," which has its source in the Big Book. And the Big Book has historical priority. Before meetings evolved as important to the program, the text stood as the prime communicator of the AA ethos. Today this influence continues and has expanded. Key themes from the Big Book, always crucial in Alcoholics Anonymous, now resound in offshoot recovery groups. In spite of the increasing admixture of eclectic elements and tensions, Alcoholics Anonymous strives to maintain the focus of its founders, expressed most fully in the Big Book.

THE NATURE OF THE PROBLEM

Reading the Big Book closely, so persuasive for so many people, is crucial before doing a theological analysis. The Big Book describes the nature of the problem from which alcoholics suffer. This description forms the basis from which responsibility can be determined. It also provides a solution. According to the AA ethos, little progress can be made until the nature of the problem is understood. The problem is presented as very much a physical condition, although it is also seen as psychological and ultimately spiritual. It is not primarily a lack of willpower or deliberate wrongdoing. This is because "real alcoholics" are seen as in some crucial way different from other people.

It Is a Physical Illness

The Big Book makes clear that the alcoholic's problem has at least three facets, the physical, the psychological, and the spiritual. Although ultimately it points to the underlying problem as spiritual, it presents the physical aspect as something especially important to understand. Dr. William D. Silkworth's understanding of "allergy" to alcohol, so persuasive for Wilson and for most AA members ever since, is crucial.[1] The physical nature of the problem affects both body and mind. This assertion is pivotal for the entire phenomenon. Even so, there is not much elaboration about the specifics of the illness. Only a few things are said: for example, that craving is a symptom and that, unlike other illnesses such as cancer, this one gravely affects the many persons involved with the alcoholic.[2] Alcoholism is understood as a progressive illness; one can only "get worse, never better." Even if one stops for as long as twenty-five years, resuming drinking puts one right back where one had been. "Once an alcoholic, always an alcoholic." Additionally, although there is mention of the "poisoning" that comes from overuse[3]; "to be gravely affected one does not necessarily have to drink a long time nor take the quantities some of us have."[4] Nevertheless, the physical origin of the problem—whether it resides in the genes, in faulty role modeling, or in neurology, biochemistry, or some other defect—is never discussed. Instead, it is simply presented both as inherent predilection (in that someone may be a "potential" alcoholic)[5] and as the result of "poisoning."

Although the Big Book does not offer opinions on the physical genesis, it does allude to some behavioral indicators common among alcoholics. "More than most people, the alcoholic leads a double life. He is very much the actor," unwilling to be honest even with well-meaning psychologists.[6] Alcoholics are "undisciplined,"[7] often enthusiasts who "run to extremes" and are handicapped by sensitivity.[8] Yet they are "energetic people . . . they work hard and they play hard."[9] Most important, however, the alcoholic is understood as someone abnormally self-concerned. "Selfishness—self-centeredness! That, we think, is the root of our troubles." Alcoholics are "driven by a hundred forms of fear, self-delusion, self-seeking, and self-pity" and "an extreme example of self-will run riot,"[10] though they usually don't think so.

Real Alcoholics Are Different
from "Normal People"

According to the Big Book, knowledge of one's alcoholic condition, although crucial, is inadequate to prevent the self-destructive behavior.[11] "The delusion that we are like other people has to be smashed."[12] In working with a prospect, "The more hopeless he feels the better."[13] This is a fatal condition, "to drink is to die," and "most chronic alcoholics are doomed." Since the only end is insanity or death, one's dire condition must be kept constantly in mind.[14] There is no permanent cure for the illness, only a "daily reprieve."[15] Alcoholics can never become like normal people; that illusion should be crushed as soon as possible. "Real" alcoholics are presented as constituted so differently that it is as if they were almost a distinct form of human being. Quite simply, alcoholics are "bodily and mentally different from [their] fellows."[16] Because of this—and partly as proof—others can almost never truly reach them, no matter how well-meaning or trained they may be.

Part of the problem, however, is that others, through ignorance, misunderstanding, or ill will, can be judgmental, "holier than thou," lacking a sincere desire to help, having axes to grind, wanting to be paid.[17] Fellow alcoholics would not have such motives, since they would identify with the sufferer. Within the grouping "alcoholic," there is equality. The illness cuts across all socioeconomic lines, and among the rescued there is an "indescribably wonderful" fellowship.[18] Because of their unique status and understanding, alcoholics are given the responsibility to reach out to fellow sufferers. "You can help when no one else can. You can secure their confidence when others fail." An entire chapter is devoted to strategies.[19]

Willpower and Morality Are Not Relevant Issues

Since alcoholics and "normal people" are different, the alcoholic predicament is not an issue of willpower in the usual sense, according to the Big Book. For "the alcoholic reacts differently from normal people," regarding both willpower and common sense.[20] For alcoholics, "that first drink prevents normal functioning of the will."[21] They have "lost the power of choice."[22] Somehow, it is contended, the will has been disabled in relationship to alcohol, though in other regards it may operate properly. Although there can be a strong desire to stop, there is no ability. Just as it is not an issue of willpower, neither is it an issue of morality. "Many of us felt that we had plenty of character. There was a tremendous urge to cease forever. Yet we found it impossible. [There is an] utter inability to leave it alone, no matter how great the necessity or the wish."[23] This, then, is how one can identify a "real alcoholic,"[24] and it also explains the seeming immorality.

The alcoholic is presented as a "Dr. Jekyll and Mr. Hyde" character. Although "he may be one of the finest fellows in the world . . . let him drink for a day, and he frequently becomes disgustingly and even dangerously anti-social."[25] The alcoholic may want to behave morally but, when drinking, simply cannot. They are "often perfectly sensible and well balanced concerning everything except liquor, but in that respect . . . incredibly dishonest and selfish."[26] Wives are especially admonished to realize the distinction, because "in nearly every instance the alcoholic only seems to be unloving and inconsiderate; it is usually because he is warped and sickened that he says and does these appalling things."[27]

THE LOCATION OF RESPONSIBILITY

Once the condition is described—and before a solution can be elaborated—responsibility must be determined. There is a tension in the Big Book between locating responsibility outside and inside the alcoholic. In relationship to these vulnerable people, the substance of alcohol is nearly reified, given an independently threatening and hostile status. Yet the description nevertheless also allows some claiming of personal responsibility. This challenges the contemporary stereotype that flatly contrasts sin and sickness. Where responsibility can be claimed, the primary failing centers on some kind of self-centeredness. Whether from fear or defiance, the alcoholic is judged someone in whom self-will has "run riot."

Alcohol as Foe

To explain this quandary, alcohol takes on a life of its own, possessing almost diabolic power. Alcohol is a "subtle foe"[28] that is "cunning, baffling, powerful."[29] Friends are "mystified," it is said, and alcoholics are "puzzled" at finding themselves drunk again. They cannot explain this inability to leave alcohol alone and to give no apparent thought for the all-too-obvious consequences.[30] It is almost as though the person is caught in a spell or has been driven insane by the substance. "Insanely trivial" excuses are used to justify drinking. The afflicted person's behavior is "absurd and incomprehensible." Yet this insanity is claimed only in relationship to alcohol. For, the writer says, "however intelligent we may have been in other respects, where alcohol has been involved, we have been strangely insane." Finally, when recovery does come, it has often been because alcohol "beat us into a state of reasonableness."[31] Many variations in contemporary practice have grown out of this approach. In one common variation, the illness rather than the substance can become the foe.

One counselor reported to me that a young man in "detox" said he felt impelled to retrieve an item stolen from him, though it would put him back into contact with addicted acquaintances. The counselor told him to ignore the desire. "That's the disease talking to you," she said.[32] I have frequently heard similar statements at addiction-recovery meetings and from my students who have experience in Twelve Step programs.

The Extent of Personal Responsibility

In spite of all this, however, the Big Book also lays a significant amount of responsibility upon the alcoholic. This element, interspersed with explanations of alcohol's power, often moves beyond tension into contradiction. The Big Book claims the alcoholic is nearly held in thrall by the substance, puzzled by lapses, driven insane, wanting to act morally but unable to do so. The alcoholic is someone unaccountably predisposed toward this problem, or at least totally out of control with it after a certain point, yet also held responsible in two ways.

First, the alcoholic is responsible for what may have befallen the family, such as financial difficulties, because of drinking. In addition, if the family is difficult, the alcoholic "did much to make them so."[33] But this is a limited understanding of responsibility and does not deny the powerlessness in or predilection toward alcoholism. It is more like an acknowledgment of the facts. This links with the kind of responsibility talked about in contemporary recovery meetings, where it is common to hear that, although addicted persons are generally not responsible for their illnesses, they are nevertheless expected to "manage" them. A standard analogy is the diabetic who must agree to take insulin.

The Big Book goes further than that. For, second, it sometimes seems to hold the alcoholic responsible for the condition itself. It baldly states that "our problems were of our own making. Bottles were only a symbol."[34] Blaming—even of God—is not appropriate, for "it is clear that we made our own misery. God didn't do it."[35] There is a nagging suggestion that "early in our drinking careers most of us could have stopped drinking." Therefore, those who became alcoholics were "crushed by a self-imposed crisis" that could neither be postponed nor evaded.[36] The root of the problem, according to the Big Book, is the overweening "self-will." Indeed, "any life run on self-will can hardly be a success."[37] But for the alcoholic, even if the self-centeredness stems from fear or over self-reliance, it is an extreme problem.[38] This is the essence of alcoholism as a spiritual disease. For it, the alcoholic must take profound responsibility.

This can be a jarring counternote when contrasted with earlier statements about the power and subtlety of the foe alcohol, the insanity, the powerlessness. Yet the note of responsibility is significant, for it dispels the stereotype that Alcoholics Anonymous promotes irresponsibility under the canopy of a disease model. This occasional accusation from outsiders is most vigorously denied by members.[39] One seminarian is a good example. Raised in pre-Vatican II Catholicism, he had heard much about sin, but as a teenager he rejected it. "I was taught that you're screwed anyway, so you might as well have fun. At 17 I forgot all that God stuff and left the church." Over the years his excessive drinking caused him to lose his successful career and his family. The government also stepped in. First, therapy was required by a social service agency, which otherwise threatened to remove his children, and then he was compelled by the court to enter treatment to avoid a jail sentence. Through this and the requisite attendance at Alcoholics Anonymous, he became convinced he had a disease and must remain forever abstinent. In detailing his history, he convincingly insists that Alcoholics Anonymous taught him, for the first time, to take responsibility. I have heard similar stories, yet there is a limit to the responsibility claimed. Even more than the Oxford Group, the focus on self effectively constrains the range, purview, and goals of addiction recovery. There is no mention of the social systems or cultural forces implicated in individual addiction.

According to Alcoholics Anonymous, laying responsibility elsewhere is inadmissible. In fact, looking for causes is not part of the program. The closest one is allowed to come to a legitimate cause outside the self is through the suggestive near-personification of alcohol. But this is not a generalized "demon rum" or a generic symbol for evil. For alcohol is only an enemy for the "real alcoholic," not for other drinkers. This is unlike the ethos of the temperance movement, which understood the systemic power of alcohol abuse and presented alcohol as inevitably addicting for everyone. In the Big Book, alcohol has become person-specific. Yet despite alcohol's power over the vulnerable, the real problem is seen as spiritual. The truth of the matter is, liquor is but a symptom of the "self-will run riot."[40] Therefore, for the alcoholic caught in this trap, there is only one solution. Complete abstinence from alcohol is necessary on the physical level. Much more important, given the source of the illness, is to turn one's will and life entirely over to God. This is a step only the alcoholic can take, according to the Big Book. The alcoholic must "quit playing God" and be relieved of the "bondage of self." Finally, "self, manifested in various ways, was what had defeated us." Indeed, it was "the flaws in our make-up which caused our failure."[41]

The Status of the Will

According to this schema, the alcoholic's will is to a great extent under personal control. Although it is disabled in regard to alcohol, it is functional in other respects. This is highlighted when the Big Book claims that "those who do not recover are people who cannot or will not completely give themselves to this simple program." There is not much of a way out given here. There are only two categories of alcoholics for whom this program does not work. One type wills not to subscribe to it. They choose to remain in bondage to self and to alcohol. The other type is not able to subscribe. These are "usually men and women who are constitutionally incapable of being honest with themselves." These "unfortunates" have less than an average chance. Yet "they are not at fault; they seem to have been born that way." Nothing can be done. Even those who suffer from "grave emotional and mental disorders" along with alcoholism are better off, the book says, since many such persons "do recover if they have the capacity to be honest."[42] To this day, these hard words are frequently read aloud at the start of many AA meetings.

Therefore, according to the Big Book, the alcoholic must personally turn his or her will over to God. This is the saving moment. For through this action on the alcoholic's part, the will is changed. Where once there was no control regarding alcohol, now there is. By turning one's will over to a power "greater than oneself," a "psychic change" occurs. The "very same person who seemed doomed . . . suddenly finds himself easily able to control his desire for alcohol."[43] Through this action, God's power is allowed in and put to work. There is now "absolute certainty that our Creator has . . . commenced to accomplish those things for us which we could never do by ourselves."[44] A turning over of one's will, then, is the main requirement. Many contemporary members explain that this action often needs to be repeated frequently, whenever a seemingly insoluble problem arises or, more important, whenever self-will reasserts itself.

The Solution and Its Results

Once the problem is understood and responsibility apportioned, a solution must be elaborated. The AA solution requires action primarily by the person but also by God. It involves a rudimentary acknowledgment of a Higher Power, the humbling of pride, and the abdication of self-will. Although the results are life-changing and dramatic, they represent only a "daily reprieve," contingent on specific activities.

The Humbling of Pride

Ancillary to the turning over of one's will, yet facilitating it, are a number of difficult actions. Primarily the process requires a "leveling" or "pocketing" of one's pride. This is done through drawing up a list of one's shortcomings ("Step Four: Made a searching and fearless moral inventory") and then confessing to a trusted person (Step Five). One's entire life story must be told with complete honesty. This is frankly required as a "humbling" process. The Big Book adds a warning. When newcomers have tried to avoid humbling themselves in this way, "almost invariably they got drunk."[45] Beyond these actions, one must "make amends" and "repair the damage" one has caused, wherever that is feasible. This step is necessary even concerning those who may have done worse harm to you, and no matter what the consequences. The preliminary goal is "to put our lives in order." Yet, ultimately, "our real purpose is to fit ourselves to be of maximum service to God and the people about us."[46] Although this sounds like a plan for wider social action, the service is never spelled out. I have noted that in practice it is usually restricted to individual "amends," service to the AA group in particular, some helping of fellow members, and recruitment of others to the program.

The Role of the Higher Power

The Big Book uses *God, Power greater than yourself,* and other such terms interchangeably. Although today many more AA members may not have a religious orientation, even in 1939 there was concern about references to God. The concern seems not so much about offending those of other faiths as about dealing with potential members who are "violently anti-religious" in general. It is asserted that half of the original fellowship "thought [they] were atheists or agnostics." Others had a negative or inadequate idea of God from childhood. Many thought it was weak to depend on God. This helps explain the placating and reasoning tone in the book. Persons are "begged" to lay aside their antagonisms, prejudices, and scepticism, to experiment with the possibility that there is a God and that religion may have some value.[47]

This also helps explain why the concept of God has little overt content, for the goal is simply to win admission that there is something outside oneself that is greater. The use of *Power greater than yourself, Supreme Being, Creative Intelligence,* and other euphemisms emphasizes this. Indeed, persons are counseled to come up with their own idea of God and submit to it. "We did not need to consider another's conception of God. Our own conception, however inadequate, was sufficient to make the approach and to effect a contact with Him." This is not such a far reach, the book implies, because "deep down in every man, woman, and child is the fundamental idea of God . . . faith in some kind of God [is] part of our make-up." These are clearly devices meant to persuade (in theological terms, "apologia"). There are also suggestions that as members progress they might practice the spiritual methods of their own denominations, join a congregation, or "be quick to see where religious people are right."[48]

The role of God in the recovery process is ambiguous. On the one hand, God does not ask any more than simple acknowledgment of the divine existence. For "God does not make too hard terms with those who seek Him."[49] One must simply entertain the possibility that there is a God and then offer whatever of oneself one can. On the other hand, God is the "Director" who wants to be totally in charge of one's life. Indeed, "we are in the world to play the role He assigns." It has been "self-will [which] has blocked you off from him." But there is "no way of entirely getting rid of self without His aid." Therefore, one must "abandon" oneself "utterly to Him." This God is "all powerful," is felt as a "presence," and, if we ask, has the ability to make us kindly, tolerant, serene, less fearful, and, of course, resistant to the lures of alcohol. However, God can only provide these benefits to the extent that we "do as we think He would have us, and humbly rely on Him."[50]

The Role of the Group

Alcoholics Anonymous was not intended originally as a group experience. The Big Book, rather than meetings, was the foundation of the program. Nevertheless, one gets a sense of solidarity through the Big Book. It speaks often of "we" and "our": that is, the shared distinctives regarding the malady, character defects, and sense of being rescued. Yet there is not much explicit theorizing on the status of the group per se. It was not basic to the original program, but it has a functional necessity now. ("You alone can do it, but you can't do it alone.") Although Alcoholics Anonymous has developed into a mutual-help program, the focus has remained on the individual. Should a generalized Twelve Step consciousness (as might spring from a growing proliferation of recovery groups) coalesce into a social movement with goals beyond itself, this might change. For now, it remains a program that promotes personal change.[51] This assertion runs counter to many who stress the community aspect of Alcoholics Anonymous and other recovery groups. In our transient and alienated society, recovery groups do serve an important nurturing and socializing function. However, even the important stress on group cohesion and discipline has an individual focus. The Big Book has always been clear that the goal is to provide Alcoholics Anonymous with maximum effectiveness for recovering and potential members. This can, of course, result in solidarity, warm fellow feeling, and informal personal help between members. The Big Book suggests that such was the case from the outset. Nevertheless, Alcoholics Anonymous and the recovery-group phenomenon are not meant as a social-change movement.

Even less is Alcoholics Anonymous presented as a modern model of the church, though many use it this way today. Tradition Two does insist that the group's ultimate purpose and direction comes from God. But this is different from making primary some acknowledgment of a source in

God, or the community as a creation of God. The Big Book does not show a higher sense of the group as a body with an eschatological goal, mission, or source. It shows no concern with common ontological origin or eternal destiny. Alcoholics Anonymous maintains that the bonds of fellowship consist in the common problem, in shared gratitude for the remedy, and in a desire to transmit the program to other alcoholics. This, however, is understood to be a demanding and time-consuming allegiance. Spouses are admonished not to be jealous of the energy that those who are recovering lavish on group members and prospects. Spouses are urged to join in this work, but to focus on the families since they are not qualified to help the alcoholic.[52]

The Results

Large promises are made in the Big Book. In return for the sacrifice of self-will, as well as alcohol, the program promises alcoholics "a revolutionary change in their way of living and thinking. In the face of collapse and despair, in the face of the total failure of their human resources," it is claimed they find "a new power, peace, happiness, and sense of direction."[53] They have "entered the world of the Spirit," sanity is restored, the desire for liquor is largely gone, they are "neither cocky nor . . . afraid." Additionally, they "will intuitively know how to handle situations which used to baffle" them. Many will find their families and finances restored. Most important, "self-seeking will slip away."[54] They will become less interested in their own "little plans and designs" and more interested in seeing what they can contribute to others.[55] Physically, many have found that, once into recovery, no marks of dissipation remain. They are "miracles of mental health." They "absolutely insist on enjoying life"; they do not "carry the world's troubles on [their] shoulders."[56] They realize that "the age of miracles is still with us."[57] They are "reborn."[58]

Yet all this is but a "daily reprieve." Continuation of the benefits is contingent on not drinking and, most important, on the "maintenance of [one's] spiritual condition."[59] They do not claim to be saints. There is no ultimate goal or destination, no generic version of sanctification at some future point. Rather, they are "willing to grow along spiritual lines." Thus the principles are simply "guides to progress." They "claim spiritual progress rather than spiritual perfection."[60]

COMPARISON TO THE OXFORD GROUP

The Big Book shows practical and theological similarities with the Oxford Group, though they are transmuted and made generic. Although specifically theological terms have been reduced by Alcoholics Anonymous, even further than the Oxford Group had done, there are some significant similarities in the spiritual processes of both groups. While the word *sin* is rarely used in the Big Book, Alcoholics Anonymous has an equivalent concept in its understanding of the alcoholic's dilemma. The alcoholic is presented as having a spiritual illness that in some important ways lies behind the physical illness of alcoholism. The dominance of self is the core problem for both Alcoholics Anonymous and the Oxford Group. Alcoholics Anonymous follows the Oxford Group in using disease language to describe this pathology.

Central both to the "soul surgery" of the Oxford Group and to the recovery process of Alcoholics Anonymous is complete surrender of the self to God. Self-will must forever be given up, replaced by a day-to-day submission to God's will. Both groups do not shy away from pushing members into despair to get them to recognize the lethal nature of their condition. Both groups believe that the will is in many respects functional. If it were not, self-initiated submission could not occur. Both believe that God's power is elicited by one's submission and automatically activated on one's behalf through this action. For both groups, the problem is unitary in nature, although for the Oxford Group it is universal and for Alcoholics Anonymous it is particularly evident in alcoholics. Neither different socioeconomic groups nor the two genders experience the predicament differently. For everyone it is a problem of self-will versus God's will. Self-centeredness or pride is the heart of the blockage. Like the Oxford Group, Alcoholics Anonymous understands women to be just as afflicted by self-centeredness as men.[61] Both groups seek a complete conversion, seeing nothing less as effective.

Both the Oxford Group and Alcoholics Anonymous seek affinity with similarly troubled others to spur identification and prompt the will. Both find the group process spiritually efficacious yet focused primarily on individual's transgressions and maturation. Both promise personal benefits as a prime result of the change. Both send out newly converted individuals to reach others. They do this out of compassion but also because it maintains the member's faith. It is also implicitly done because of the inherent truth claims of the message. This includes rudimentary arguments for the existence of God. Both remain quite individualist by stressing that this evangelistic activity is especially beneficial because it solidifies one's own conversion. Neither group stresses social action, although the Oxford Group eventually moved in that direction without giving up its individualist focus. They both see the individual will at the heart of all change and the only legitimate place to work. Both offer fairly limited definitions of God and God's character. Yet they see a God who is interested in exercising total control over an individual. Both believe this process must begin through the individual's action. Recurring submissions of individual self-will are necessary. Only this can sustain one's reception of God's power. Only this can change individual behavior.

Certain important aspects of this spiritual process, however, have been modified by Alcoholics Anonymous, certain aspects dropped, and a few new elements added. The Oxford Group had been intent on explicitly seeking and receiving direct guidance from God; Alcoholics Anonymous significantly reduces this. Although the Twelve Steps still advocates "prayer and meditation to improve [one's] conscious contact with God," the lessons learned from the Oxford Group made Alcoholics Anonymous shy away from what were perceived as grandiose claims about explicit guidance. Also, there is a more individualist focus, so that group "checking" is reduced to group-preservative functions. Therefore, although it is more subtly expressed in the Big Book, in practice at meetings "advice giving" or "cross talk" is eschewed.

The affinity principle practiced by the Oxford Group has been heightened into the dominant ethos for Alcoholics Anonymous. Throughout its history, AA focus has resolutely stayed fixed on fellow alcoholics. Whereas in the Oxford Group affinity was used as an aid to evangelism and conversion, for Alcoholics Anonymous it is its sole purpose. This has major theological implications—though pragmatically it has been quite effective. It reduces the universal understanding of the human predicament to the unfortunate disability of a particular group. Though there are a few suggestions that self-will is a universal malady, Alcoholics Anonymous has never expanded that thesis to invite persons with other manifestations of this core problem to enjoy the benefits of its fellowship. It took the burgeoning recovery movement to expand, or reexpand, this principle into a more universalistic mode.

Also modified was the perfectionism of the Oxford Group, but not as much as other commentators have claimed.[62] A total break with sin was transformed into a total break with alcohol. The Oxford Group "absolutes" were reduced to a goal of complete abstinence. Nevertheless, positive behavioral changes sounding very much like the Oxford Group's standards are expected to grow out of this primary sacrifice. There is even some hope for behavioral "perfection" if the person becomes *entirely* ready to have God remove *all* character defects (Step Six). In Alcoholics Anonymous, sobriety means more than simply abstaining from alcohol. Those who stop drinking but do not pursue the further behavioral standards are known as "dry drunks." Knowing the particular needs of the population, however, the Big Book is clear to claim "progress, not perfection" to avoid undue pressure. But, equally important, the avoidance of "absolutes" was also simply a pragmatic move to break any outward identification with the Oxford Group.

Some other very significant changes signaled the break with the Oxford Group, not just on the pragmatic but on the conceptual level. Most obvious, neither the somewhat vague Christology of Buchman nor the more focused and theologically pervasive Christology of Shoemaker was retained by Alcoholics Anonymous. No matter what Wilson's understanding had been, there are clear omissions of earlier themes. There is no mention of Christ. There is no salvific work external or prior to the initiatory action of the alcoholic. There is no transformation into a community through spiritual incorporation into divinity. An "insertion" of Christ would radically change the AA program. If one did this, the entire transaction between the alcoholic and God changes; it would be reconstructed on another foundation.

Additionally, in spite of Shoemaker's influence on Bill Wilson, certain important factors did not transfer. Shoemaker's love for the church, concern for its mission, and intentional connectionalism did not carry over to Alcoholics Anonymous. Instead, the connections to the wider church were thoroughly dropped. In this, Alcoholics Anonymous more closely follows the Buchman Oxford Group pattern, although carrying it further. This was probably done for a variety of reasons: to appease those hostile to religion within AA's early circles, to broaden its appeal to a wider variety of alcoholics, to avoid denominational conflict, and possibly also because Wilson's conversion never completely broke his earlier skepticism of religion. In any event, the outward connections with religion have been severed. Only a few remnants remain. There is an effort to elicit a friendlier attitude toward religion, especially from those members who are hostile. There is a respectful nod at the good intentions and influence of the clergy. And there is a pragmatic recognition that many alcoholics will have had church backgrounds and might be personally helped by reinforcing or reconnecting with them.

Indeed, some persons do eventually return to their religious affiliation after some years in Alcoholics Anonymous. This happened for some in the Oxford Group as well. Yet for many, AA membership does not promote greater church participation. Nor does it necessarily work to prompt religious affiliation for those with no religious background. As with the Oxford Group, AA meetings and companions often assume the function of religion. As one writer commented, "When I would question some AA members why they did not include the church in their spiritual life, their response was, 'I don't need that. I have my church here in AA.' "[63] Perhaps, like the Oxford Group, much of the outcome is determined by the earlier religious experiences of members and by the outreach of church leaders.

Finally, Alcoholics Anonymous introduced a very different approach to the will and to evil. Rather than a will that is functional but misdirected, the group presented a will that was partly disabled by its vulnerability to alcohol. In this, Alcoholics Anonymous was much closer than either Buchman or Shoemaker to understanding what theologians have called "the bondage of the will"—that condition referred to in Paul's letter to the Romans (7:14–25) where even the things he knows he should do he cannot, because he is a slave to sin. For Alcoholics Anonymous, this is only a partial paralysis, which represents a curious blending of the evangelical Arminianism (the will is totally functional) of Buchman and Shoemaker with a more Augustinian understanding of the inability of the will to seek after good.

This blend grew out of their personal experience with alcohol. Yet this potentially productive insight led in an unexpected direction. It has offered a resonant note to contemporary culture with its increasing fears of powerlessness and disorder, and sense of biological determinism. This, too, has contributed to the attractiveness of Twelve Step recovery groups that broaden the types of behavior over which people feel powerless. Yet Alcoholics Anonymous and these other groups understand bondage only of specific persons to a specific physical substance or process.

Finally, Alcoholics Anonymous took more seriously the element of radical evil, unlinked from personal sinfulness, than did either Buchman or Shoemaker. The foe alcohol, and some people's vulnerability to it, cannot be explained. Neither can it be totally traced to personal waywardness. The problem is that this radical evil is objectified and contained in a particular physical substance. The substance is made to stand for the tempter, the foe, the diabolic power waiting to ruin one's life if one succumbs. While an element of radical evil is thus recognized, it is effectively externalized. One may be vulnerable to it, but there is a way to block it out. This schema implies that the power of God can prevail over the enemy, yet there is little sense that this divine power is sovereign or that God may use it freely. This divine agency is only unleashed by human cooperation. In this worldview, human agency precedes divine agency. Additionally, its scope is narrowly presented. Although the drama is captivating, the symbolic battle between good and evil is not fought on a cosmic scale. It is primarily restricted to the arena of alcoholism.

7

THE EXPANSION OF THE
ADDICTION–RECOVERY MODEL

Thousands have attested, over many decades, that the Big Book is a good description of one type of alcoholic condition. Many insist that it describes their circumstances very well. But the model offered by the Big Book has been adapted to problems far beyond the intentions of early Alcoholics Anonymous. It is now used to describe and treat a wide variety of disparate behaviors grouped under the expanding umbrella of addiction. More broadly, some suggest the model provides an apt description of the human predicament in general. It is true that the AA description has distinctive theological roots. From this perspective, a simple doubling back, a return of this model to a frankly religious context, may seem appropriate and easily accommodated. If Alcoholics Anonymous emerged out of a particular theological description, why cannot it be used that way again? But the situation is not that simple, for many changes have taken place since the AA description was originally conceived. There are now significant differences in the way society views alcoholism and addiction, which color how the essential AA message is heard in contemporary groups. These changes radically affect the use of the addiction-recovery situation as a paradigm for the human condition. They also affect the use of this description in the church as a theology or form of spirituality.

The addiction-recovery field is a rough sea, especially as one moves beyond the bounds of the AA program. The field is filled with conflicting theories, business operations, professional tensions, socioeconomic issues, and various critiques. This state of affairs has complicated the world of addiction recovery. It has also highlighted conceptual silences in the AA program that many have tried to fill. Some of these gaps have prompted science to discover explanations of addiction as illness. Some have given rise to a proliferation of addiction diagnoses and treatments. Some have prompted the church to bring Alcoholics Anonymous and its relatives back within a more frankly religious structure. Nevertheless, the AA description is still fundamental. It is a prototype for addiction recovery, and it is still the main approach that seriously considers the spiritual issues in addiction.

The church still hears important resonances in the AA program. Yet these resonances are now coming through a filter that contains many elements originally uninvolved in the development of the AA approach.

ALCOHOLISM AS A DISEASE

The Big Book was clear in presenting the alcoholic as someone sick. But it was also somewhat restrained in doing so. It never used the word "disease," preferring instead the looser terms *illness* and *malady*. It realized it needed to keep clear of the purview of the medical profession, and it was generally silent on biological factors and causes. Nor did Alcoholics Anonymous ever fully leave its Oxford Group roots. It understood this disease as ultimately spiritual, not simply physical and psychological. Nevertheless, the Big Book's distinction of alcoholics as somehow different, and definitely ill, cooperated with contemporary understandings, including the increasing medicalization of human difficulties. A disease understanding of alcoholism preceded the emergence of Alcoholics Anonymous. Thus the AA understanding of the alcoholic as ill in three ways blended fortuitously with the "solid, largely uncritical, popular 1930s acceptance of alcoholism as at least some kind of 'disease.'"[1] This probably aided a more rapid public acceptance of AA ideas.

Today, the assertion that alcoholism is a disease is "sacred."[2] It has achieved a level equivalent, in theological terms, to dogma: a fundamental, non-negotiable, undergirding belief. Alcoholism as disease is so foundational that one cannot deny it without effectively distancing oneself from the believing community. People involved in addiction recovery understand this implicitly, in spite of the "take what you like and leave the rest" dictum. The most automatic and visceral reactions are often encountered if one suggests that there are other ways to view alcoholism or that alcoholism may not be a disease in the usual sense. Many consider the disease model a new, benevolent approach to the problem. To suggest otherwise is to be considered unenlightened or inhumane. It is sometimes claimed that, in practice, AA members take varying approaches to the disease concept. Thus, while many do believe they have an actual medical condition, some members virtually ignore the disease concept, and others simply use it metaphorically.[3] Nevertheless, frequent strong reactions to questions regarding the disease concept of alcohol addiction point to its dogmatic status. The idea of addiction as disease is fundamental even if the interpretations vary. In addition, the contemporary connotations of addiction as disease differ from early AA's views. They are often less nuanced, less focused on the spiritual aspect, or much more medically based than the AA "illness" view.

HISTORICAL FACTORS IN
THE DISEASE THEORY

In some ways, the disease approach is a "renewed" way of looking at alcoholism. New groups often seek to gain credibility by claiming historical precedence for their existence or major contentions, and the recovery movement is no exception. Many writers reach back to the late-eighteenth-century doctor, Benjamin Rush, or to earlier thinkers. They claim that enlightened people have always recognized the lack of control that may be experienced regarding alcohol. This lack of control is the baseline for the disease concept of alcoholism.[4]

Yet an overfocus on the disease concept's historicity obscures some important points. Understandings of illness before the rise of the modern medical profession were quite unlike our own. In many ways, today's understanding of disease is a construct that both emerged from and helped form a new political and socioeconomic structure.[5] It is not surprising to find evidence of this paradigm change in writings about alcohol abuse, for they reflect changes going on around them. There is a clear thread of disease theory running through discussions of alcoholism, from Benjamin Rush through the Washingtonians, the Good Templars, and finally the temperance movement. These writers lived during the paradigm change, used it, and contributed to it. If the disease aspect became submerged during the later years of the temperance movement, with its hopes that Prohibition would end the problem, it reappeared again when that experiment proved a failure.[6] This history does not prove or disprove that alcoholism is a disease. It does, however, point to the growing acceptance of the disease concept in nineteenth- and twentieth-century American society.

USES OF THE DISEASE THEORY

While it is helpful to examine the meaning of the disease theory, it is even more important to understand how this concept is used. It has been a strategy as much as a tenet. From the start, the disease concept was presented as the new enlightened alternative to a moralistic, punitive, and judgmental way of viewing the problem of alcohol abuse. Contemporary anecdotal experience confirms that many people assume that the church is aligned on the moralistic side of the dichotomy and that the disease theory was developed primarily to counteract that influence. The disease theory is often still used as a way either to reprove the church or to distance from it. This attitude has clear roots. In the early rhetoric of the alcoholism movement, "the primary counterfoil to the new 'scientific' approach was the old 'moralistic' approach of the temperance movement." And in transmuted form, it carries on today, as new scientific breakthroughs are used to "neutralize moral connotations" regarding alcoholism.[7]

There was some advantage in this strategy, but it is not the whole story. The moral and illness views are to a certain extent compatible, making the stereotyped dichotomy much too sharp. Also, early Alcoholics Anonymous was not specifically responding to or opposing religious moralism. The Big Book was considering numerous other factors in early twentieth-century America as it sought to present a new view of the alcoholic's plight. For one, under the influence of psychoanalytic theory, many professionals had begun to view alcoholism not as a primary condition but only the symptom of an underlying neurosis. Seemingly in response, the Big Book insists that this problem only affects an individual's will and sanity in relationship to alcohol. Also, early Alcoholics Anonymous probably wanted to direct the problem away from the criminal justice system, which had long used punitive measures to deal with the social disruptions caused by alcohol abuse. This would be of special concern to its many middle-class members, who sought to maintain or regain a professional life and place in society. Anonymity also helped in that goal.

In addition, alcoholism had become identified with many social problems arising out of industrial capitalism and immigration. Many had come to assume alcoholism was hereditary and connected with racial degeneration. The Big Book would thus want to show it as an "equal opportunity disease" in the hopes of garnering attention for the many middle-class nonimmigrant sufferers. Yet also, coming so close to the repeal of Prohibition, the "illness" view of the Big Book was a reaction against a temperance movement that had become more judgmental and punitive toward alcoholics, falling finally into a neglect of them once Prohibition was enacted. Early scientists of alcoholism, such as Edwin Jellinek, assumed that this punitive attitude had been dominant among temperance reformers from the outset. Yet, as sociologist Harry Gene Levine points out, that was not so. A compassionate approach was characteristic of the earlier stages of the temperance movement.[8]

CHANGING PUBLIC OPINION

It took considerable time to change public opinion about alcoholism. Renewed interest in the disease approach began with positive publicity about Alcoholics Anonymous. This was aided by the work of such groups as the Research Council on Problems of Alcohol and the Center of Alcohol Studies (first located at Yale, then at Rutgers), starting in the late 1930s and 1940s. In many ways Alcoholics Anonymous provoked this research; their success stories made studies on alcoholism interesting and fundable. Research on Alcoholics Anonymous was crucial to E.M. Jellinek's idea of "phases" of alcoholism. Jellinek went on to publish one of the earliest and influential treatises on alcoholism as a disease, yet his earlier work was built on the evidence of only 98 questionnaires prepared by and for members of Alcoholics Anonymous.[9] Some critics, including Jellinek himself, have questioned whether this was adequate scientific data. In addition, he excluded the data of women informants.[10] Yet his work was pivotal in the scientific grounding of the disease theory.

Some legal and socioeconomic changes also worked to promulgate and then expand the disease concept. Alcoholism took several decades to be legally recognized as a medical condition. In 1935 the American Medical Association (AMA) said alcoholics were "valid patients," in 1952 the World Health Organization noted that alcoholism's "interference with mental and bodily health" required treatment, and in 1956 the AMA defined alcoholism as a slow, progressive, and incurable disease, thus prompting legislation to force hospitals to accept alcoholics for treatment. Alcoholics were to be admitted to hospitals on a par with patients with other diagnostic conditions.[11] In the 1970s civil rights legislation allowed alcoholism to be considered a disability. This opened the doors to funding, insurance coverage, and even mandated treatment. The result was a "mad race" in which "a new industry sprang into being," according to historian and interpreter of Alcoholics Anonymous Ernest Kurtz.[12] By the late 1970s professionals and the public firmly believed that alcoholism was a disease. "As a 'health education' campaign in the United States, the disease conception must be judged an astonishing success," insists sociologist and addiction specialist Robin Room.[13] These perceptions were then expanded to define other life problems as addiction. The stage was set for an addiction-recovery movement that was burgeoning by the 1980s. With it came a proliferation of diagnoses, mutual-help groups, huge book sales, and ancillary businesses serving an increasingly interested public.

MEANING AND CONFLICT
IN THE DISEASE THEORY

Many people now confidently assert that "alcoholism is a disease." But the meaning of this phrase can vary considerably. There is surface agreement but underlying conflict. In its most generic sense, disease is simply "a disturbance from normal functioning," or "dysbehaviorism." Functionally, disease is simply "whatever the medical profession recognizes as such." However, there are certain specifics in alcoholism as disease. Both in treatment and among the public, the tenets of the classic or "dispositional" disease theory of alcoholism predominate.[14] Although these tenets are not officially promulgated anywhere, they are widely known. The theory makes assertions about alcoholism's physical aspects, as well as indications for policy and attitudinal change.

In the classical disease theory, alcoholism is understood to be a distinct clinical entity and a unitary disease. It is not presented as the symptom of something else. This state is said to be qualitatively different from normality. Either one is or is not an alcoholic. Alcoholics thus will always be different. They can never drink "normally"; indeed, they should never drink again. According to the classic theory, the causes of this condition are rooted solely in biology, primarily genetically determined factors such as abnormal brain chemistry and metabolism. Other factors, such as dysfunctional behavior and personality, are symptoms and not the primary problem. The chief characteristic of this disease is understood as loss of control in regard to drinking. Proponents insist this is an irreversible condition; it can never be cured. Thus the alcoholic's genetically and physiologically based differences always remain. Both attitudinal and policy factors follow from this. This approach stresses its humanity and modernity. It is contrasted with a moral or religious approach impugned as antiquarian and unenlightened. It insists that alcoholics should not be treated as immoral or criminal. It demands treatment for alcoholism as an urgent priority for society. Finally, according to the classic theory, this is the best and only way to handle society's alcohol-related problems.[15]

The classical disease theory heavy influences public perceptions as well as those of treatment providers. Especially for those in the alcoholism movement, alcoholism as disease "is a Platonic entity rather than a human construction" as sociology understands it. This is not restricted to movement members because "clinical thought in the modern era has generally been dominated by Platonic assumptions about disease entities."[16] The disease theory seems widely accepted and unilateral. However, under this surface agreement there is conflict.

One factor behind this conflict—or perhaps because of it—is that understandings of addiction on the professional level are still in a "preparadigm state."[17] For decades there has been continuing disagreement on the theory or aspects of it. In fact, challenges started as early as the 1950s. Over time they increased rapidly. Serious critiques of the disease concept have made many experts step back and refine or defend their understandings of alcoholism as disease.[18] Some have retreated so far as to adopt a pragmatic, almost skeptical approach, where the concept is not so much believed as used because it works. Thus, although the impression is of scientific agreement, in fact the disease theory has always been somewhat vaguely and variably expressed. This has not proved to be a serious problem, for the theory has largely functioned as a way to get a better deal for the alcoholic.[19]

Public attitudes are not simple, either. The classic disease theory holds sway for those who are unaware of professional conflict. Professional disagreements have "remained lost on the general U.S. public."[20] Yet for many people, several apparently conflicting theories seem to exist simultaneously. The public intermingles moralistic attitudes with its acceptance of alcoholism as disease. (Data suggest that professionals do the same.)[21] It is harder to separate illness and moralism than is usually realized. This is probably intrinsic to the modern use of the illness category.

Even beyond its connection with addiction, illness as a larger metaphor often removes guilt with one hand only to return it with the other. As Susan Sontag in *Illness as Metaphor* points out "Illness expands by means of two hypotheses. The first is that every form of social deviation can be considered an illness. . . . The second is that every illness can be considered psychologically. . . . These two hypotheses are complementary. As the first seems to relieve guilt, the second reinstates it."[22] This paradox holds true for alcoholism as illness or disease.

At least four often conflicting elements are combined in U.S. beliefs regarding alcoholism. First, the dispositional disease model is firmly held. Here, alcoholics are understood to bear no responsibility at all. They are seen as incapable of rational decision making, thus needing social intervention and coercion. Opposite that is the still influential moral-volitional model. This stresses personal choice and presents alcoholics as willfully aberrant. A personality model exists alongside these. It claims alcoholics "have a consistent and abnormal personality." And finally there is the AA model. It has elements of the moral, the medical, and the psychological, yet it primarily presents the problem as "a reflection of a human need— gone wrong—for spiritual life and growth."[23]

With these conflicting views often held simultaneously, it is no wonder that confusion reigns on this topic. Surface agreement on addiction as disease hides this. This underlying confusion is widespread. It will be present when a church adopts an addiction-recovery model as a spirituality, or simply as a mode for helping troubled persons. A church cannot avoid this underlying conceptual confusion. It will transfer over when the addiction-recovery model is adopted as a spirituality or theology. This situation causes considerable obstacles to the forming of a cogent theological statement regarding addiction, or human dysfunction in general. This confusion inevitably has practical consequences. Action is firmly intertwined with belief. For better or worse, we cannot "take what we like and leave the rest."

EXPANSION OF THE THEORY AND METHOD

There have been many changes in public perceptions and scientific views since Alcoholics Anonymous first promulgated its approach. Not only has the idea of alcoholism as a disease gained widespread acceptance, there is increasing attention paid to its physical aspects. Subtle shifts in the understanding of the addictive predicament have occurred over time, as focus has increased on biological factors. Since the 1970s, science has tended to look for the responsible genes and other seemingly entrenched physiological, biochemical, and neurological factors in behavior. Our perceptions have changed gradually until there has been "a geometric increase in publications pronouncing the genetic basis of such disparate phenomena as shyness, rape, mental illness, alcoholism, crime, even social and economic position."[24]

Shifts in Focus

There has been a perceptible shift in public focus to the more biological aspects of addictive disease. This has been far greater than early Alcoholics Anonymous ever intended, with its simple analogy of "allergy." The public often understands genetic studies to prove particular problems are intractable, inevitable in certain persons, and unamenable to substantial change.[25] This influences Alcoholics Anonymous as well as other recovery groups. In their loose structure, they have little provision for "quality control."

Because of this, an unexpectedly strong attitude of biological determinism often accompanies an addiction-recovery model for spirituality. On the one hand, a frank recognition of the tragic and deep proportions of human difficulties can lead to greater compassion. On the other, this can be accompanied by a subtle pessimism regarding divine grace and power and a sense of despairing helplessness impeding human action. The recovery movement may wane as other popular movements have eventually done (and some people question whether its popularity has already peaked[26]). Even Alcoholics Anonymous may loose its hegemony someday. Nevertheless, changes in public perceptions will inevitably linger on.

The Proliferation
of Twelve Step Groups

The successful public education campaign about alcoholism as disease was accompanied by what Philip Rieff calls "the triumph of the therapeutic."[27] Attitudes about alcoholism expanded to include other problems. There was acknowledgment of drug addiction and the problems of families of alcoholics. Alcoholics Anonymous helped form such official offshoot groups as Al-Anon for families of alcoholics (in 1951) and Narcotics Anonymous (NA).[28] In time, some people began to attend multiple meetings to deal with their different "issues." It would not be unusual to find "double winners," who attended both Alcoholics Anonymous and Al-Anon, to deal with their own and their spouse's drinking, or "dually addicted" persons with both substance and alcohol problems who went to both Alcoholics Anonymous and Narcotics Anonymous. Eventually, many began to claim they were "multiply addicted."

For those who decided their parents were alcoholic, Adult Children of Alcoholics (ACOA) was formed in the 1970s. This group was not under AA's official umbrella, although the members often were familiar with Alcoholics Anonymous and Al-Anon. Eventually some people began attending the various alcohol-related meetings with less specific problems. Some had a strong desire to be part of an active support group. Some initially attended to help a friend or relative or participated in a family program at a treatment center and became converted to the model. There were others who subsumed many personal difficulties under the umbrella of alcoholism and found there a way to consolidate their problems like so many outstanding debts. In the process, many of these people found themselves unexpectedly drawn into the addiction discourse.

In the 1970s and 1980s—apart from the direct influence of Alcoholics Anonymous—a growing number of other human problems have come to be seen as addictions and treated with the Twelve Step method. The issues identified by this expanding movement range beyond substance abuse; they have moved into the more ephemeral world of "process addictions," including such behaviors as eating, sex, shopping, work, and strong emotions, all considered as problems that are out of control. One offshoot that is very influential with women has been a substrate dealing with "addictive" relationships and compulsive dependency, "codependency."[29] By the 1990s, an average-sized city newspaper might list some twenty such "Anonymous" groups meeting during one week,[30] not counting the official AA and Al-Anon meetings. A large city might have scores of AA groups available in any given week, and nearly as many different recovery meetings.

While the Twelve Steps might be retained in these groups, the careful governance process expressed in AA's Twelve Traditions, a set of organizational principles that guide the life and work of the AA fellowship groups and national office, generally is not. Sometimes staunch AA supporters privately decry this proliferation. They believe it is a watering down of the AA message and diverts attention from a truly life-and-death matter to deal instead with less urgent problems.[31] They say it commercializes it, often allows more blame than responsibility, and divorces the Twelve Steps from its programmatic safeguards in the Twelve Traditions. Some ideological aspects of these new groups do not fit the AA ethos, such as the individualism and externalization of causation taught in the codependence movement. Some people see this as the inevitable downfall of the wider recovery movement. Others claim that Alcoholics Anonymous itself is at a decisive point because of these disparate influences.[32]

The proliferation has gone even further, for its real influence has been in an attitudinal change, well beyond the purview of Alcoholics Anonymous. This affects those who do not attend Twelve Step meetings, not just those who join the new groups or those who stick with the more traditional format. There has been an increasing acceptance of a generalized addiction-recovery mentality or "Twelve Step consciousness." This new and expanded "sobriety" is akin to a type of religious asceticism and perfectionism. More things are understood as addictive, more people search for their own "addictive patterns," more things get restricted. More people are willing to self-diagnose, and more are willing to claim their problems are out of control. This modern moralism lends a tinge of fear to things previously considered either enjoyable, within the range of normalcy, or simply aspects of human nature. This can even extend to the prosaic church supper. One time, when I commented to an AA friend that I had attended a church potluck dinner, he responded, "That's the only place where addictive eating is religiously promoted."

A pastor I know returned from a visit to her parents and announced that her mother was "in denial." Her parents, actively involved all their lives in liberal Protestant professional circles, known and respected widely, had always felt free to enjoy alcohol in moderation. But the daughter now decided her mother was an alcoholic, and she was angry that her mother refused to admit it. She attempted a professional "intervention" to get her mother to recognize that she had a problem but was unsuccessful. Although she did not cut off contact with her family, subsequent visits were the source of much anger and frustration for her. Formerly a moderate social drinker, she feared the problem might be genetic, though she had never had problems with alcohol. She began to search for her own "disease process." To purge herself from temptation and promote a purer lifestyle, she first banned alcohol, then sugar, and then meat from her home. Attendance at various "Twelve Step groups" became an essential part of her life and the principles a part of her preaching.

Restrictions can become complicated and pervasive. Some people elect to place increasing limitations on their eating habits. They restrict not just alcohol, drugs, and tobacco but also, as with the pastor just described, such things as sugar, coffee, and certain animal products. Others are wary of repeating "addictive patterns" in close relationships or family dynamics.

They tread fearfully in these areas or avoid them altogether. The result is an often intense preoccupation with personal behavior akin to a pursuit for ritual purity. It is possible this attitude of inward cleansing is one reaction to the social changes, drug experimentation, and failed social hopes of a generation. Others feel it draws on the best of an earlier period. One writer in the recovery movement was pleased to find she had joined "a cultural movement that incorporates much of the spiritual exploration, group energy, folk wisdom, and effective anarchy that I had loved about the '60s."[33] For many, there is no doubt this is a spiritual quest. But it often begins and ends with human behavior. Divine grace is lodged somewhere in the middle, functioning more as means than end. There is also an economic element involved, for a lucrative industry has emerged. There are often "recovery sections" in bookstores, large seminars and popular conferences devoted to recovery themes, and professional meetings to train providers in new theories and methods. Whole stores can be devoted to the literature and paraphernalia of recovery: greeting cards, medallions, plaques, even prayer cards.

From another perspective, the increase in small support groups—many of which make some use of addiction discourse—is an important grass-roots response to societal changes such as increased transiency and institutional instability. In this the recovery movement is strikingly similar to the history of the Oxford Group, where increasingly global-sized problems in the late 1920s and 1930s inspired despair and retreat in many. For them, group meetings provided at least a feeling of personal efficacy and morality again. But the expanding application of the addiction metaphor is also a response to a theological vacuum created in part by the insecurities and resulting silences of religious communities as such core concepts as sin became unacceptable in public discourse.

In all of this, the AA influence, however inadvertent, has been determinative. The proliferation of recovery groups was conceptually undergirded by the AA ethos. The transmutation of the sin conversion dynamic into an addiction-recovery model—although it has multiple contributing factors—could not have happened without the pioneering pattern of Alcoholics Anonymous. Although some AA members disavow the generalized recovery movement, the expansion of the addiction metaphor is a logical outgrowth of the AA program. The group maintains its insistence that the underlying problem with alcoholics is spiritual. It has continued the Big Book's contention that this is only a worse form of the problem that afflicts others.

The Addiction Paradigm and the Church

Alcoholics Anonymous itself has indirectly helped to spread the idea that the alcoholic predicament is somehow related to the human predicament in general. Ernest Kurtz has summed up AA's overarching message as "not God," that is, human finitude. He claims that "the phenomenon of alcoholism replicates the essence of the human condition."[34] This is similar to the Oxford Group's understanding of sin as a universal condition, rooted in pride, requiring surrender of self-will to God. Although the recovery movement does not follow this complete course, when the church is attracted to the Twelve Steps or to an addiction-recovery paradigm, it senses better than others the resonances left over from the more traditionally Christian Oxford Group program.[35]

This may be one reason why church-related publications have paid increasing attention to addiction issues. This attention spans the spectrum from liberal to mainline to conservative.[36] Much of the writing deals with specifics and types of addiction and the fact that persons with such problems are hidden in the churches.[37] Many claim that the church has not been attentive to chemical dependency issues. Some writers complain the church's ministry often goes no further than to offer space, although in many communities it is mainly churches that have opened their doors to Alcoholics Anonymous and related groups. Writers do, however, welcome the new awareness. They call for more pastoral attention to persons with substance abuse problems.

Many such writings reveal distinct presuppositions. True to the addiction paradigm, the sufferers are often identified solely by their problem ("the addicted"). Many writers broadly assume addicts have been hurt by the church or harbor negative attitudes. The church is stereotyped as well. It is reproved for wrongly considering the problem as a sin, fruitlessly appealing to the will, and being a place of "denial, judgmentalism, passivity, and simplistic thinking" inhabited by "closed minds and cold hearts." There can be a tone of bringing enlightenment to an unreached place, "equipping" churches by giving them "an understanding of the basic dynamics of addiction and a few elementary instructions on how to begin doing effective addiction ministry." The church is considered to be "in denial" similar to addicted persons. Sometimes addicted persons are judged, too, called "very difficult to love" or manipulative.[38] But other writers point to persons "in recovery" as potential spiritual healers for a congregation.[39]

Many churches are interested in the recovery model. Many also look to addiction-recovery support groups as ways to promote growth and revitalization. Some churches have thoroughly restructured their ministries or have been created around a Twelve Step approach.[40] This interest is not solely a late-twentieth-century phenomenon. Shoemaker himself, in the 1950s, suggested with his sermon "What the Church Has to Learn About Alcoholics Anonymous" that the church could copy Alcoholics Anonymous. He claimed that, in contrast to the church, Alcoholics Anonymous demanded much more of its members and got it. (Yet two decades earlier Alcoholics Anonymous had claimed that the Oxford Group expected too much.) To make this strong connection with Alcoholics Anonymous, though, Shoemaker had to modulate his beliefs. He considerably reduced his Christocentrism and his idea of church as the Holy Spirit's abode.[41] He narrowed his focus specifically to sin or its replacement and issues relevant to this, such as the will, bondage, responsibility.

What happens when this model is brought into the churches today? AA's borrowings from the Oxford Group do not involve method only; content is inevitably included.[42] Nor was the borrowed content restricted to seeing the problem (whether sin or alcoholism) as selfishness, combined with an illness model to describe sin or addiction.[43] The Oxford Group had distinct positions on key theological issues. For them, conversion only happens through surrender, sin is primarily ego-centeredness, community is built on mutual confession, God wants to control one's minutest acts, and evangelism is primarily personal life-changing. Yet these are not the only explanations of sin, grace, and conversion. Rather, these are distinct choices from a broader theological spectrum. When the addiction-recovery model is simply replanted in the church, all these positions are implicitly brought in as well. There are theological trajectories carried within the model and structuring the methods.

These implicit theological trajectories do not mean other cultures and religions cannot use the addiction-recovery model. There is some indication that they can.[44] Alcoholics Anonymous is justly proud of its worldwide expansion. It would be fascinating to examine how AA methods affect, say, Buddhist content, and vice versa, but that is another topic.[45] The origins and majority membership of Alcoholics Anonymous, and certainly of the generalized recovery movement, is still in the United States. The expansion of Alcoholics Anonymous beyond the United States cannot hide the fact that there is something distinctly American about this program, in both method and content. The model of the reformed sinner has a distinctly American appeal, and conversion testimonies have long fascinated us, largely because of our Protestant revivalist heritage. It would be ironic if the worldwide proliferation of AA-type meetings had an unintended Americanizing effect similar to the earlier Christian mission impulse.

Especially in the United States, recovery groups have become for many people fillers of a spiritual vacuum or replacements for rejected religious backgrounds. Society needs to understand what sort of anthropology is being expressed and, concomitantly, what sort of personality is being formed. The culture has impugned the ideas of original and actual sin as needlessly negative, even disabling. It would be ironic if the very type of theological position on human dysfunction discarded by the majority in American culture was coming back to society now in another form.

The thematic has thus come full circle. What was originally understood as the universal condition of sin, then reduced to the pathology of a particular group, and then expanded into a proliferation of addictive diagnoses has simply become another name for a universal human predicament. From a cultural studies point of view, this circular path of an idea makes for an interesting story. But from a theological angle, there are significant disparities that need attention. For in its long journey, this understanding of addiction and recovery, or sin and redemption, has acquired a slant different from its theological roots. In addition, AA's theological roots were themselves only one interpretation of the drama of human conversion.

Part 3

THEOLOGICAL REFLECTIONS ON THE ADDICTION–RECOVERY MODEL

8

THE NATURE OF THE PROBLEM

As a Christian theologian attending various AA and addiction-recovery meetings, I am often fascinated by the discussions taking place. It is striking how many of the issues have been the subject of theological inquiry for thousands of years. I have often wanted to exclaim, at certain points, "Oh, you're talking about the problem of evil" or "That's an interesting slant on the concept of original sin." But this always seemed beyond the acceptable bounds of discussion.

It has been particularly frustrating to hear people in Alchoholics Anonymous and other groups insist they are "spiritual but not religious." Although they desire some kind of communion with God, they wish to be neither doctrinally nor institutionally bound in this quest. Yet the resultant distancing from the spiritual traditions of centuries effectively cuts off a natural avenue to dialogue. Many religious thinkers have pondered similar problems of volition, finitude, and powerlessness. Their insights could alert contemporary persons to some options other spiritual seekers have considered through the ages.

Christian theologians would also benefit from dialogue with persons focused on a difficult problem like addiction. Such interaction would aid the reconstructing of theological positions in light of contemporary insights. Although all faiths have believed something is not quite right about the human condition, Alcoholics Anonymous and its derivatives have posed the problem and the solution in a way particularly amenable to Christian categories. This is not surprising, given AA's roots in the Oxford Group and its location in a culture still very much influenced by Judeo-Christian modes of thinking. Alcoholics Anonymous could be a productive dialogue partner for theology and church. Why has this not happened with any regularity? Some recovery members may feel they have arrived at an improved version of spirituality, have little to learn from traditional views, and have moved beyond theology by being "spiritual but not religious." Yet dialogue is also short-circuited when Alcoholics Anonymous is perceived simply as an anonymous reflection of the

Christian message. Christians may believe a reintroduction of explicit theological terms is all that is needed. They thus may not take the time to hear deeper contributions, challenges, and discordancies.

I believe intentional dialogue could be productive and is essential. Many issues raised by the addiction problem are relevant to theology and to lived faith. Belief continually informs and structures action, even when we are not fully conscious of it. Actions double back to restructure beliefs. In the case of addiction, the conceptual issues underlying the recovery method are of great significance. Ultimately we are dealing with the nature of the human condition, its limitations, potentialities, and ends. Though the outward focus in Alcoholics Anonymous is pragmatic ("Keep coming back; it works"), dedicated members realize they are not simply dealing with behavior modification or physiology. Alcoholics Anonymous understands it is touching issues ultimately spiritual in nature. The questions many addicted persons ask have distinct theological implications.

When addicted persons ask such questions as "What is really wrong with me? How did I get this way? What can be done about it? How much change can I expect?" they can be given purely biological or medical answers. Alcoholics Anonymous itself avoids explicit answers to these questions, except to insist the problem is multifaceted. But the methods and explanations they do give, if followed out, have very definite theological implications, or "trajectories." The following discussion provides a map, an aerial view, suggesting the directions to which certain explanations and options point. Many of these theological trajectories are not new; Alcoholics Anonymous and the recovery movement are not sailing an uncharted sea. Important theological trajectories recur from different vantage points throughout the Big Book's presentation. It is well worth tracing these complicated issues, for each has practical consequences for our sense of efficacy, our ability to hope, and our enthusiasm for life.

THE PROBLEM AS PHYSICAL

The Big Book is clear that the alcoholic's dilemma is ultimately spiritual, while also being at least partly psychological. However, the physical nature of the problem is presented as an especially enlightened and helpful piece of information. Sufferers expect that genetic markers, biochemical components, or other discernible physical anchors for the alcoholic's particular vulnerability can be found. The AA approach thus gives the impression of partnership with science. A perceptual advantage is gained, especially when theology is thought to be skeptical of or out of touch with scientific developments. Many newcomers find this stress on the physical nature arresting. Alcoholics Anonymous still takes seriously Dr. William

Silkworth's advice to "give them the medical business, and give it to them hard."[1] Addiction is portrayed as a seemingly permanent and intractable vulnerability. Although it sounds determinist, many newcomers often find this aspect empowering because it relieves them of some responsibility for the origin of the condition. Additionally, this emphasis is descriptively powerful. It depicts the almost visceral sense of powerlessness that many alcoholics and addicts feel.

Stressing the physical aspect of addiction is not antithetical to a theological understanding. The addiction schema is a contemporary way of addressing many long-pondered issues about our physicality. Theology has long reflected on the way being physical and finite affects the human ability to know and serve God. However, contemporary theology does need to better integrate the increasing discoveries regarding the genetic and biochemical bases for behavior.

The specific focus on addiction as physical has both advantages and problems for theology. One advantage is that the physical emphasis seems to describe in a graphic way what earlier thinkers called the "bondage of the will." This is the feeling the apostle Paul describes in Romans 7:19 when he says, "I do not do the good I want, but the evil I do not want is what I do." Alcoholics Anonymous wavers on whether this bondage is preventable. Within Christian tradition, however, there is insistence that the bondage is self-imposed at a certain early point, both historically and personally. This is a very important caveat, for it preserves human freedom to turn away, even in the face of God's sovereign love. Both Alcoholics Anonymous and Christianity more or less agree that once the path away from God is traveled for a time, there is no turning back, short of the intervening power of divine grace. One is habituated into sinning; the longer it is practiced, the more a bondage it becomes.

Original Sin and Willpower

Another advantage of the physical stress is it revives discussion about original sin. The concept of original sin offers an astute observation of the seemingly inevitable corruption of an inherently good, God-created human nature. It explains why human beings display an almost inherent predilection for disorder, even while yearning for wholeness. Addiction as physical disease makes a similar conceptual move. The idea of addiction as physical is as close as the modern mind may come to a descriptive picture of original sin, especially when genetics or inherited characteristics are stressed. Those who see addictive vulnerability as inborn or intractable implicitly make a similar claim about the power and bondage of human dysfunction. Thus, one is not responsible for the vulnerability, but one nevertheless chooses how to deal with it. There are similar images of intransigent and/or inherited predilection. These include the deep conditioning power of addictive vulnerability and the readiness to accept the existence of genetic and biochemical factors in alcoholism.

Addiction as physical disease becomes especially like original sin when it is extrapolated to cover everyone, as some in the wider recovery movement do. This focus can get out of hand, however, sending everyone on a search for an individual and unique pathological condition.[2] Yet the return of this insight is intriguing and ironic. The idea of original sin, even more than actual sin, has been decidedly disowned by American culture. It is striking that the dynamics, if not the specifics, of this culturally despised Christian doctrine should return in the guise of addiction.

Another advantage of stressing the physical aspects of addiction is that it prevents an inordinate dependence on willpower. The Big Book's stress on the powerful physical nature of the alcoholic's problem, I suggest, may be an unwitting reaction to the Pelagian focus on willpower in the American church. Pelagianism is an ancient problem, one against which Augustine's work on original sin was focused. Pelagius, a British monk of the fourth century, did not deny the necessity of grace. However, he did stress human responsibility for righteousness. He believed persons possess fully operative wills and thus freely choose either virtue or vice. Augustine, the North African bishop, countered by stressing the binding power of transmitted sin. Yet he also saw a voluntary element and thus held that humans are nevertheless responsible.

Although this presentation has dominated much Western thinking, American Christianity has put an increased stress on willpower. It was a distortion of doctrine but it had pragmatic utility. This emphasis well suited America's first two centuries, undergirding its drive to mobilize human effort in the land-settling and industrialization processes. But it also made the American church distinctly uncomfortable with physical limitation, seemingly willful impediments to progress, or anything that cannot be overcome through our "can do" attitude. Alcoholism, then, so observable and seemingly self-induced, has come under serious criticism. An American over-focus on willpower may contribute to the common fear, outside the recovery movement, that if addicts believe they have a disease they will abdicate responsibility for their problems. Alcoholics Anonymous works to avoid this reaction by discouraging the externalization of responsibility. Nevertheless, it still claims alcoholism as a vulnerability seemingly inborn, or acquired very early. AA's claim that one is powerless over alcohol no matter how much one wills otherwise is a distinct challenge to this Pelagian mind-set. In fact, the argument sounds something like Augustine's. This gives the AA message persuasive power both in and out of the church.

But this bold move against American Pelagianism may not be so necessary today. Since the Big Book was written, the focus on willpower in American religion has lessened considerably. Devastating world wars, stock market crashes, ecological crises, and unstable economic, social, and political conditions have made us doubt the salvific power of human reason, effort, and science and our formerly strong trust in progress. Determinist explanations increasingly gain popular attention. The strong current of biological determinism in popular thought may suggest that the opposition to Pelagianism has gone too far.

Human Finitude and Pessimism

There is a pressing danger to the emphasis on addiction as physical. It can foster the opposite theological problem. When one opposes the optimistic Pelagian way of looking at human willpower, the temptation is to fall into its opposite, a pessimistic Manichaeanism. These are the two "natural heresies."[3] In the Manichaean schema, simply being human—being a limited, finite, historical, temporal creature—is functionally equated with evil. The potentially good and free human spirit is thus locked in a constricting material reality. Creation is not good but evil, and human beings bear no individual responsibility for their bondage, although they suffer in it. Here, constitutive human limitations are equated with sin.

This is highly problematic. Although human beings are by definition limited and finite, it is a mistake to equate this finitude with actual wrongdoing. When this is done, finitude becomes characterized by ignorance, weakness, and suffering and is seen as the real problem. Sin becomes merely a smokescreen. Going further, a stress on physical aspects of addiction can cause an overlooking of sin entirely. Instead, the entire dilemma of human nature is understood as tragedy. Culpability becomes irrelevant. Human limitation becomes so prominent that the human condition is seen solely in terms of its finitude. In stressing the limitations inherent in being human, there is a danger that persons will be pushed to extrapolate from their situation. They may so focus on their particular weakness, pain, or vulnerability that they come to regard it as just one instance of the overwhelmingly tragic human condition per se. While this reflection may help some people to relax from inordinate effort, others may be weighed down by a pervasive hopelessness.

The addiction-recovery schema can promote a Manichaean pessimism in persons, no matter how much it is immersed in a sea of serenity. People may adopt a passive, resigned, or limited view of life. Acquiescence to one's plight—giving up "denial"—can be guilt-relieving and comforting in a way. Yet it can also be tinged with despair and resignation. At the least, it can confine action to a constricted and low-risk mode. I remember being sincerely praised by a meeting participant because I had "made it out of the house with matching socks." Persons in crisis often do need to move forward slowly, allowing themselves to be encouraged by seemingly small survival-oriented gains. Nevertheless, the risk is that sights will be permanently lowered and vision dimmed.

I have seen this in the faces and demeanor of persons who—while they finally feel accepted and loved for who they are—yet feel confined to a pathological identification indefinitely.[4] They are confronted with a seemingly intractable vulnerability, inherently linked to their particular physical nature. They accept that they are not responsible for this disability, but they believe there is no complete escape, simply management. No doubt some find a welcome serenity in the acceptance of such a hard reality, and some celebrate the tragicomic status of being finite. But many others quit struggling and become increasingly quiet in their desperation. For those who want to generalize the addictive dilemma into a modern metaphor for the human predicament, this presents a serious theological problem. The bondage of sin is more seriously acknowledged than the power of grace. Finitude becomes more determinative than freedom. Focusing on limitation more than on grace is always a temptation in Christianity, and one to which many succumb.

While the addiction-recovery ethos does not say that finitude is the same as sin, there is a danger that this message will be implicitly conveyed. The ritual repeated introductions at AA meetings—"Hi, I'm Sue, and I'm an alcoholic"—can work a subtle change on one's self-identity. Slogans like "Once an alcoholic, always an alcoholic" confirm this. Presenting the addictive vulnerability as integral to the person skates dangerously close to the Manichaean picture of human nature. Although this may seem similar to a Christian understanding of original sin, it is similar only to common distortions of it.

On the contrary, original sin is "inevitable but not necessary."[5] It is not part of God's creation of or intention for us. The Bible presents an originally good creation by God. It promises the restoration or re-creation of that status through the salvific work of Jesus Christ. Christian theology has generally held that finitude is not, per se, evil. By definition, to be human is to be limited. Through these contentions, it works against a perennially potential pessimism about the human condition. The biblical account presents all the material world as a good creation of God. Human finitude, our inherent limitations as physical creatures, is part of that originally good creation. In this paradigm, the corruption of that good, through both inherited and chosen sin, is credited to human responsibility. Otherwise, God would be made the author of sin. The tension between our human finitude and our God-imaged freedom presents the occasion for sin but is not sin in itself.

It is a particular contribution of the Judeo-Christian tradition to separate the sin problem from the tragedy of human limitation. Through grace, we can gain some control over sin. Ironically, a frank admission of sin allows more room for hope and change. When explicit reference to sin is eliminated, the danger is that persons will be led to focus primarily on the finite (tragic) aspect of their condition. Although they will not feel liable for this condition, they may feel even more inextricably and tragically bound to it. The human situation is then seen as ontological, that is, a "tragic fate." Against this, the Christian tradition assures persons that it is instead a "historical" problem, that is, an "addressable bondage."[6] There is something that can be done about it—life does not have to be an endless cycle of repeatedly acknowledging one's particular weaknesses, hurts, and limitations.

The Big Book never falls explicitly into these particular theological problems. With its Oxford Group roots providing ballast, and also the general theological milieu of the times, it seems to have struck a tentative balance between powerlessness and responsibility. It manages this even while stressing the physical nature of the alcoholic's problem. In fact, the Big Book, Alcoholics Anonymous, and the general recovery ethos are all helpful in reintroducing the element of tragedy. This hard reality has tended to get lost through our historical focus on sin and effort. But without explicit intellectual underpinning to maintain this tension, and without the spiritual guidelines religious traditions can implicitly provide, the danger is it will break down. This is especially likely for persons who now practice this ethos in a different cultural milieu.

Recovery members contend they deal with the tension between responsibility and powerlessness when they pray the "serenity prayer." In this frequently ritualized prayer, often attributed to theologian Reinhold Niebuhr,[7] members ask for guidance in determining what they can and cannot change. But what principles beyond this basic act will give individuals clear intellectual guidance in discerning the difference? The group provides support and comfort but offers few concrete principles by which to evaluate cultural influence or the shifting values of the majority. For groups as well as individuals, when we are left to our own devices, or to moral standards of our own making, we are apt to get our bondages and our freedoms mixed up. The collective experience of the group—especially if not submitted to studied discernment—can just as easily confirm as overrule us in this confusion. As Niebuhr has said, "There is . . . less freedom in the actual sin and more responsibility for the bias toward sin (original sin) than moralistic interpretations can understand."[8]

Still, the addiction-recovery schema must be taken seriously. It has generated a large and ready audience of people who find resonances with their own experience. This schema addresses the fact that particular types of physical limitation—once understood primarily as failure of willpower—feel inherent, condition choice, and seem to predate conscious action. Theology has not yet made sufficient place for specific genetic or inherited vulnerabilities—or even socially induced ones—which seriously jeopardize the extent to which the bondage is freely chosen. Our general understanding of sin as somehow transmitted through the generations needs to be refined. Theology must integrate the fact that individuals may be impaired in differing and physically conditioned ways. Nevertheless, in doing this, our understanding of God-imaged human freedom must be preserved. It is essential to love God out of choice rather than coercion, if we are to grow in grace.

Beyond this, we must all take seriously the extent to which genetic and other scientific studies push so many people toward a despairing biological determinism. The church must consider that, at least in part, this is a continued reaction against the inherited Pelagianism in much American religion. But this pervasive determinism is also an odd unintended collusion between fund-seeking scientists, sensationalist media, and an acquiescent public overwhelmed by a rapidly changing world. The result is that social injustice and human limitation appear inevitable.[9] The church must also acknowledge the tragic element in life, areas in which there is true powerlessness. Not everything we suffer is the explicit result of sin. Both theology and church need to work through a presentation that considers new scientific data and the widespread resonance to the recovery focus on powerlessness, yet still holds to a God loving enough and a salvation thorough enough to restore or re-create human nature. The recovery movement must take very seriously the cultural drift into a pessimistic, almost Manichaean biological determinism, since it can unwittingly contribute to it.

REAL ALCOHOLICS AS DIFFERENT FROM "NORMAL PEOPLE"

The Big Book makes a distinction between a heavy drinker and a "real alcoholic." Alcoholics Anonymous is meant for the latter type. Related recovery groups, too, work to gain a membership of individuals caught in various and specific forms of bondage. If a newcomer to an AA meeting believes he or she qualifies as a "real alcoholic," that person learns there to feel vulnerable to alcohol in a unique way. Officially the diagnosis is left up to the individual. But informally, many members will help the newcomer search out identifying marks in personal experience or behavior. Alcoholics Anonymous officially accepts anyone with "a sincere desire to stop drinking." Informally, I often have heard in and out of meetings that if one believes one has a drinking problem, one does. Many believe that if one has enough curiosity to attend a meeting, one probably qualifies. A researcher offered an illustrative vignette.

> One cold evening [the author, visiting an AA meeting] sought the comfort of the fireplace. . . . She was huddled by the fire shivering when an AA member approached her and asked, "How long is it since you've had your last drink? I know the shaking gets pretty bad at the beginning." The investigator responded . . . she was chilled. This response was denied and more advice was offered about how to control physical discomfort during the early stages of detoxification. On another occasion [the author] told her sponsor that she was not really a bona fide alcoholic. . . . The confession was rejected. . . . "You may be doing research, but obviously your interest in this area is because you and your colleagues are really alcoholics."[10]

Some may want to discount this story because the reseacher's position obviously was not completely clear to members. However, my own experience confirms this dynamic. Although I did attend AA and Al-Anon meetings out of real concern for a heavy drinker, I found the same interpretive screen placed over everything I said and did. No matter how often I explained I was ultimately doing research and writing a book, I was assumed to be "in denial" about my own "disease process." This can be stretched even beyond Alcoholics Anonymous in the recovery movement. One of my students had been divorced for five years but could not break out of her malaise. Trying to help, recovery-group members lent her books, suggesting she might have some sort of addiction. Nothing "felt right" until she was given a book on grandchildren of alcoholics. She decided perhaps her grandparents had been addicted to something, although there was no outward evidence. Through this assumption, she felt qualified to become a part of a recovery group. Professionals, the court system, families, and friends too may encourage a persons to regard themselves as alcoholics or addicts. This is at least in part because a structure exists which can then absorb and help the troubled person.

A Bond of Unity

An outsider might see this embracing of a new status defined by a pathology as an onerous burden. But the recovery process—experienced through regular attendance at meetings, voluntary identification with the common vulnerability, and willingness to practice the method—makes the identification process a source of significant and useful benefits. One gains support, communal solidarity, consistency, acceptance, and a definite program that promises results. When newcomers attend their first AA meeting or other recovery meeting based on Twelve Steps, many attest to experiencing an unusual amount of acceptance, welcome, and identification from the outset.

One member who experienced this was an ex-nun who had joined a religious order right out of high school. Although she had consumed alcohol at home and her father was a heavy drinker, the first time she got drunk was in the convent. "At a Christmas party I finished the dregs in everyone's glasses, got drunk, and then got sick. Because of that they took away my first home visit." After twelve years she left the order, married, and continued drinking. But it was not until her father and brother died of alcohol-related causes that she began to question her upbringing. A priest friend recommended a retreat: "Healing the Wounded Child in the Adult." Another priest recommended she join Adult Children of Alcoholics (ACOA) and gave her several books to read. A Protestant minister eventually took her to AA meetings. When she attended her first ACOA retreat, "It was just like coming home. Here were other people who had experienced the same things I had. It was wonderful!"

She, like many others, was amazed to find herself among a group of people who openly acknowledged what she had long denied. Both officially and unofficially, the newcomer is welcomed and made to feel accepted and valued. Some groups read a set "welcome to the newcomer" speech at the beginning of each meeting. Newcomers are often asked to identify themselves, and later members speak with them. Especially in our increasingly alienated and transient world, it is unusual to feel so readily noticed, accepted, and wanted. This positive experience is a crucial factor in motivating a person to return to subsequent meetings. The dynamic is not unique to recovery meetings. Minority religious sects, too, often work to make newcomers quickly feel part of the group. This is sometimes done by stressing the common destiny that brought them together or by asserting that a providential divine hand set them apart and led them there.[11]

In recovery groups the focus is on a particular pathology, vulnerability, or experience. The newcomer's problem is interpreted as part of the common difficulty these particular people experience, which the newcomer is encouraged to see as their common identity. A bond of unity is thus forged between all persons present. Providing the newcomer is willing to admit to suffering from this specific problem, he or she is incorporated into the communal identity. The compassion and identification practiced by members through this process is deliberate, effective in gaining members, and often learned. Entering a room of "instant friends" may be repellent to some people, but it is often desperately welcome to others. This sort of up-front compassion and acceptance is expedient, too, in an era where the normal processes of friendship formation are often aborted or never begun because of our extreme geographic mobility. This makes the proffered compassion and comradery no less valuable and unusual a gift.

At first glance all this may seem to have little to do with theology. It may seem to affect the church only in the area of conflicted loyalties or competition for members. It may seem important only on the ethical level, implicitly incriminating a church that believes it should provide help for troubled persons but often fails in this task. Yet it is not simply an ethical issue. It is profoundly theological to ask: What is the basis of your common bond? Should we consider addiction the common, even universal, human problem? Or is this a unique status held by a particular group of people?

Theological Tensions

The Big Book's presentation contains a tension. It claims a distinct status for "real alcoholics." Yet elsewhere it claims this is just one instance of the common human problem of pride or self-will ("self-will run riot"). My suspicion is that the tension was better maintained within the AA structure when the organization was closer to its theological roots. Separating out the alcoholics was pragmatic and phenomenological, but it was built on AA's understanding of the universality of sin, inherited from the Oxford Group. No matter how narrowly the Oxford Group defined sin or its remedies, members understood clearly that it was a universal condition. To them sin thus equalized rich and poor, famous and unknown, native and foreign. Alcoholics Anonymous took this theme and adjusted it. Everyone was seen to have a weakness for self-will, but for some reason alcoholics fell into this trap especially hard. This kept the tension productive.

The contemporary world has a harder time maintaining this tension. Today universals regarding human behavior are increasingly rejected. Theological consensus is gone, and many spin-off groups based on distinctive shared victimization have arisen. The addiction issue now rests unknowingly on the cusp of a contemporary intellectual debate with many practical ramifications: Are there universally common or shared elements, problems, and solutions for human behavior?[12] On the one hand, Alcoholics Anonymous welcomes the question. It pragmatically avails itself of contemporary criticism of universals in favor of the particularity of experience. Alcoholics are different, it is claimed. They cannot entirely be judged by standards that are appropriate for nonalcoholics. Yet at the same time Alcoholics Anonymous stands against the contemporary position.

Ultimately, it understands the spiritual disease of the alcoholic as a magnification of the spiritual disease of us all. It implicitly follows its theological roots by claiming the alcoholic's place in a universal human dilemma. This tension has made the AA description flexible and has gained it members. But it is internally unstable, especially as the culture changes. Drifting further from its theological roots, it will need something else on which to pin its understanding of spiritual disease. Otherwise, it opens itself up to increasing cultural influence.

From a theological perspective, there are some congruences with and some problems in the dual claim. The most obvious problem grows out of the claim that alcoholics are somehow different. People do suffer from particular biologically based vulnerabilities. However, difficulties emerge as each category of sufferers is separated out into a unique group based on physical limitation. Although this may work therapeutically, it becomes problematic theologically. It can deny that this particular behavior is in any way part of that universal condition of brokenness. A group may so identify with its unique vulnerability that compassion, understanding, and communion is largely restricted to those within the special group. One member relished relating his therapist's remark that "normies haven't even been around the block," much less experienced anything like the sufferings of alcoholics.[13] Although Alcoholics Anonymous may not promote this outgrowth, it can result when the distinctiveness of the condition is stressed. Alcoholics are informally advised to associate frequently with people in recovery. Whole social networks are formed based on addiction-recovery themes. Frequent meeting attendance, work with prospects, seminars, parties, and informal contacts take up much time. This can all be as identity-forming as any sectarian lifestyle.

There is another, more subtle, issue. Alcoholics Anonymous claims that alcoholics simply have a serious version of the common human spiritual disease. This seems congruent with theological tradition. AA's Oxford Group roots are noticeable. The Big Book does not claim that everyone is addicted, although it suggests we share in the spiritual aspects of the disease. But AA's success has helped encourage a variation, the claim that nearly everyone is addicted to something. Others go further to posit addiction as the universal human predicament. This is another ironic twist in a culture that rejects its theological heritage. Nevertheless, it seems we are—depending on one's perspective—either doomed to repeat it, driven to clothe it in a more contemporary guise, or longing to recapture a way to speak broadly of human experience. It is not surprising that as cultural consensus about human nature has broken down, the addiction metaphor has increasingly been broadened to help explain more problematic behavior. This aspect helps attract a wide audience, both in and out of the church.

Theology and church can be sympathetic with the effort to find a universal human spiritual malady. Theology is openly in the business of universals, searching for enduring characteristics of, problems in, and remedies for human experience. This task, of course, continually needs critique and revision. Doctrine must be responsive to and aware of its own cultural context. Also, it is a fact that the doctrine of sin has been used sinfully, to separate, judge, and condemn. There is no doubt that the Christian positing of sin as a universal has led to hegemonic distortions and oppressions. Nevertheless, theology does attempt to posit an ontology that holds for human nature per se.

Sin in Christian theology is a broad-based description and diagnosis of human brokenness. Although there are many definitions of sin—such as idolatry, usurping God's role, disruption of order—no one is exempted from the condition. Sin can be described as our inherited and chosen vulnerability to alienation. Primarily this alienation is a turning from God's actuality, presence, providence, and grace, but it is inextricably related to our relationship with others and with ourselves. Although it can be worked out in different ways, everyone is immersed in and cooperating with a broken situation. It is, therefore, an equalizing factor in the faith, setting no one under or over another.

THE ISSUES OF WILLPOWER AND MORALITY

The claim that willpower and morality are not issues has a clear descriptive power. It ably depicts the situation of people who become so habituated to heavy drinking that they feel they can do nothing to stop, no matter how much they want to change. Alcoholics Anonymous identifies this feeling and relieves a large burden of guilt. It explains that what looks like perversity is in fact out-of-control behavior, since the "real alcoholic's" will becomes disabled by and concerning alcohol. This explanation can also work to deflect the anger and impatience of friends and family over the alcoholic's destructive behavior. It can motivate the alcoholic to depend on the group's joint desire for and experience with change. By simply going to meetings and trusting the group's communal intentions and strength, alcoholics are encouraged to rely on group energy as their own will is being empowered.

There are really two different, although interlocked, issues here. One, the person is presented as having no control regarding alcohol. The will is so disordered, in relationship to alcohol, that it is not even a matter of willing wrongly. Instead, it is a compulsion or bondage, such that the will is not free. Second, the person is understood as neither inherently immoral nor guilty for having the disease, though out of this disease all manner of destructiveness arises. Although he is responsible for whatever he has done, even when "under the influence," he acts out of the disease, not out of choice. It is as though he were two persons. Both my AA students and professionals would frequently explain to me, "Don't expect the unrecovered alcoholic to listen to reason or even to hear you. You are not talking to a person, you are talking to a disease." Although Alcoholics Anonymous does stress the responsibility for all actions, there is a partial separation here of actual causality and inherent moral culpability. The person is responsible for his actions, but not for the disease. Yet from the disease spring the actions. Although this is a subtle distinction, it is a crucial one theologically.

ORIGINAL SIN BUT NO ORIGINAL GUILT

The most salient theological issue has to do with original sin and actual sin. Original sin is our inherited predilection for disorder and our emergence into a world already bent by evil. Actual sin is our individual response to this predicament. The AA explanation inadvertently but persuasively adds one more crack to the continued dismantling of the Augustinian schema, which links original guilt with original sin. The AA ethos does promote an idea of original sin, in that it stresses intransigent and inherent vulnerability. This is a partial borrowing from the pervasive Augustinian schema. Yet Augustine linked the power of original sin with an equally strong judgment on the person (original guilt). He insisted that although we could not do otherwise, we are still held guilty. Augustine made this connection through stressing the solidarity of the human race. Thus, guilt has been passed down from Adam through the generations. Augustine connected original sin and original guilt. He did this by insisting that both our inherited predilection to sin and our guilt for it comes through our biological solidarity with Adam and Eve, transmitted through sexual intercourse. One does not need to accept the historicity of the account or the particular biological transmission theories to be affected by its symbolic power and emotional import. Although Western culture has been in the process of rejecting this schema for well over a century, residues of guilt linger on. Another reason for the persuasiveness of the addiction-recovery metaphor is in part, I contend, its implicit dissolving of these residues.

Our focus on biological predisposition today may be an experiment with a contemporary and secularized version of original sin divorced from original guilt. American culture's growing biological determinism leads persons to feel inextricably led into dysfunctionality. This intriguing throwback to original sin could well push us back to entertaining thoughts of original guilt too. In other words, is guilt hereditary, as Augustine thought? In modern terms, are we somehow inexplicably responsible for our genetic makeup, the faulty role-modeling given us, or our family history that predisposes us to destructive action? On the surface, in our assured individualism, we reject this intellectually. Yet vague feelings of culpability can remain. Alcoholics Anonymous stops this train of thought by denying the link between our obvious diseased bondage and our responsibility for it. Alcoholics Anonymous does not *deny* the facticity of the alcoholic's destructive actions. It does hold him responsible for these. But he is not morally responsible for the disease itself. AA's presentation emerges out of a culture which rejects inherited guilt, preferring instead to hold each person responsible only for his or her own actions. The addiction-recovery movement thus owes part of its popularity to eradicating emotional vestiges of the Augustinian schema. Additionally, it is attractive because it also helps prevent a return to the old connection in a climate that could logically move in that direction.

There is a problem, however. This dismantling of the Augustinian problem has not provided an alternate way to eradicate the bondage. The Augustinian schema made sense because it claimed a solution for the otherwise unbearable tension it raised. The effective and historical work of Christ broke both the inherited and the chosen bondage. It restored people to the ability to choose the good, to turn toward God. If today people learn not to feel guilty for their inherited vulnerabilities, it does not prevent them from feeling in bondage to them. It may exacerbate that feeling, especially if the inherited weakness becomes linked with tragic finitude as the determining factor of the human condition. Nor does the dissociation of bondage from responsibility provide an effective solution beyond eternal vigilance. Indeed, wariness can become habitual for persons who fear they may "slip" or trigger a particular addictive vulnerability inadvertently.

Responsible but Not Culpable

A second issue involves current choices, actions, intentions. The Big Book claims that the disordered actions of the alcoholic are not morally blameworthy because they were done without consent and sometimes even without knowledge. Many insist they have had "blackouts." These are times during a drinking bout that the alcoholic cannot remember, particularly when embarrassing or destructive actions may have been taken. I have heard many use the evidence of blackouts as a test of true alcoholism. This links with the Big Book's distinguishing of responsibility for disordered action from inherent immorality and responsibility for having the disease.

Theologically, this distinction might allow us to distinguish between two types of actions. It might separate actions done with evil motivation, and thus morally blameworthy, from disordered actions done either inadvertently or from good motivation but erroneous activation. Works on alcoholism sometimes explain that drinking can initially start with positive motivation, as for a shy person who wants to improve her sociability.[14] Wilson is often attributed with the phrase "we were trying to find God in a bottle."[15] In general, however, Alcoholics Anonymous avoids discussion in this area, focusing more on the bondage that inevitably happens when someone with the inherent vulnerability begins drinking. Yet in both cases, the point is that the motivation, and perhaps even the basic character of the person, was not disordered at the outset.

This difference in assessing a wrong action has a theological history. It is similar to the distinction in traditional Roman Catholic moral manuals between material and formal guilt. Material guilt simply points to the actuality of a wrongful action. Although the person did perform a wrong action and is responsible in that sense, it is not true sin. The person either did not intend harm or was ignorant of the consequences. An action is truly sinful—thus qualifying as "formal" guilt—if it is deliberate, conscious, and voluntary. Alcoholics Anonymous makes a similar point by insisting that persons are materially responsible for actions done while "under the influence" but are not thereby sinful or bad. They were in the thrall of a disease. They either did not know any better or could not help themselves even if they wanted to. They are guilty in one sense (materially) but not in the other (formally). People educated in the Roman Catholic church can understand this distinction. This may be one reason why many Roman Catholics have felt comfortable in Alcoholics Anonymous.[16] The AA perspective is salutary for those who are in the grip of a long-standing compulsion. It is also compassionately realistic for those few so biologically vulnerable that they had little choice almost from the outset. Similarly, it is helpful for people so formed by their destructive habits that they reach a point where they can no longer choose right actions. But the way this distinction is used in Alcoholics Anonymous is too broad, universalized, and unnuanced. It lumps together whole groups of people whose motivations, intentions, knowledge, and choices are vastly dissimilar.

The distinction between material and formal guilt parallels the modern concern to distinguish between goodness and rightness. Goodness refers to one's motives and intentions. Rightness refers to the right or wrong quality of one's actions. One can intend good, but act wrongly. One can intend bad, but act rightly. Goodness is "antecedent to any action; [it] expresses whether the agent moves toward love or away from it," toward or away from God and neighbor. "Sin or badness is the failure to respond to the Lord who calls us to move forward." Thus sin, too, comes before actual choice and action. It is simply "the failure to be bothered." It is the failure to respond to the love of God. One's goodness depends on whether one wills the good, even if one ends up acting wrongly. Ultimately, willing the good is not a self-initiated action. It comes as a response to God's initiative. For God in grace reaches out toward us, shown best in the sending of Jesus Christ.[17] For us, orientation and intention are more crucial in determining goodness than is action.

The AA ethos can be persuasive when placed over against an oppressive and unnuanced use of the religious moral tradition. Many church persons have automatically equated sin with wrong actions, and wrong actions with badness in general (whether bad motivation, bad character, or spiritual "badness," a deliberate turning away from God). Alcoholics Anonymous gains a ready audience by addressing persons harmed by this misuse. It insists that abusive drinkers do not intend wrong. In other words, they are not bad. Part of the roots of the false dichotomy between sin and sickness lie here. However, there is a problem. Not only does the AA approach lump together many different motivations and actions, it ultimately falls into the same trap it earlier condemns. There is a great divide between problem and solution. When addressing the problem, Alcoholics Anonymous usefully distinguishes between goodness and rightness. But after the "enlightenment" of recovery, the solution becomes fixed on acting rightly. In this it is similar to the moralistic Oxford Group.

Alcoholics Anonymous begins with a distinction between goodness and rightness when explaining the character of alcoholics. But it soon discards this distinction when it proposes the solution. For sobriety—abstinence plus right action—becomes the main goal. Once one crosses the great divide between denial and recovery, less attention is paid to proper motivation or intention. This could be counteracted by the emphasis on gratitude in Alcoholics Anonymous. One has gratitude toward the program and for one's sobriety. Ideally and hopefully, one is grateful for God's grace in delivering one from the evil substance. One's prime motivation is then to serve God and to want good. But the process does not always work that way. It can become simpler to focus on sheer behavior: abstinence and sobriety. This was the same standard earlier rejected as a test of goodness. Yet it can become its main identifying mark. The celebration of anniversaries of sobriety are a common part of AA meetings. Additionally, the achievement and maintenance of sobriety can become less a relaxed, trusting, and confident response to God's initiatory goodness and more a white-knuckle avoidance of temptation.

The tension in addiction recovery over the extent of responsibility is probably another aspect of its anti-Pelagianism. Especially in areas of seemingly obvious self-determination, such as drinking or taking drugs, a church tendency has been to address the problem by urging self-control. Anything less is sometimes interpreted as deliberate perversity. Alcoholics Anonymous insists that for alcoholics self-control with alcohol is not possible. The person is thus not inherently immoral, it is claimed, because she or he is not willfully aberrant. Yet this is fighting Pelagianism with the tools of Pelagianism.[18] Pelagianism says the will is neutral regarding evil and good, not predisposed either way. Wrongdoing is sinful, then, because it proceeds from a free will that could go either way. Alcoholics Anonymous turns this around, in effect saying, " In our particular case, our wills were not free, thus our actions were not sinful. We are not sinning, we are sick." Yet it is agreeing with Pelagianism that essentially—except for certain people regarding alcohol—the will operates freely and one is fully responsible for one's choices. In the end, Alcoholics Anonymous becomes similar to what it is fighting.

The AA caveat regarding will (and, implicitly, intention) has expanded considerably since the writing of the Big Book. The range of things called addiction has grown, pointing to the attractiveness of this view. It preserves the cultural orientation toward individual responsibility. At the same time, it selectively allows echoes of the "bondage of the will" to reverberate. These echoes have clear explanatory power when intractable human failure makes a Pelagian explanation sound discordant. If you are told repeatedly to "buck up" and you do not, there may seem only two reasons: either you are willfully perverse, or you really cannot help yourself. I suggest that Alcoholics Anonymous originally functioned as a way to help a certain troubled group get back in step with the American penchant for self-control. However, the opposite unexpectedly happened. The experience of powerlessness known by alcoholics became generalized to explain more lapses from the American ideal. The Big Book schema relieves guilt, but, perhaps more important, it offers an alternate explanation of dysfunction that accords with many people's experience. It also accords, to a certain extent, with one thematic in the theological tradition. These factors help explain its attractiveness.

Alcoholics Anonymous claims that the problem "is a disease, not a disgrace," that one is not sinning but sick. Although this is not especially useful for detecting true motivation, it is effective in getting the attention of those burdened by an unnuanced moral view. Yet Alcoholics Anonymous significantly rescinds this offer of grace. For it claims that although the alcoholic has an illness that in effect takes over, at base the person is inordinately self-willed. This serious antinomy in the schema can cause many practical problems for members. It especially affects them as they try to decide where they can and must change and where they have truly been victimized. Ironically, it can also return us—at least on the emotional level—

to the Augustinian discomfort of being both inherently in bondage and yet personally guilty.

What About Those Harmed by the Addict?

A third issue involves those who have been harmed by the alcoholic's or addict's destructive behavior. These friends and family cannot be put off indefinitely. As much as they are told the person is sick and not sinning—and as much as their own behavior may not have been exemplary—they have usually experienced true harm. It is true that the Twelve Steps ask for examination of behavior, confession, and the making of amends. This could be effective in restoring relationships, but certain of AA's emphases short-circuit this. The sharp focus on the alcoholic's vulnerability and the "Dr. Jekyll and Mr. Hyde" situation can work to trivialize or distract from the harm done. The bracketing of willpower and morality for the alcoholic under the influence can subtly affect the focus of any restitution. Our gaze and concern are shifted away from those harmed. Alcoholics Anonymous here is similar to the theological standard that makes consciousness of sin a criterion for culpable wrongdoing ("formal guilt"). The Big Book functionally lessens the import of the harm done others by focusing on powerlessness, the disabled will, the alcoholic's ignorance of his or her true condition.

When Alcoholics Anonymous claims "this is a selfish program," friends and family may wryly agree. This is especially poignant when the ultimate goal of restitution is viewed primarily as self-healing. "Making amends" with this as the key objective gives the process a certain off-taste for the harmed. It does not inherently promote compassion and empathy. Nor does it make the act a true and impartial work of justice. In this and other ways, the solutions to broken communion that emerge out of the Twelve Step method can work to hinder fully restored relationships. For those on the receiving end of these "amends," an inordinate amount of selflessness, mercy, compassion, and tolerance are required if they want the relationship. It should not be surprising that these recommendations were originally made with wives in mind. Not only had women of that day been socialized to forgive and sacrifice, they often did not have many alternatives. Economic opportunities were limited, outside child care often nonexistent, and divorce stigmatized. But there are some alternatives today. Alcoholics Anonymous cannot lean as much on socialization and cultural reinforcement. Much of this once came through religious channels, but this is a source that can no longer be assumed for members and spouses. Nor can they depend as much on women's economic and cultural limitation. The problems of this method have come home. As a result, I contend, the road to recovery is littered with broken relationships.[19]

Stressing prerecovery ignorance of the alcoholic's true condition creates another problem. It downplays the fact that lack of consciousness can be a choice, though a habituated one, to avert one's eyes from reality and to move away from the good. Theologically, conviction of sin happens when a person acknowledges a long-standing alienation and culpability. Alcoholics Anonymous seems to echo this with its efforts to bring members to full awareness of their diseased condition (breaking through denial). But by its bracketing of morality, the theological import is quite different. The emphasis is not on awakening one to one's cooperation with a broken situation. Instead, the recovery ethos suggests there is a point before which the person, because ignorant, is not inherently culpable though objectively responsible. Sin is then equated with deliberate intention and consciousness, rather than being both a generalized state into which we are born and also a true decision to turn away from God, love, and others.

Lack of consciousness has generally been accepted as moral excusability in those emotionally undeveloped, such as young children or the mentally incompetent. Claiming this as the state of the adult alcoholic who is as yet unaware of his true condition is subtly demeaning. To limit lack of consciousness to the state of being "under the influence" or only in relationship to alcoholic bondage, seems at first an improvement. Yet it has problems. It segments the person's will, requiring that we posit a state in which the will is only partially disabled, yet fully functional in other respects. From a theological perspective, this is an inherently untenable explanation. It denies the pervasiveness of our broken condition. The fact that some contemporary recovery-group members seem drawn toward a more generalized theory of impairment may be a tacit acknowledgment of the difficulties of the AA explanation.

9

WHO IS RESPONSIBLE?

In the Big Book, alcohol is the main enemy, "cunning, baffling, and powerful." Insisting that alcohol is the chief foe has an important effect: It makes the battle clear and manageable, for one has an identifiable adversary. There is a definable substance to avoid, there is a recognizable behavior to shun. For a newcomer, this limited focus can summon energy. Group support, frequent meeting attendance, and thought control through slogans and reading can all help. But ultimately one must begin to use one's own will. Focusing all effort on shunning this one substance may provide just the exercise the sick will needs to improve its strength. This can be like physical therapy that isolates and works a weak muscle. Until the head clears, until the body has dispelled the substance fully, and until the person can make it from day to day without a drink, there is little else that can be done. No talk of "character defects," making amends, or helping others can make much impact until the person stops living to drink. The device of claiming alcohol as the chief enemy thus often works well at this stage.

THE CLAIM OF ALCOHOL AS FOE

There is an intuitive theological wisdom in this labeling of alcohol as foe, for it implicitly raises the problem of evil. On the positive side, it recognizes there is extrinsic evil. It makes a useful graphic picture of the fact that although there is evil (alcohol) outside the person, the vulnerability to it (biological predisposition) resides within. The language itself, calling alcohol "cunning, baffling, and powerful" calls up popular images of the demonic. It is also a striking and partial contemporizing of a biblical theme. The Bible presents evil as a power that lures or seduces. Once one lets this evil in or responds to it, its insidious work begins on the inside. A craving or inordinate desire ("concupiscence") is set up, which ultimately becomes a bondage. In the garden of Eden story, evil is already there in the character of the serpent.[1] The serpent represents radical evil. Humans do not create it, but yielding to its temptation is their own act, one with protracted and horrible repercussions. Alcoholics Anonymous and the recovery movement thus implicitly note the interplay of radical evil and human cooperation. This is a useful reminder for a church that either focuses on the power of the will to resist evil or remains silent in simple fideism. The addiction issue thus provides a welcome chance to discuss openly the difficulties and uncertainties we experience in the face of evil.

The AA explanation can be useful in dealing with alcohol and drugs, substances not essential to human life. But with other addictions, especially those called process addictions, we move away from an external chemical substance and a possible biologically imbalanced response to it. It is harder to make an enemy of food, relationships, emotions. Some may stretch the chemical imbalance or allergy theory with, for instance, sugar, white flour, chocolate, coffee. (This reaction is not unusual—remember the story in chapter 7 of the pastor who banned increasing numbers of things from her home.) Even here, many people focus on an assumed biological vulnerability in all kinds of addiction, or such things as ingrained neurological responses as the results of previous trauma.[2] Yet it becomes much more difficult to shun, demonize, or attack something in this category of addiction. Although it is not completely clear-cut even with alcohol and drugs, in so-called process addictions the lines between will, freedom, compulsion, and bondage become even more blurred.

It is not necessary to delve into the many explanations for extending the addiction metaphor into these other areas. What is most striking is the way these often elaborate efforts point to the persuasiveness of the original AA schema, as well as to our culture's increasing biological determinism. The AA schema is attractive because it fills a gap in the contemporary culture by dealing seriously with human dysfunction and its interplay with evil, without acknowledging any explicitly religious explanation.

Yet the strategy of demonization is not novel. Rather than protesting a problematic aspect of Christian practice, it seems to secularize it. Especially in the case of alcohol, it echoes a strand of the temperance movement that set up "demon rum" as the chief enemy.[3] There was precedent for this. In earlier ages, the flesh, sexuality, or women served as the focal point for demonization. Christianity, in its beginnings and for long afterward, felt at home in a world that attributed evil powers to demons and personified the forces of evil. An undercurrent of this attitude has remained, even after Enlightenment success in dispelling the more extreme forms. Alcoholics Anonymous has carried this strategy on successfully—though restricting it—by blending the medical aspect of allergy or chemical vulnerability with demonization. The strategy promotes some familiar behavior, however. For although the language may be more scientific or therapeutic, the behavior is strikingly similar to the restrictions of religion. Three vignettes will help illustrate how mundane, yet familiar, this can be.

A recovering alcoholic student refused to eat a slice of cake served her at a party until she could confirm no alcohol was used in its production. She insisted on scrutinizing the list of ingredients. Others assured her that no alcohol had been used and that, even if it had, it would have been dissipated by the baking process. She was not reassured and decided to play it safe and not eat the cake.

A recent seminary graduate was a longtime recovering alcoholic who had no trouble being around alcohol. When he took his first associate position, however, he was upset to find some members having a drink at a church function. He considered this highly inappropriate and clear evidence of underlying "dysfunction." When staff and others in the congregation did not respond with equal shock, he denounced the whole church as clearly "in denial," "sick," and addicted. Relations deteriorated and he was soon transferred.

A student who consulted her doctor about low energy was given a liquid vitamin supplement. As she took her teaspoon a day, she said she began to look forward to it. She interpreted this as evidence of incipient addiction and called the doctor to ask about the liquid's contents. A small amount of alcohol was present. She stopped treatment and expressed outrage at the doctor. But she was even more worried that she would have to forfeit the credit she had won by keeping "clean" for several years. She called her AA sponsor in great distress. Much to her relief, she was told that because she had been ignorant of the medicine's contents, she was not at fault and could continue celebrating her anniversaries of sobriety.

Such problems magnify when the demonization process expands into exclusivism. A person in recovery may judge or refuse to associate with those deemed "in denial." Or one may see individual finitude and limitations as the core enemy, having the potential to lure one back to the old bondage. A quest for personal purity, the illusion that one can keep evil at bay, a judgmental attitude toward others less enlightened—these too can happen. In any case bondage, even if of a more socially acceptable sort than outright substance addiction, is the result.

Therefore, demonizing alcohol, drugs, or even certain foods, settings, and types of people may have some immediate benefits for addicted persons. But as a long-term model it falls into familiar traps. What is more important, such a strategy does little to help persons explore the very complicated relationship between free will and determinism.[4] How much has the person, whether through inattention or deliberate malfeasance, cooperated with the "evil power?" And how much has been predetermined through rearing, circumstances, biology, trauma? Theology has long discussed this dilemma. The modern therapeutic version is hampered by its generic or secularized tone. It cannot place the evil force in a framework of cosmological source and cause that could account for its power. Nor can it frame the problem in a sociological version of "principalities and powers" that would locate evil in systems that inextricably hold persons. Both the addiction-recovery ethos and the theological tradition agree that evil has a luring power. But the ethos functionally limits evil to a particular substance. It is not an improvement to confine it to an internal "disease process," divorced from any cosmological or philosophical context that situates good and evil in a larger framework. The result of these limitations is a truncated or domesticated version of evil that does not explain—and can implicitly underestimate—both its power and our cooperation with it. The opposite can also happen: Evil can take on such proportions that it assumes an equal status with God, thus severely minimizing divine power.

In the recent past, people feared God and expected divine wrath for their disobedience. The rejection of this causal relationship has not reduced human anxiety. Instead, many have simply displaced this fear onto various substances and processes. Now, instead of understanding our complicity with sin, sin has become a preexisting condition and we are its victims.

THE EXTENT OF PERSONAL RESPONSIBILITY

The Big Book creates a tension in the area of responsibility. On the one hand, although alcoholics must acknowledge the harm they have done because of their addiction, they are seen as powerless to stop. Therefore, they are more sick than bad. On the other hand, the alcoholic's real problem is presented as "self-will run riot." This suggests alcoholics are blameworthy, even morally guilty. "Self-will run riot" can mean many things. The Oxford Group would have understood it as a shunning of God's rule in favor of self-rule. Today it can simply imply that there was an early point when the alcoholic could have stopped acquiescing to his or her vulnerability but chose not to and fell inevitably into bondage.

This tension has some of its roots in the sin tradition and can be translated into theological terms. The inclination to sin resides within a person. It is hard to resist, yet we have a certain measure of choice in fighting it. In a sense, sin is "inevitable but not necessary."[5] Anxiety results from the inherent human situation. Humans are weak and limited, yet they have potential freedom and self-transcendence. Evil is not inherent in humanity. Instead, we find it already present in the world. Yet it tempts us with the illusion that we can resolve this tension, transcend our weakness, or alleviate anxiety. It is inevitable that in one way or another we will succumb. Here too, Alcoholics Anonymous makes a creative stab at breaking the connection between original sin and original guilt, though only for this restricted population. The AA schema would be especially attractive for those who have lived unhappily with our inherited interpretation of original guilt. This is heightened in a culture that rejects communal culpability and favors individual responsibility.

Yet the reprobation the Big Book schema takes away with one hand, it returns with another. Alcoholics Anonymous relieves guilt by claiming a version of "material" but not "formal" responsibility. ("I did it, but I'm not bad. I didn't intend it. I was sick and powerless.") Yet it hands it back again by claiming that, at base, the alcoholic is actually *too* self-willed. This is why the problem is said to be ultimately spiritual. The alcoholic recognizes neither personal limitations nor the greater Power. This identification of "self-will" as the source of the problem is perhaps the clearest meeting point with the theological tradition. It is a definite contribution of the Oxford Group. They, too, worked to turn over self-will to God's will. The connection goes further. Understanding the source of sin as "pride"— meaning assertion of self against God's claim—has long been a dominant strand of Christian theological thinking. This similarity is probably what attracts many Christians to the AA schema. Yet this thematic has come under increasing theological and secular challenge, particularly regarding gender, as chapter 10 discusses.

The Big Book presents alcoholics as the equivalent of "the chief of sinners." Echoing the Oxford Group, the Big Book asserts that *any* life run on self-will can hardly be a success. The Big Book contends alcoholics represent an extreme incidence of the perennial problem of self-will. Translated into theological terms, this is a devastating indictment. A dominant interpretation of sin in Christian tradition sees lack of submission to God's will, putting self in the place of God, or turning away from God and toward idols as the most basic and serious sin. Alcoholics, accused of extreme "self-will run riot," are thus doubly indicted. This heinous charge is accepted so often because, unfortunately, it accurately reflects the inner self-assessment of many alcoholics. It thus has both descriptive power and a striking resonance with inner experience.[6] This inner despair reveals an unverbalized deep knowledge of the reality of sin. Yet the implicit judgment leveled by Alcoholics Anonymous is as serious—or more serious—than the charges it fights from outside. Newcomers may experience serious tension over this incongruity. They are welcomed by being told they are physically sick rather than bad. But then they are confronted with this underlying cause of their sickness.

Alcoholics Anonymous may be making an implicit contract with society by focusing on personal responsibility. In this unspoken agreement, the previous destructive behavior of alcoholics is atoned for through the asceticism of complete abstinence, permanent identification as an alcoholic, and continuing responsibility to "work the program" and attend meetings. There is a payoff, though, in a sense of moral superiority. To make the move "from the derogated status of active 'drunk' to the morally superior—even somewhat prestigious— status of 'recovered' or 'recovering alcoholic' demands not only that the alcoholic disavow and purge himself of his past life—as in the confessional of the AA meeting— but also that he be seen to be giving up something which, by the definition of his condition, he has valued above all else."[7] There are at least two potentially negative consequences.

First, it can subtly elevate the self or at least prolong an intense focus on it. Alcoholics Anonymous tries to keep this in check by actively discouraging "grandiosity," although it admits to being a "selfish program." The Big Book also warns that the alcoholic in Alcoholics Anonymous may now feel "he has become a superior person with God on his side."[8] But this dilemma is built into the framework. Religion learned long ago that the temptation of inordinate self-abnegation is a perverse and oddly disguised self-elevation. This form of spiritual narcissism is especially endemic to our age.[9] It may be an interesting consequence of the "therapeutic ethos."

Second, the recovery movement often includes those involved with the addict under the therapeutic umbrella. They can be considered inherently impaired as well. I have heard many women say in Al-Anon and other recovery groups, "I have to realize that I am sicker than the alcoholic." Others lamented, "Why would I have chosen him if there wasn't something wrong with me?" Although strictly speaking Alcoholics Anonymous and Al-Anon do not promote this, they cannot systematically counteract it, such is the pervasive effect of cultural influence.

The Big Book does imply that anyone living with an alcoholic will be inevitably injured by the experience. The entire family, to a certain extent, is ill. The book also distinguishes between dysfunctional behavior on the partner's part that results from living with an alcoholic, and such behavior that comes from a particular partner's own inherent pathology.[10] This latter aspect has become an influential thematic in the culture since the book's publication. In the late 1980s and early 1990s the codependency movement[11] and debates over "self-defeating personality disorder"[12] became prevalent. This focus can result in a search for one's own particular pathology, rather than an effort at restoring a healthy communion.[13] Again, our culture may be wrestling unaware with theological shadows. For this sounds like a distant echo of the biblical dictum to attend first to one's own culpability before criticizing another, transposed to fit a more individualist and medicalized context.

THE STATUS OF THE WILL

The usual dividing line between the sin and addiction concepts is in the area of will. The conventional dichotomy asserts that under the old sin rubric, the alcoholic was considered a freely willful person, thought to continually choose to drink excessively and destructively. Or the alcoholic was seen as someone who, in choosing drink, chooses sickness and bondage. The will is considered fully free, at least at the outset, and sin is thus presented as free choice used deliberately perversely. This is believed to accurately represent the sin concept, and it is roundly rejected regarding alcoholism.

Under the new addiction rubric, the alcoholic is seen as under the control of an illness. In this sickness, the will is gravely affected. It is disabled by a powerful substance (and—in the original form of the rubric—primarily or only in relation to that substance)[14] to which certain individuals are especially vulnerable. There is a kind of determinism here. The person is in the grips of a pathological condition and cannot exercise the will to do otherwise. Concerning alcohol, then, the alcoholic has no free will. But this is a "soft" rather than a complete or "hard" determinism, for the will, though affected, is not totally bound.

Therefore, in spite of all the stress on powerlessness and lack of free will, elements of free choice appear in the addiction-recovery schema. For instance, there is a suggestion that some choice may have been present at the outset of the illness, even if it was soon lost. There is also a hint that members believe a more enduring level of free choice remains. Members sometimes speak with regret of those who "do not want to want to stop." The Big Book stresses that nothing can really be done until the desire to change breaks forth in the person's own psyche. I have heard many recovery group members say that nothing can happen until the person "gets sick and tired of being sick and tired." Sometimes there is a judgmental edge to this, implying the person is unwilling to change.

The Big Book thus presents a seeming contradiction. First, it claims the alcoholic is powerless, will-less, in the face of alcohol, and yet free choice is not affected in other areas. But, second, it also suggests, in seeming contradiction to the first assertion, that even regarding alcohol, the person can choose to change. In the first contention, then, the will is segmented into sick and healthy parts. In the second, there is a level of physical determinism that somehow does not affect a person's spiritual freedom to call for help and accept it.

The Big Book holds, at base, to only a partial paralysis of the will. But in so doing it blends two quite disparate theological themes. On the one hand, the will is seen as functional. Otherwise, it could not "want to want to stop" and it could not accept God's help. This evangelical Arminianism is borrowed from the Oxford Group. But it is combined with a strong traditional (Augustinian) understanding of the inability of the will to seek the good. This insight clearly grew out of the founders' personal experience with alcohol. In an earlier age, this thematic may have strengthened resolve and promoted self-efficacy. Today, however, it often leads in an unexpected direction by contributing to a cultural drift into biological determinism. Many have embraced it because it confirms contemporary culture's increasing fears of powerlessness and disorder and nascent sense of fatalism. This, too, has contributed to the rise and attractiveness of Twelve Step recovery groups that broaden the types of behavior over which people feel powerless.

Modern recovery practice often moves more in the direction of determinism, with much less segmenting of the will. Many members extend the effects of the disease quite far—sometimes implying that a level of "insanity" exists in this disease that touches virtually all areas of life. After a meeting, one solid-looking business-suited member explained that he distrusted his own and other members' opinions. "Alcoholics are contentious and hostile. Everyone in this room is crazy." At first, he said, he thought he was just powerless over alcohol, but still had control over his recovery and other things. During ten years in recovery, however, he has learned that he is powerless over everything.[15] Another longtime AA member said in a seminary class that lapses in general moral behavior—not necessarily resuming drinking, but such things as domestic violence or dishonesty—can happen even after years of sobriety. He explained, "We're just a bunch of drunks and we do silly things sometimes."[16]

These claims regarding the status and efficacy of the will seem tangled. However, they can be unraveled by looking at some theological aspects of this tension. Theological inquiry sheds light on the seeming mystery of a will that is bound but still free to seek change. It helps explain the dramatic change and strengthening that can happen when a person reaches out. And it highlights the means by which this transition happens. In addiction recovery, the will is believed to experience a dramatic change when help is accepted from one's Higher Power. This is similar to the contention that in spiritual regeneration we are given a new or restored will. In some limited ways, it is an analogy to the Christian view of salvation. Indeed, many members do experience a spiritual quickening through this program. Explaining how this change happens, however, is difficult within the recovery schema.

The idea that the will is segmented into healthy and sick parts is one solution, but it is an awkward one. From a theological perspective, it denies the full extent and pervasiveness of the world's "fallen" or damaged condition. The fact that modern members do see the more extensive effects of spiritual sickness may be a recognition of this fact. But the enduring tie to biological determinism is a weak link in the schema. It can lead to immersion in the tragic dimension of life, with permanently lowered sights or the perpetuation of a fearful self-protective mode. Although it can lead to relatively successful coping, it cannot justify full healing or full regeneration. In the biblical account of regeneration, the new creation is everything (Gal. 6:15). We are created new and made part of a new creation.

Another insightful observation with theological roots is the program's focus on the need for human cooperation with divine power. No matter how pervasive the powerlessness, an element of human choice and cooperation remains. Although God's power is the ultimate change agent, the Big Book recognizes that without human willingness nothing can be done. Many traditions in Christian theology, too, agree on the ultimate need for human beings to choose for or against God. Room is always left for human cooperation, no matter how strong the view of God's sovereignty. However, the transition of human beings from one status to another has two additionally key aspects that are not present in the Big Book's schema. First, traditions within Christian theology assert that God's grace ultimately "goes before" or is perpetually present to inspire, move, or transport the person to the new status. This is most graphically depicted in the incarnation of God in Christ. Second, this is not just a symbol but a reality. For there is an objective act, encapsulated in the sending, life, death, and resurrection of Christ, which makes this transition possible. It is not dependent on human decision but instead is historically grounded outside individual will, actions, or desires. It has the firmest foundation, being rooted in God's intention, intervention, and love. God's grace always goes before our actions (it is "prevenient"). Our actions are both made possible by God's grace and are a response to it. That is the essential message of Jesus Christ.

Because the recovery schema offers no explanation for how this change in status is navigated, it is too limited as a ground of faith. Members may consider this a mystery or insist that explanation is unnecessary when the reality is present. But something firmer is needed to support hope for the long term. The secularizing of a theological theme may be efficacious while the religious tune continues to play in the collective memory. But over time the strains will become distant. At bottom there is a Pelagian cast to recovery when members believe the will must make its first move toward God unaided. In this case, although grace is praised and its mysteriousness stressed, it is functionally subsequent. It comes after the change in status, change in will, and appropriation of God's power. Some members do understand grace to precede their actions. But there can still be problems, unless that change is grounded in a God-initiated objective event, tangible reality, or something enduring and trustworthy, efficacious for oneself, others, and all of history.

Ultimately, the doctrine of sin has been rejected for the wrong reason. At the root of this rejection is a misunderstanding of the freedom of the will. The various strands in Christian tradition agree that freedom remains even in a corrupted world. There is freedom to make choices. But this is different from the biblical "freedom of the children of God"or "Christian liberty."[17] This is the freedom to choose the good and God. Both church and culture operate today with a serious misunderstanding of the relationship of sin to freedom. Many talk about free choice in the formal sense. They set this in opposition to being determined by "a pathological condition." But the doctrine of sin is not talking about the "formal capacity of free choice." Rather, it speaks more about the agent's telos, the ability to "shape desire and set direction."[18]

To place addiction within the category of sin does not imply that a person can easily choose to stop. Both the recovery schema and the doctrine of sin understand the unaided human will as able only to turn away from the good. But theology adds that the first move of that will toward God can only come about through the indwelling grace of God, present before all time. The doctrine of sin preserves the spiritual freedom of the will to respond to that grace. There is moral culpability when that grace is resisted. Even so, the will's bondage is not minimized. On the contrary, it is fully appreciated in the theological picture of the human predicament.

The Big Book, however, has other strategies to motivate the will. Newcomers learn from the Big Book that there are a "few unfortunates" who are "constitutionally unable to be honest" with themselves (about their true alcoholic condition). New members may be shocked at this, given the concomitant stress on the inherent, powerless, and in many ways blameless condition of alcoholics. But persons must somehow be impelled to exert their own wills, rather than giving in to the disease. This becomes especially necessary when members are not given clear explanations of God's presence, desire for the person's well-being, and infusion of grace. Allowing the person to hit bottom or inculcating a fear of being one of the lost, the inherently dishonest, can be used to impel the choice to change.

The emotional import of this strategy is similar to a misuse of the doctrine of "double predestination." In this, some are consigned from eternity to salvation, and some to perdition, through the sovereign election of

God. In this tradition, one's presence among the elect, especially through church membership, and one's observable progress in sanctification, are the chief consolations against this horrible status. Similarly, if certain individuals are both powerless over alcohol and yet constitutionally unable to admit it—the first and essential step to getting help—their situation is genuinely tragic. An alcoholic's only hope is that he or she is not among the "constitutionally unable." To reassure oneself one must practice the program and continue at meetings. A problematic effect of this approach, whether done religiously or therapeutically, may be to "scare one into the kingdom." It can also be used to label others not similarly awakened. Predestination holds a legitimate place, if not a universally accepted one, in Christian theology. But its full theological import is more an assurance of God's firm intention to save than God's design to condemn. For all the practical difficulties it may cause, it differs from the AA schema because it hinges on God's choice. The danger in the AA presentation is that, without a clear and ultimate reference point in God, it may move close to determinism or even blind fate. From this perspective, the will is not really free. For the ability of the will to change is set, and motivation only works on those already predisposed to respond.

Nevertheless, many find the addiction-recovery metaphor an attractive way of describing human dysfunction. I have been contending there are some crucial theological reasons that help explain why the movement appeals. Alcoholics Anonymous and similar groups are tapping into some long-standing debates about the human condition. Since this is done in a way that is both accessible and well suited to a transient, pragmatic, and unstable age, it successfully engages people to think about these perennial problems. The fact that these issues are immersed within a consistent program of help and hope makes it even more appealing. But it is a limited presentation that can fall into some identifiable theological difficulties.

THE HUMBLING OF PRIDE

We all crave clear explanations for our troubles. But the power of the addiction-recovery schema is not simply that it provides a succinct explanation of the addiction problem. This would not be enough to hold people. The addiction-recovery ethos is especially compelling because it offers both a resolution of the problem and a well laid-out plan for reaching it. An important part of the plan is the humbling of pride.

THE HUMBLING OF PRIDE

The AA goal of humbling pride often sparks considerable discussion within addiction-recovery circles. But its theological roots also connect it to the contemporary discussion about the nature of sin. The Oxford Group, Samuel Shoemaker, and early AA members all insisted the troubled person needs to be humbled. The first AAs sometimes required prospective members to kneel and request God's help before being allowed to meet with a group. "On our knees" was written into the original Twelve Steps but was later eliminated.[1] Kneeling is not usual today, but the program still closely follows the Big Book and Twelve Steps in urging a "searching and fearless moral inventory" and sharing this with a trusted person. Earlier practitioners may have stressed the examination of character defects. Today, however—perhaps as an accommodation to current stress on self-esteem—this inventory usually involves an assessment of both positives and negatives in a person's character. Yet the goal of humbling is still part of the process. This may seem unbelievable and even distasteful in an age that values a positive self-image, but it has remained a core aspect of the program.

Since the program aims to be nonauthoritarian, humbling is not put forth as a requirement. Nevertheless, various ways are used to prod people into this difficult step. The Big Book warns that those who avoid the inventory almost invariably get drunk again. Peer support and the counsel of sponsors is a goad. Constant repetition of the Twelve Steps can be persuasive. Once the step is taken, the Big Book implicitly expects that a "leveling" of pride will result. Behind this is the assumption that inordinate self-will ("self-will run riot") is the underlying spiritual problem. Following the moral inventory, the person is to ask God to remove the "defects of character" revealed. Where feasible, they are to try to repair the damage caused. This process of taking "personal inventory" and admitting wrongs is expected to continue indefinitely. Undergirding this whole process, and the chief humbling act, is to turn one's "will and life over to the care of God," as the person understands God.

From a theological perspective, this humbling process draws on a traditional understanding of what separates us from God. Rebellion against God has long been considered the primal sin and source of alienation.[2] This diagnosis results from a standard framing of the human predicament. The traditional theological schema explains that God is the author of our existence and deserves our obedience. Humans were created as "image of God" with a significant measure of freedom. However, since we are creatures, we are by definition limited. Our primary sin, according to the tradition, is trying to defy our limits; this is "pride." God made us human— that is, limited—so these limits are not sin. Instead, defying God, trying to decide one's own limits, refusing to let God be the Lord of one's life: These are sin. God did not cause this, or God would be the author of sin and the divine goodness would be impugned. But human beings invariably choose to use freedom wrongly, and this causes separation from God. God takes the initiative to rectify the situation, especially in the sending of Jesus Christ. We can accept or reject this grace. In this traditional schema, our misdirection has been traced back to the primal misuse of freedom by Adam and Eve depicted in Genesis. This predisposed the human race ever afterward.

This theological schema has a long lineage, reaching back to the apostle Paul. It still provides an influential theological backdrop to contemporary understandings.[3] Its residue pervades the culture, though it is at odds with other more contemporary cultural themes, such as the quest to establish a unique human identity and the duty of self-fulfillment. Contemporary theology also has modified the traditional schema. The primal sin is now understood more as an existential, individual, yet inevitable choice.

Alcoholics Anonymous closely follows the older schema in significant ways. It is traditional theologically in its talk of inordinate self-will as the main spiritual problem. The Big Book shows this strong influence when it suggests that self-will is the source of human difficulty ("any life run on self-will can hardly be a success"[4]). But Alcoholics Anonymous also departs from tradition in claiming alcoholics especially exemplify this chief human problem. This is a strong assertion, but it is unclear how inordinate self-will links with the alcoholic's physical vulnerability. Alcoholics Anonymous is silent on the origin of the problem. It does not posit a historical or even symbolic primal "sin." It does not describe the conditions of the human predicament that would predispose us all to this sin, alcoholics in particular. All it says of origin is that some people seem inherently vulnerable to alcohol. This is problematic, because it makes their predisposition part of their nature, rather than involving a measure of choice or freedom. Logically, this seems to implicate God in their disability, although at one point the Big Book does explicitly reject this implication. Although there is compassion in acknowledging the very real bondage alcoholics face, the program offers no reason or starting point for the "inordinate self-will." Since this is seen as the primal spiritual disease, it poses a difficult dilemma for the alcoholic. Both exonerated and blamed simultaneously, the alcoholic suffers from an inherent weakness but is also too self-willed.

In determining the nature of the problem, the recovery ethos straddles science and theology. But the resolution of the alcoholic's problem follows a dominant strand of traditional theological thinking. Although abstinence is essential, it is not enough. God must rule one's life. We must "turn our will and our lives over to the care of God" (Step Three). Acknowledging God's authority and submitting to it is the only way to rectify the problem. The ultimate goal is service to God and others. Given this traditional format, it is ironic that many believe the recovery ethos is a more palatable and modern understanding of human difficulty than traditional Christianity's. It also seems discordant in a purposely nonauthoritarian movement that eschews traditional religious structures, hierarchies, and doctrines. Yet by stressing divine authority and human submission, Alcoholics Anonymous in effect has adopted the traditional basis for authority in the church.

For many there is a comforting familiarity about the Big Book's claim that inordinate self-will is the basic problem. However, more than mere familiarity accounts for the attractiveness of the "pride" theme. From the start, this theme was effective for early Alcoholics Anonymous, as it had been for the Oxford Group. The Group had appealed to those people aspiring, logically expectant of, or already enjoying worldly success. They were counseled to give up self-will in favor of God's will. Understanding false pride or self-will as a source of alienation from God was probably an apt diagnosis for many. Similarly, many early members were white middle-class men, down on their luck for various reasons, not the least of which was the Depression. Yet most had probably expected to follow the reigning American formula for success through self-motivation and self-assertion. If they found failure, rather than success, through this formula—and their alcohol vulnerability only exacerbated this—perhaps the problem was the formula.

The prescription can be as salient today as in the past. It is still an accurate diagnosis for many who find their way to recovery meetings. It may be especially captivating for those suffering from a desperate striving after, and/or failure to live up to, the cultural expectations of their particular status and socioeconomic situation. Alcoholics Anonymous recognizes the spiritual quickening that can result when people acknowledge God, opening themselves to divine presence and authority. In this sense Alcoholics Anonymous may serve, in Bill Wilson's terms, as a "spiritual kindergarten" opening up the possibility of God, especially for those hostile to religion in general.

The AA strategy of self-loss also echoes a theme from Christian practice. Many Christians have claimed to be transformed through a similar paradox. Following the biblical dictum that one must lose one's life to find it, many have discovered that in sacrificial obedience to God they find new life. Christians have taken the divine obedience argument further, using it to propel not just personal action but social action as well. They have defied human authorities by claiming obedience to the higher authority of God. Women's suffrage, the abolition of slavery, and the civil rights movement all received invigoration in this way. This trajectory is not evident in the Big Book, although Al-Anon may use, in a limited way, the theme of submission to a higher authority as liberating. One precept says that "all of us are, in the last analysis, subject only to whatever Higher Power we choose as a guide for our lives."[5] Generally, however, this is an unplumbed potential in the recovery schema. Activating it would require a loosening of self-focus and a social analysis of systemic structures that help produce addictions. But it would also require a coherent and agreed-upon understanding of God, some objective standard of behavior by which to test action, and a strong sense of guiding empowerment through God's spirit. Otherwise, the action could become the source of internal dissension and could be fragmented, coercive, or destructive.

To be valid, all self-giving in service to God must be voluntary. It cannot be induced through coercion. It is not freely chosen when it springs from exhausted, resigned, or fatalistic acquiescence. Although Christianity has always had its own set of logical and psychological persuasions, its sorry episodes of legally impelled conversions have, one hopes, been relegated to the past. Alcoholics Anonymous began in the spirit of freedom. Early Alcoholics Anonymous insisted that alcoholics might be persuaded, if they were willing to listen, but they were not to be forced. As much as the early AAs believed alcoholics often needed to hit bottom, they did insist one must work to get recovery for oneself. Today, however, not everyone comes to the program by deliberate personal choice. External coercion can come through court-mandated treatment, school referrals, spousal threats, pressure from employer-assistance programs, and interventions.[6]

SIN AS SELF-LOSS

The theme of surrendering self-will to God has a long legacy within the Christian tradition. It has often been used in a liberative way. Alcoholics Anonymous closely follows this by linking rebellion against God primarily with self-will and pride. Like much of Christian tradition, Alcoholics Anonymous posits inordinate self-will as a univocal diagnosis. It is considered equally true for everyone. But this presupposition has come under criticism from both secular and theological perspectives.

Some reject the "submission to God" aspect of the program as oppressive or as enforced religion. Others simply want all reference to God and religious overtones eliminated in a recovery program.[7] Those more sympathetic to the "spiritual" angle sometimes consider turning over power to an external or transcendent God as the specifically oppressive element. Instead, women and other disempowered persons are urged to claim the God/ess "within." Some critics have rewritten the Twelve Steps to redress these problems.[8] Critics of the self-will motif often stress socioeconomic factors. Some argue it is counterproductive to urge an admission of powerlessness from women, people of color, and others forced—through social, economic, or biological circumstances—to disavow personal power and self-actualization. One African-American pastor expresses it graphically: "People of color, women, and homeless folks have always known they are powerless. When some White person stands up and reads the first step in a twelve-step program, a Black person hears the call to powerlessness as one more command to lie down and take it."[9] This implicitly questions AA's presupposition that inordinate pride and self-will are the ultimate source of addiction.

Some committed recovery group members and practitioners accept the critique in part. They allow that "AA's initial members were argumentative, self-willed men who needed to accept limitations upon their behavior and then subsequently make amends for the damage they had caused. It does not make sense to ask women who have been overly submissive to follow the exact same steps."[10] But they respond that the solution is a paradox. In admitting powerlessness over something harmful, one unexpectedly gains personal power. This response simply reasserts the spiritual power of voluntary self-sacrifice. Christians have long argued the same. However, the univocal diagnosis of self-will or pride as the primal sin is still problematic. There are strong theological reasons to question it. Sin can be two-sided. One need not sin only through self-elevation; one can sin also through inordinate self-abnegation or denigration, as women have generally been led to do. I have called this "the sin of self-loss." One can fall into ungodly despair through refusing to be a full self as much as through defiantly trying to assume Godlike proportions. This sin of sloth can be equally destructive in prompting alienation from God.[11]

The sin of self-loss is equally important and equally as damaging as inordinate pride. It is equally able to alienate one from God, self, and others and to cripple one's true potential as image of God (*imago dei*). This sin is aptly characterized by "triviality, distractibility, and diffuseness; lack of an organizing center or focus; dependence on others for one's own self-definition . . . in short, underdevelopment or negation of the self."[12] An entire audience is left unaddressed when the traditional focus on sin as inordinate self-will is stressed. Women and other disempowered people are then implicitly assisted in the sin of inordinate self-loss. They may also be blamed for succumbing to oppression. In either case, they experience further guilt and shame, rather than forgiveness and acceptance. This happens as their legitimate efforts to actualize the self are both punished by society and further discouraged through one-sided preaching against pride. Consequently, the real sin of self-loss is not addressed. It cannot be confronted, confessed, or touched with the message of divine forgiveness.

The two sides of sin do overlap. For the sin of self-loss contains a measure of defiance, and the sin of inordinate self-will contains a measure of passivity.[13] Yet the church has focused its primary attention on the self-will aspect of sin. This is at least partly because the tradition was largely shaped by those who understood personally the temptations of status and power. Alcoholics Anonymous has followed theological tradition in focusing on the same aspect. It is sometimes expressed today in terms of control, as many members are led to focus on their "control issues," areas where they refuse to accept their powerlessness.[14]

There is a problem in continuing this one-sided approach. While it may be salutary for many members, it leaves other people untouched. Those who suffer from inordinate self-loss, or even simply from depression, may find the humbling motif and group influence counterproductive, even devastating. Wilfred Sheed makes this point about depression in his autobiography. He entered treatment for a drinking problem and, like most patients he met there, was also emotionally depressed.

> The Valley had only four weeks to cut us down to size, which in my case would reduce me from about three inches tall to barely visible. A diet of humility designed for knocking the stuffing out of a monster of arrogance can make short work of a borderline depressive, and most of the time I neither agreed nor disagreed but just lay there and let

the bulldozer do its deadly work. If I didn't have low self-esteem when
I got there, I'd sure as heck have it by the time I left.

Earlier he says that "accusing us of low self-esteem at this point was pretty
much like shooting fish in a barrel. Anybody who felt good about himself
at this particular time and place [in treatment for alcoholism] must be self-
deluded indeed, not to say nuts." Although he is describing treatment, not
Alcoholics Anonymous per se, the treatment center closely modeled itself
on the AA program.[15]

At the least, those who have a strong penchant to conform to others' standards will not be emboldened to strike the self-motivated course
necessary to promote maturity, responsibility, and identity. What can result is a lowering of vision and expectation, a resting content in minor
victories. As for the church, the danger is that it will continue to ignore
the inadequacies of the traditional overfocus on sin as pride and self-will.
This motif may promote a hopelessness that becomes sinful. Temptation
then "consists not so much of the titanic desire to be as God, but
in weakness, timidity, weariness, not wanting to be what God requires
of us."[16]

There is a further problem. Not everything that appears as the sin of
self-loss is actually sin. Inordinate self-loss may be the tragic result of having been sinned against. For the societally disempowered, then, an admission of powerlessness may not be an antidote but an exacerbation of the
problem. "The victims of various types of wrongdoing express the ineffa-
ble experience of deep bitterness and helplessness. Such an experience of
pain is called *han* in the Far East. [It is] the critical wound of the heart generated by unjust psychosomatic repression, as well as by social, political,
economic, and cultural oppression." The despair that comes from victimization should not automatically be characterized as the sin of self-loss.
This despair "is entrenched in the hearts of the victims of sin and violence,
and is expressed through such diverse reactions as sadness, helplessness,
hopelessness, resentment, hatred, and the will to revenge." Although this
may set up the precondition for sin, it is not always sin itself.[17]

Thus inordinate self-loss is not always simply another form of sin, as
some feminist argument claims. Rather, it may be the *han* of women. "Sin
is the volitional act of sinners (oppressors); han is the pain of the victim of
sin. Thus, women's sin as 'diffuseness' and 'triviality' is a misnomer.
Women's lack of an organizing center is not sin but han." Although a letting go or turning over of self-will may indeed be liberating for some people, for others it may merely be the resignation of *han*. In both cases a letting go would result, yet when all effort is directed toward impelling a

troubled person to let go, the crucially different motivations could easily be ignored. "While positive letting go requires self-control, its negative form derives from the loss of self-control. Negative letting go is resignation, self-renunciation, and self-abnegation."[18]

Our inherited focus on self-will has caused a misunderstanding or ignoring of the problem of self-loss. Yet self-loss is probably a more common source of despair in the modern era than inordinate self-will or pride. The conditions for loss of self are built into modernity. Our bureaucratic age promotes an inherent facelessness and erosion of self. Persons easily get lost in the crowd. Sometimes this kind of self-loss becomes pathological, and an even more complicated situation results. Pathology can result from victimization, tragedy, or adverse social conditions. Yet it can also set up the preconditions for sin. For instance, narcissism may be one unhealthy or pathological reaction to bureaucratic facelessness. This increasingly common problem is frequently condemned as inordinate selfishness or self-regard. Instead, it may not be too much pride or inordinately self-confident will but an unhealthy self-focused reaction to the loss of self prompted by our age. Feeling inadequately noticed, narcissists become their own cause. This drive is fueled not so much by an overblown self or a misuse of freedom as by the simple *quest* for a self. However, it sets up the conditions for sin when, for example, the person manipulates and misuses others, feeling guiltless and entitled to special treatment.[19] Separating pathology and victimization from sin is both necessary and extremely difficult, because they can overlap or one can prompt the other.

The recovery ethos is presented as an apt approach for victims and persons who are sick. It aims implicitly to deal with victimization, pathology, and responsibility, and this helps account for its popularity. However, members are presented as victims not of oppressive social structures but of a disease. The program of addiction recovery gives few clues for telling the difference between systemic and personal sin, between victimization and sin. It offers one central tool to all. Its method, developed by and for persons who could potentially wield power in society, has been inappropriately expanded and applied. It can thus fall into the same difficulties inherited from the theological tradition, by being similar to a one-sided usage of sin. It may be that, in some respects, "it is the doctrine of sin itself that is self-centered; it is concerned about and focuses almost exclusively on the sinner/oppressor."[20]

It is an improvement to realize there are two sides to sin. Including inordinate self-loss along with inordinate self-will advances our understanding of individual sin. It is even more helpful to know we must distinguish *han* and sickness from sin. Nevertheless, the distinctions are rarely clear-cut. Victims can sin, sinners can be victims.[21] Further help is needed in distinguishing a sinful response from a victim's helpless reaction. Much hinges on this important difference, both for theology and for the recovery ethos.

Even so, learning to make distinctions is still a limited goal. There is evil that does not come primarily from individual sin. Systemic sin cannot be adequately addressed by focusing only on the particular sins of individuals. Societal systems and structures can carry a destructive force that is often more than the sum of individual wrong actions. Reducing our focus to the level of individual action can be an ironically self-centered way of approaching evil in the world. Warped social structures precondition individual behavior. Change must happen on both the structural and the individual level.

Persons committed to the recovery ethos often argue that personal change must happen before larger structures are addressed: "Change has to start within me." This echoes a traditional Christian emphasis on spiritual growth, or sanctification. Growth in grace and developing Christlikeness is an important theological theme. Yet it does not and cannot stand alone. It is connected with a larger agenda and is part of a holistic theological perspective. Individual believers grow in grace to emulate and live more fully in Christ. But this places them inside a much larger effort. The work and message of Christ are for the whole world, not just for individuals. Alcoholics Anonymous makes a selective borrowing of this theme. It partly resembles evangelism in its offer of a group "mission." Step Twelve assumes that recovering alcoholics will "carry this message" to other alcoholics. Sometimes, in practice, this simply becomes an extension of the diagnostic umbrella. It is a valuable mission to seek out hurting people, but it is limited; it avoids the rest of the theological picture: the global, cosmological, and eschatological perspective that a world-concerned Christology provides. Individuals joined-together-as-church work within this larger mission. Bill Wilson specifically rejected this aspect of the Oxford Group's work.[22]

The result, however, is that larger social problems can be minimized in importance. People can be prompted into an endless chase after the elusive goal of personal improvement or down in an endlessly spiraling discovery of deeper and deeper levels of pathology. Instead, they need to be deliberately and programmatically impelled to move beyond both themselves and their fellow sufferers. Healing cannot be successful and sufficiently widespread unless we vigorously challenge societal structures that are exacerbating or promoting addiction problems. Other forms of suffering, too, must be compassionately recognized and healed.

CODEPENDENCY

Some may wonder whether the diagnosis of "codependency" offers a solution to the traditional minimization of the problem of inordinate self-loss. Codependency is presented as the disease that comes from growing up in a so-called dysfunctional family. Originally, this was especially directed at the alcoholic family. But the definition of *dysfunctional* became broadened to where some insist that 96 percent of American families fit the definition.[23] Codependency is generally described as an inordinate, compulsive, and harmful dependence on another, or the uncontrollable giving up of one's self in service to some cause, organization, group, or person. Ego boundaries are blurred, denial is endemic, excessive sensitivity to others reigns, shame is pervasive. Although it is said that men can "have" it, it is most often identified as a particularly female ailment.[24]

The diagnosis has a genius to it. It highlights the problem of inordinate self-loss and deals specifically with gender issues. In many ways it critiques traditional female sex-role socialization, which helps account for its success in capturing public attention. In spite of its wide diagnostic net, the identification of codependency may seem to correspond well to the feminist claim that inordinate self-loss is as damaging as inordinate self-will. In fact, the creation of this diagnosis may be simply one more reaction to our inherited absorption with inordinate pride and self-will. It seems, like feminism, to critique the feminine stereotype, and it extends the practical techniques of Alcoholics Anonymous to a much wider audience. This diagnosis grew out of Al-Anon, the offshoot of Alcoholics Anonymous that strives to help loved ones cope with a family alcoholic's behavior and especially to focus on their own difficulties. But it has reached a wider audience through the work of Adult Children of Alcoholics (ACOA), Co-Dependents Anonymous, and a body of literature on the topic. Today both Al-Anon and ACOA warn about the pathology of self-lessness, whereas previously Al-Anon worked primarily within the AA identification of selfishness and pride as the chief defects for both women and men.[25]

The genius of this diagnosis also becomes its liability. Codependency is probably the most far-flung of the behaviors labeled addiction. The problem is defined broadly enough to fit a myriad of disparate behaviors. It is difficult to argue convincingly that it is physical, like substance addictions, or that it is a unitary disease. It is especially suspect in its pathologizing of female socialization: What was once an assigned and sanctioned role becomes a "disease process." The increasing use of the diagnosis means that many partners of alcoholics assume they have this disease and need treatment. Even those with no discernible relationship to an addict, but who complain of relationship problems, may find themselves included. Most of those so diagnosed will be women.

Although it appeals to some aspects of the feminist critique and finds wide resonance among women, codependency is a cooptation of some feminist aims. In actuality, it grounds "women's experiences and difficulties in heterosexual relationships in a profoundly conservative set of psychological and political premises."[26] When Al-Anon first experimented with the concept of "enabling"[27] (helping the alcoholic continue to drink heavily by covering up, minimizing, rescue, and support), later to be called codependency, it presupposed traditional gender roles. Consequently, it found the wife of an alcoholic in the socially unacceptable situation of having to control the home. She had to do this "unnatural" thing because drinking prevented her husband from assuming his "rightful" place. An important goal during the group's early years was to bring the proper authority and role differentiation back to families in recovery. Beyond this, the codependency construct is reductionist. It pathologizes and homogenizes what are really a differentiated and complex set of sociological and psychological issues, and ultimately spiritual ones as well. Thus the relationship-addiction model represents "a reified, reductionist rendering of depth psychology, packaged for mass marketing. To accept this world of social and psychological equivalents, where victim and perpetrator, addict and caretaker, are no different pathologically, is to accept an undifferentiated world."[28]

From a theological perspective, the codependency construct does little to help delineate certain crucial distinctions. It does not provide tools to differentiate victimization from sin or to distinguish externally coerced self-surrender from self-oriented and manipulative self-loss. Guidelines are also needed for distinguishing either of these from the passive sin of self-loss. There must be a way to sufficiently differentiate pathological or sinful self-loss from voluntary and loving self-giving. This latter distinction is crucial, since love as voluntary self-giving is an essential element in the Christian faith. The Big Book also alludes to this value, so the later-developed codependency construct can cause problems for Alcoholics Anonymous as well.[29]

It is especially striking how much the codependency diagnosis reverts to the focus on inordinate self-will as the chief problem, though it begins with the problem of self-loss. One expert claims that even though the codependent may "voluntarily dismantle" her ego strength in order to connect with others, underlying the problem is the "secretly willful and manipulative nature of the co-dependent's relationship to the world."[30] This in itself is a uniquely will-oriented way of describing self-loss, I contend. Thus, forms of both pride (as ego strength) and self-will—the traditional components of sin—are identified as core in what otherwise may pass as a problem of inordinate self-loss. It is true that one's assertion of power and another's submission to that power contain elements of ambiguity and paradox. There is often some percentage of hidden symbiosis between parties, although the "submitter" may have had little choice in the arrangement. Yet with the AA motif of "self-will run riot" ever in the background, discussions do not always focus well on the "sin of self-loss." Nor is there stress on developing tools to distinguish victimization from sin. A dominant theme in recovery members' discussions as I have encountered them, in Co-Dependents Anonymous for example, is that the codependent is actually using self-giving behavior as a controlling device. Therefore, what at first may have looked like a productive though purely psychological diagnosis—with potential linkages to a theological understanding of self-loss—turns out to impale itself again on the same sword of inordinate self-will.

This diagnosis does not help distinguish between controlling behavior and survival tactics. Yet this is an essential distinction in such problems as domestic violence.[31] Here a woman's apparently manipulative behavior may arise not so much out of self-assertion as out of fear of violence. She may delude herself into believing she can prevent or ameliorate the abusive event. But she is not operating out of inordinate pride or a desire to exercise sheer power. Instead, she usually is trying to protect self and family. The codependency diagnosis can be especially counterproductive when sin and victimization are homogenized. The perpetuation of guilt, a common strategy of abusive partners, is only reinforced when the woman is told she is sinning—or even sick. This accusation from three directions makes it even more difficult for her to evaluate her actions properly. Even though a few writers are more sensitive to feminist concerns, when the diagnosis of codependency is fitted back into a Twelve Step program, the danger is that, like a compass needle, the emphasis will gravitate back toward the reigning metaphor of inordinate self-will. The new awareness of inordinate self-loss, whether seen as sin or victimization, will thus be subsumed beneath the metaphor of self-will.[32]

THE ROLE OF THE HIGHER POWER, THE GROUP, AND THE RESULTS

From the start, Alcoholics Anonymous was sensitive to people who were distant from or actively hostile to religion. The Big Book accommodated the antiauthoritarian bent in American culture by reducing any teaching about God to the bare minimum. Today, AA's light hold on God-talk still can be expedient. Many persons have come to Alcoholics Anonymous alienated from religion but, through the program, have considered the existence of God. Many have reoriented their entire lives. Like those who used the Oxford Group to galvanize and refocus their spiritual energies, many pass through Alcoholics Anonymous to go on to wider service and usefulness to society. A number become chemical-dependency counselors or work in other social services. Some find their way to the church. A few even enter the ministry.

THE ROLE OF THE HIGHER POWER

A budding awareness of God is often the first step in this reclamation process. Not everyone understands the Higher Power as God, however. Some simply choose the group or other tangible entity outside the self. The founders of Alcoholics Anonymous hoped that eventually each member would find the way to God. The chief route is through giving up self-will for God's will.[1] Teaching members to recognize their problem of inordinate self-will is the AA method to gain an admission of God's existence. The pivotal point in an AA conversion is admitting that there is something outside oneself that is greater. Those who have turned away from God through pride, self-assertion, or a desperate striving after Godlike control can find this move liberating. It is not always so liberating, however, for the societally disempowered, for here nearly everything outside oneself is already presumed to be greater. A more liberating admission is to recognize that one is created in God's image, has unmediated access to God's grace, and a divine mandate to live as a full self. The standard AA program is geared more to the first type of liberation than to the second.

Nor does Alcoholics Anonymous provide much content about the Higher Power. This restraint was originally useful, because it allowed people from various backgrounds and with various attitudes about religion to coexist and focus on their common problem. Even today, this relative silence about God's nature can stir curiosity. It may drive persons back to a formerly followed faith tradition or foster consideration of another religious form.

But Alcoholics Anonymous also provides a shortcut that bypasses this route. First, it insists that "we did not need to consider another's conception" of God, for "our own conception" is enough as a starting point.[2] On the surface, this is attractive because it appeals to American antiauthoritarianism and pragmatism. Samuel Shoemaker used a similar approach as the first step in an apologetic process. However, Shoemaker worked to help believers move toward a fuller understanding of God. Echoing this somewhat, the Big Book suggests that members may want to explore religious tradition as they move on in the program. But today this can be subverted as recovery group members stress that they are "spiritual but not religious." This can cooperate with the declining influence of organized religion in America to keep members from taking seriously the Big Book's suggestion. People often stop instead with the minimalist spiritual help provided by Alcoholics Anonymous.

Second, Alcoholics Anonymous contends that "deep down" everyone has faith and a conception of God.[3] In AA's early years many still accepted the idea of God as a "categorical imperative" of human reason (Immanuel Kant). Many were influenced by theologians who explained that a common human impulse—such as the "feeling of absolute dependence" (Friedrich Schleiermacher) or "ultimate concern" (Paul Tillich)—can lead to knowledge of God's existence. Religious resources were available to carry further the effort begun in Alcoholics Anonymous. While these themes may still be persuasive for many today, they are less supported by contact with religious tradition. They can lead as much to idolatry as to worship. This can happen when people set up a God of their own imagining and stop there.

One pamphlet available at a renowned treatment center well known for its Twelve Step perspective takes this to its logical conclusion. It urges women to "shape an image of her Higher Power that appeals to her." Later, it adds, "What you want to achieve is the gift of a blank slate, with a pencil poised in your own hand to redraw the image. . . . What do you need to draw a new image, your *own* image of a Higher Power? . . . What does a Higher Power need to do for you? . . . What form should that Higher Power take? What's best—most comfortable—for you?"[4] Thus the shortcut to God that Alcoholics Anonymous provided in one era—

where resources were readily available to deepen and situate the God-image—can become problematic in another. It encourages people to define God for themselves, to set up their own image of the divine. God is thus crafted in agreeable, malleable, and manageable proportions. Those who should be worshipers are turned instead into artisans.

When we do this with persons—seeing them or allowing them to interact with us only in the ways we want and need them to be—we know, ultimately, that it is wrong. If this route denies the fullness and complexity of a human being, it is even more antithetical to the character of the living and free God. God is the one who confronts us and creates us, rather than the other way around. As in a marriage, one cannot have a true and full relationship with a person or a God we tailor to fit our own needs. In that sort of situation, one can never really know the person or the God.

Additionally, given our perennial bent to move away from God and toward ourselves—or toward idols of our own choosing—it is ultimately not we who can effectively seek God, but God who seeks us. Otherwise, no reconciliation would be possible. Even our knowledge of God depends on God's initiative, not on our curiosity or drive. God is not a God of our own creation. We are a creation of God. We are not, then, required to go on an arduous journey in search of God. Many are not willing, some are not able, and even those who desire to do so can rarely sustain the effort. It is too easy to lose one's drive when the inevitable roadblocks appear. Ultimately, we are not capable of discovering the true God on our own. Instead, we must turn around and recognize the God who is seeking us. The Big Book says, "God does not make too hard terms with those who seek Him."[5] This can encourage a turning toward the seeking God. Just as likely, however, it can give the misleading impression that most of the initiative rests with us. Worse, it can foster the spiritually prideful attitude that those who have sought and found are somehow more advanced or especially chosen. In other words, the same dangers exist here as have always existed in organized religion.

Additionally, it is hard to keep one's focus on God. It is far simpler to turn toward a tangible idol. For some members, the program assumes this function. The clear sets of steps and traditions, the supportive fellowship, the regular meetings—all can interpose themselves between the member and an initial turn toward God. Public testimonials from members about the program explain how *it* saved their lives, how grateful they are to *it*. Meetings end with "Keep coming back, it works." When I visited the book and gift shop of a much-celebrated treatment center, one greeting card read on the outside, *Congratulations on your fifth anniversary of sobriety.* On the inside it proclaimed, *You are living testimony that the program works.* Some might say that this is a euphemism for God in a skeptical age. But later two dedicated AA members, also elders in a church, commented, "No doubt about it, the program becomes an idol for many."[6] For psychological purposes, it may be advantageous to replace a clearly harmful chemical dependency with a benign or even beneficial substitute. But for spiritual purposes, any replacement is fraught with its own danger.

On the surface, the Big Book offers a nonauthoritarian and minimalist presentation of God to encourage belief. Underlying this, however, and seemingly in conflict, is an ultimately monarchical conception of God. God is the all powerful Director who wants to be totally in charge of our actions. This God assigns the role we are to follow and can only work with us if we surrender totally. Another card in the treatment center shop took this to its logical conclusion. It showed a distraught person on the cover. It opened to reveal a director's chair with GOD written across on the back. *Relax,* the text said, *God is in charge.*

It would be irresponsible to judge a program or an ethos based on reductionist one-liners and marketing concerns. Nevertheless, items such as greeting cards hold significance. Like the holy cards, medalions, and popular talismans of folk religions, they ultimately both reflect and exert an influence. Theologians should not ignore or disdain them, leaving it to the social historians of a later age to find them worthy of consideration. They reveal a system conflicted between contemporary antiauthoritarian experientialism and traditional monarchical views. This allows members to move indefinitely between two essentially incompatible views, with no guidelines for knowing whether they are obeying an independent God or a product of their imaginations.

This view also assumes that God in fact works like a monarch. But this is only one theological view of God, more a product of a previous hierarchical and authoritarian age than a nonnegotiable principle. True, scripture speaks of God as King and Lord, and there is a strong theme of sovereignty and rulership. But there are many other varied metaphors for God to make the description richer and more complex. The traditional emphasis on monarchy and unity can work to distract from the more vibrant understanding of God as triune. This uniquely Christian view of God as Trinity involves a God who is internally interrelated and independent, yet also indwelling and interactive with humankind toward the goal of partnership.

God takes on human form in the person of Jesus Christ. We are gradually assumed into the divine life as we are incorporated into Christ's body, healed and sanctified. This culminates when God restores all (apocatastasis, Acts 3:21), becomes all in all, and reigns over all. It is God who takes the initiative in reaching out to us. All our lives, we are surrounded by

God's grace. Still, the choice is ours whether to recognize and acknowledge it. Many imbibe but do not credit the source. Through the incarnation, God fully and compassionately identifies with our condition. Therefore, this image of God is far removed from the authoritarian monarch who regally inhabits a distant heavenly throne, autocratically demanding servile submission and slavish dependence. While elements of obedience, dependence, and surrender are part of the process, it is a more complex matter of reciprocity, mutual commitment, and growth toward maturity through partnering service. Alcoholics Anonymous, for all its modern appeal, nevertheless perpetuates an essentially outmoded and narrow understanding of God that makes a maturing growth in grace much more difficult to understand and effect.

THE ROLE OF THE GROUP

Given how pivotal group life is for most people today in the addiction-recovery movement, it is intriguing that this aspect was not part of the founders' original intention. They expected alcoholics to read the Big Book, imbibe the program, practice the steps, and perhaps speak with a few persons who had been longer on the path. At base the program was meant for individuals and helped individuals one at a time rather than society as a whole. But dependence on the program, rather than on particular individuals, was key. Although sober alcoholics might feel grateful to those who show them the way, a key tradition has remained "principles before personalities." As one member affirmed to me, "individuals are fallible, the program is not."[7] Although this is a rather bold claim, the point here is that, at base, neither individuals nor the various groups are considered effective in themselves but only to the extent that they effectively communicate the program.

Still, over time, group experience has assumed a key role. Persons often have a "home" group, the one they attend most regularly. They are encouraged to choose a "sponsor," often from this group. But it is not the particular group that is considered efficacious. Members are usually encouraged to visit as many groups as they can, and many find they join several different ones. Many members hold an almost sacral attitude about meeting attendance. A belief widespread is that all meetings, no matter how different, are valuable.[8] Although members may feel attachment toward their home group, the recovery group experience is the consummate modern portable environment. It does not require covenanting with a particular set of people in a particular place, as monastics do who take a "vow of stability," seeing the same faces for a lifetime. Instead, the recovery ethos in many ways is a product of our mobile society rather than an antidote to it. When one moves, or even simply becomes tired of a particular group, one can easily find another to attend. Presence equals membership, and one can usually count on the faces around the circle changing frequently. Even so, a significant number find the group experience both attractive and rewarding, even quintessential to the meaning of recovery.

It is understandable that, in an age of transiency, facelessness, and bureaucratically impelled self-loss, these groups should be compelling for so many. People are brought together who might ordinarily never mix.[9] Identification and compassion are promoted. Mutual confession and group acceptance can be relieving and reassuring, especially since gossip is officially repudiated. Some suggest that here is one of the few places where contemporary persons are allowed faces, personalities, and individual care and concern. To a certain extent, these groups have become part of the glue that holds society together.

But, ironically, some of its most "modern" impulses are actually factors tending to make this phenomenon a palliative rather than a cure for impersonality. They can contribute to the decline in community, stability, and commitment in society. The essential interchangeability of persons in groups, and groups with groups, promotes less individuality, not more. Also, the fact that group members relate intimately for a set period at a set time and then go their separate ways is quite different from normal human community. In typical communities, persons share many things—such as common relatives and economic resources, land, or material things—and are bonded together in ways that cannot easily be broken.[10]

While the American impulse toward antitraditionalism and mobility makes recovery groups attractive, in the end they can exacerbate the facelessness that many persons join recovery groups to escape. They can be more a group of individuals meeting to help with individual sobriety than a truly communal effort toward mutual freedom.[11] These groups may also exacerbate our loss of communal responsibility and mutual accountability, since confessions made within the room—including distinctly illegal activities, even murder—are meant simply to be heard, not addressed and certainly not disciplined.[12]

But is all this so different from the contemporary church? Denominational loyalty is at a low ebb. Many persons choose a church based on convenience or attractive offerings, rather than traditional loyalty. Mainline church membership is down and holds less meaning than it did to earlier generations. Persons easily join and leave churches when things do not please them anymore. Many frankly do not find what they are looking for. Those who do not fit the "typical" respectable nuclear family model often feel out of place. Many churches stress service or committee work rather than more holistic communal relationships. Even more important, mutual accountability and church discipline, once a hallmark of church life, is now minimal. In this milieu, recovery groups seem an improvement, with their apparent intimacy, tolerance, informality, mutuality, one-to-one sponsorship, and flexible meeting times.

Many have hoped that recovery groups would bring something modern, necessary, and yet complementary into the church. Small groups for Bible study, prayer, education, service, youth, and social purposes have long been integral to church life. That recovery groups have been readily incorporated into many churches shows the smooth fit. Small groups do have a history of revitalizing the church, as Wesley's class meetings demonstrate.[13] Some pastors who bring in recovery groups do so to reinvigorate their churches. This indicts much of the contemporary church, which should be helpful to individuals in ways similar to recovery groups. Churches need to again promote mutual confession, tolerance, accountability, service, and nurture of one another. Recovery groups look attractive and are admired and copied precisely because church life today does *not* live up to its theological import and practical potential. However, none of these factors get at the heart of an essential theological difference between church and recovery groups. Their bonds and foci are quite different.

Although we must all readily acknowledge our common and our particular weaknesses, it is risky to place one's primary identity in a group bound by a shared pathology or biological vulnerability. No doubt groups can be heterogeneous in other ways (perhaps socioeconomically) and bound together through shared gratitude and mutual joy for each one's recovery. Still, the heavy focus on disability weighs on many members.[14] I have heard, more than once, "We're all crazy or sick here. We're alcoholics." While this is not exactly a sin obsession (even when translated into theological terms), it is nevertheless a pull to continue focusing on weakness and vulnerability. Many in the church, too, have long seen the Christian life as a continual fight against temptation.[15] This can become especially problematic in our determinist age. Focus on individual weakness, even if common characteristics are believed shared, can eventually further an alienating individualism, rather than a creative individuality within community. Alternatively, it can also gloss over real differences in experience and personal makeup.[16] There are serious difficulties in making human weakness a significant common bond.

Although our shared finitude and universal condition of sin is a fact, we sin and are weak in differing ways. Since our strengths and weaknesses differ, we are mutually valuable and differently vulnerable. Unfortunately, this often makes us mutually intolerant and uncomprehending. These factors cannot be the primary focus of the church. Instead, the church is bound together through divine strength, promise, and intention. Our focus and grounding must be in our common worship of God in Jesus Christ. We are bound together by our common indwelling by the Holy Spirit and our common empowerment for global mission, service, and healing. Sin and weakness are impediments, but they are ones we ourselves cannot defeat or transcend. Groups or ministries that focus on specific problems may be useful and even necessary, but they cannot become a primal source of identification.

Therefore, although weakness, finitude, and fallibility are endemic to the human condition, the goal and focus of the church are different. Through the Spirit's power, the church is to envision and actualize the human condition, as it is meant to be and as it is becoming. We are meant to cooperate with the divine mission to restore the world to its rightful shape. God is bringing the world into partnership with God, through incorporation in Jesus Christ. This may seem grandiose and unrealistic in light of the very realistic and often graphic focus on human frailty that recovery groups have. Nevertheless, it is both a divine mandate and a divine promise. Our world suffers tragically from lowered sights. Therefore, this vision is more necessary than continued centering on dysfunction. Such a vision is one important factor in motivating us to work against the drag of sin and toward a life activated by God's grace. Such a comprehensive vision may also be a prime aid in preventing the slip into addiction in the first place.

Since humans carry the divine image and bond wherever they go, in a sense the church too is portable. While stability often characterized the church of the past, modern mobility does not have to eviscerate the church's deepest meaning and function. It is true that meaningful relationships take time and the church could preach helpfully about the advantages of stability. Yet we need also to stress our overall relationship and responsibilities toward one another as members of the global body of Christ. We are brothers and sisters in the same faith family. Churches that welcome newcomers and help them feel quickly situated and appreciated, or ones that take special care with singles, nontraditional families, the displaced, and the lonely, all do this on more firmer footing when our eternal bond as the family of God undergirds this mission. The church should recognize both the need and the theological mandate to provide, with firmer grounding, what many seek from recovery groups.

The Results

The images and metaphors regarding the recovery program's promised results are often frankly religious. It does not take a theologian to notice this. The Big Book offers much hope and optimism for those who follow the program, at times using images very similar to those of Christian salvation. Persons are told that, if they follow the program, they can expect to have new power, restored health, and new sanity. Fear, self-seeking, and craving for alcohol can be nearly eliminated. Not only that, but they will be "reborn" and "enter the world of the Spirit." In a phrase almost directly from the Oxford Group, they will realize that "the age of miracles is still with us."[17] This is a Joblike scenario, where although one's fortune and family may be virtually destroyed, the promise is that one may well prosper again through trust in God. Although there is some implicit protest against Oxford Group perfectionism, by claiming "spiritual progress rather than spiritual perfection,"[18] the promises are nearly as bold. But there is a key difference. The Oxford Group worked for the revitalization of the world's morality. The recovery program limits its sights to individual restoration. Nevertheless, on a limited scale, it is a scenario of salvation. Most obviously, of course, in the minimalist AA version there is no Christ figure, no objective act of redemption done for humankind, no concern for eternal life, no divine plan for the world, no cosmology to situate evil and good. These differences make the two plans ultimately and radically different.

The Big Book warns that this new life only represents a "daily reprieve."[19] At meetings and in informal conversation, one hears stories of persons who started drinking again, after a period of sobriety. The common moral is that they ended up worse off than before, even dead. This may be a useful, protective strategy regarding the consumption of alcohol or drugs for those who have had serious problems. Only a small minority claim that some people can learn controlled drinking, "mature out" of the problem, or spontaneously stop.[20] But when translated into a spiritual principle, the idea of salvation being only a "daily reprieve" can be counterproductive. It can put the onus back on human effort, rather than situating one's assurance in God's faithfulness.

If salvation were primarily our work, then eternal vigilance would be essential to maintain and further any progress toward holiness. Instead, salvation rests entirely on the action and promises of God. One will surely slip, sin, doubt, fall, again and again. This need not doom one to inevitable destruction. It need not consign one's fate to the strength of one's own grip, even with the help of friends. The one assurance against this is that we are grasped by the divine hand. That hand will not let go. Many recovery group members will agree that God holds them. But if one takes the idea of a daily reprieve seriously and lets it inform one's spirituality and theology, fear and human effort can become focal points, rather than the trustworthiness of God. As with religion, the danger is that a goad of fear will become predominant instead. If one does not rely on an external and dependable action of God, effecting one's transition from death to life, one's hold on hope can be extremely fragile and necessarily self-generated.[21]

The idea of recovery only being a daily reprieve contributes to the loyalty of many members of recovery groups and to the discomfiture of others who slacken. One woman, a former active member of Alcoholics Anonymous, came up after a lecture. In an apologetic tone, she explained that, although she did not go to many meetings anymore, "I still work the steps, meditate, read the literature." She insisted it was enough, but added fearfully, "They tell me I will relapse because I'm not going so much. What do you think?"[22] Fear of losing or of not proving one's salvation has functioned similarly to keep many in the church and others worried. Nevertheless, Alcoholics Anonymous has a practical advantage, for it and many other recovery groups are amazingly tolerant and compassionate in welcoming back those who have slipped, even grievously. In this they excel over a sometimes judgmental and intolerant church, impatient with weakness and disbelieving of the endless mercy of God. But unlike the church, recovery members' slips are also useful. For members' failures reinforce the recovery ethos, proving that one is chronically or perpetually ill and in constant need of the program. Wilfred Sheed noticed this from his own treatment and recovery experience. He says:

> Never has an organization had such a soft spot for fallen sinners—and why not? The disease, as they describe it, is so overwhelming, and its victims so weak and helpless in the face of it, that defeat is almost to be expected. Every fall from grace is a testament to the fierceness of the enemy and incidentally to the absolute necessity of their own role as therapists. [23]

How much can really be expected from the recovery process? On the one hand, the promised results are dramatic and life-changing, offering images reminiscent of Christian salvation and sanctification. These groups "attempt to restore a sense of the potential for goodness in people and a commonality of purpose through which members can transcend the limits of individual experience." On the other hand, however, addicted persons must live with the equivalent of "once an alcoholic, always an alcoholic." Often, neither vision nor expectation is allowed to soar too high. One is always kept "realistic" by constant reminders and group discussion of the communal vulnerability. Any behavior deemed "excessive" can become suspect, evidence of reemerging addictive tendencies. "Recovery groups establish unity against the 'exciting, bad' objects of desire, i.e., alcohol and other people, by idealizing self-control and by shunning 'excesses.' In AA, being a 'dry drunk' means exhibiting expansiveness and excessive, unrealistic optimism members come to associate with the alcoholic state." Most recovery groups assume a commonality in the addictive process and "the futility of a final cure."[24]

From this perspective, the recovery method of managing problem behavior can appear both "puritanical" and "regressive." The groups can model some of the negative dynamics of religion. Groups can work to contain the "disturbing 'bad' impulses," expel them "ritually," and get members to "yield to an imagined perfect parent who can protect us from the torment of our own desires and limitations, the damaged humanity of other people and our own disappointing efforts to change them." Some feel, then, that this process has a drawing power "much like the appeal in a great deal of religious thought."[25]

How similar is this to Christian understandings of human growth and potentiality after salvation? Some may see the recovery tension between vulnerability and potential as simply a useful variation on the *simul justus et peccator* theme. In other words, after salvation one is both justified and a sinner simultaneously, and one remains so throughout life. Others may find the recovery ethos to be a modern way of expressing humankind's pull between finitude and freedom. It is true that a careful interpreter can use the addiction-recovery ethos analogously in these ways. Nevertheless, the analogies are limited because there are significant differences. Although there are dichotomies set in scripture between good and evil, flesh and spirit, and Satan and God, ultimately salvation in its fullest eschatological sense is not essentially a matter of purification and expulsion but of restoration and fulfillment.

Sacrifice and dislocation will inevitably happen in the maturing process as believers grow in grace. However, salvation is not primarily a matter of shedding our past, disavowing former connections and preferences, living in fear, and guarding against all incursions of previous pleasures. Although Christians often live this way, salvation has a much richer sense. It is the consummation, actualization, and redirection of a life gone astray. But it is also a life meant to reflect the divine image from start to finish. It is both a refocus of and a maturing into our potential for partnership with God. This does not imply equality with God. But it does imply God's intention and ability to raise us beyond the status of "slaves" and to the status of friends. To accomplish this, complete healing is necessary. Whether this is fully consummated in the present life or the next, we are promised to be "a new creation." This includes our complete wholeness and health, that is, a total transformation. This does not stop with individuals but encompasses all of creation. This goal may seem unrealistic. It is especially discordant in light of the modern focus on deep social conditioning, intractable behavioral problems, and enduring physical vulnerabilities. Yet it is a chief promise and outcome of faith in Christ.

IS ADDICTION A GOOD ANALOGY FOR SIN?

In spite of the differences noted, cannot addiction be used as a good analogy for sin? After all, sin and addiction seem often like close cousins. One can lead to the other, or the two can have areas of overlap. Sin, like addiction, is luring, progressive, easily habituated, highly resistant to change. Christian tradition has long affirmed—through its doctrine of original sin—that sin is something like a hereditary disease, passed down from one generation to the next. These similarities seem to bless the analogy. Additionally, many today are attuned to the addiction-recovery discourse. So here seems to be an incomparable opportunity to communicate the faith in familiar terms. Why not develop addiction as an analogy for sin, or encourage the work already begun in this area?

In the hands of a skillful interpreter, addiction can have some usefulness as an analogy for sin.[26] Yet, like all analogies, this one will only work within a limited range. When it is used to cover too much territory, to explain too much, it stretches thin and breaks, just like other analogies. A key determinant is what gives weight and grounding to the analogy. Is it primarily rooted in a deep understanding of sin, or is it primarily based in the current construct of addiction? Unfortunately, the primary grounding of the sin/addiction analogy today is, for most hearers, the medical and therapeutic framework so widespread in modern Western culture.

Given this, using addiction as an analogy for sin pushes too close to a determinist (or Manichaean) perspective, encouraging hearers to equate sin with human finitude. Although the doctrine of original sin has been heavily and repressively used, it was never meant to deny the original goodness of creation. It was never meant to question the inherent integrity of humankind as it reflects the image of God. Sin has always represented corruption, not essence. Thus, to liken sin to a genetic defect that makes a particular individual vulnerable to addiction can call into question sin's universality. Expanding the addiction construct into a metaphor that covers all human dysfunction, likening that to the universality of sin, locks us in a different vise. " 'Hereditary' sin has a hopelessly naturalistic, deterministic, and even fatalistic ring."[27]

However, the difficulty of analogizing sin and addiction is not due solely to the current preoccupation with science and medicine, its determinism, and immersion in the therapeutic mentality. Biological or illness images have always been of limited value in describing sin. Although they have been used from time to time, they function best when used sparingly and along with a range of other ways to describe the problem. Even when helpful, they cannot be restricted to only one form of illness. Scripture, which has images of sickness and healing, expands the analogy as far as possible. As Blaise Pascal has said:

> The figure used in the Gospel for the state of the soul that is sick is that of sick bodies. But, because one body cannot be sick enough to express it properly, there had to be more than one. Thus we find the deaf man, the dumb man, the blind man, the paralytic, dead Lazarus, the man possessed of a devil. All these put together are in the sick soul.[28]

Analogizing sin simply as addiction, then, is too narrow to depict sin's full range. Additionally, analogies of illness obscure some important aspects of sin. They focus too heavily on physical limitations and lessen the aspect of choice. Piet Schoonenberg reminds us that in sin

> the sinner clings to his own sinful choice, he keeps himself imprisoned in it, enslaved to it. That is why the biological images of a wound or of an illness seem to describe the sinful state less sharply than the images of bondage or imprisonment, because the latter show more clearly that life and limbs are unimpaired.[29]

Therefore, addiction is very problematic as an analogy for sin today, in spite of some common roots and existential overlap. Difficulties abound. There is widespread confusion about the doctrine of sin. Our society's common usage of medical and therapeutic modes as primary points of reference slant connotations away from theological categories. These combine with the inherent difficulty in the analogy itself. Yet there is a strong predilection to analogize these two problems. Whole churches and many ancillary ministries have been structured around addiction-recovery themes. The fact that this has become a significant impulse highlights the problem.

I suggest that in a culture that has lost its theological moorings, the penchant to analogize sin and addiction may have a deeper meaning. It may well be an inchoate attempt to deal with the perennially troublesome and unavoidable question that suffering raises: "Is all suffering the result of sin?" Throughout its history, Hebrew and Christian thought has been concerned with this dilemma. It is one theological question that can never remain theoretical. It confronts us at all levels of human existence, as persons struggle with the uncertainties, upsets, and inevitable tragedies of life, looking for meaning, looking for causes. Earlier thinkers answered the question affirmatively: All suffering is brought about by sin, whether ours or another's. Contemporary theologians lean toward the reverse answer. Persons today more readily think that sin—although not to be equated with the human condition—does spring out of our tragic predicament and the suffering it engenders.

The addiction-recovery schema is modern in implicitly choosing the second explanation. When translated into a theological mode, it depicts sin as a response to anxiety and suffering. The schema meets one particular type of suffering head on, tries hard to ameliorate it, and gives persons helpful coping techniques. This is its triumph. However, the particular way this is done can come at significant cost. First, the cost is conceptual, for theological trajectories exist that lead in problematic directions, including a narrowed and problematic view of God. Second, the cost is practical, for actions can become hampered by determinist attitudes and restricted vision. Third, interpersonally, the cost can come in terms of damaged relationships and the debasing of mutual history.

Therefore, in summary, this schema conflates many different forms and levels of human suffering, subsuming them all under the therapeutic paradigm. It also seriously distorts and repudiates a long-standing theological diagnosis of the human predicament, in the interests of its own schema. It does this by making sin out to be a purely volitional matter. But this is too narrow a reading of the doctrine of sin, in any of its variations. As a result, a rich, holistic way of conceptualizing the human dilemma— one that functioned to steady and inform thousands of generations—is misunderstood and unreflectively cast aside. In a culture that prides itself on being open to a variety of perspectives, this hegemonic stance is ironic.

Last is the tendency to force sin into the "free will" or voluntarist box. Doing this conflates the first question about suffering with a question of another sort: whether, and to what extent, we have free will. Sin is not about the formal category of will, and it is nuanced about the tension between bondage and freedom. It is, then, a confusing situation, filled with excessive conflations, conceptual difficulties, serious misunderstandings, and muddy categories. In this setting, analogies must be chosen very carefully when spiritual and theological matters are discussed. When addiction is too readily and broadly used as an analogy for sin, it is too easy to fall inadvertently into this conceptual conundrum and help spread the confusion.

12

GRACE AND RECOVERY

Sin and addiction have many things in common. Just as people feel trapped in the hopelessness of addiction, sin too looks like a hopeless situation. It is incredibly pervasive, prevalent, and deep in our systems and structures. We meet it early, and we contribute to it almost before we know it. We quickly fall into the habit of acquiescing and then do not easily change. It does seem a trap, a bondage, out of our control. But that is not the whole of human reality. We were not meant for this life of loneliness, alienation, distraction, and destruction. We were meant to live in communion with God and others. Indeed, we can only find our true selves when we place ourselves there. Our bondage is not constitutive or inviolable; it is a perversion. And there is a way out, for the one who made us is the one who can free us. God *must* take the inititiative, because we cannot save ourselves. Often we do not even realize we need saving or have any inclination to pursue it.

It is good news that God can free us. But the news is even better than that. For God *wants* to free us. God's grace will not let us rest in our inertia and complacency. Inklings of a better way, fleeting moments of joy, periods of frustration when we are sure life should mean more—these graced moments prick us unexpectedly. We realize we were made for more. Our restlessness has a reason and a resolution. Finally, the best news is that God works constantly for our freedom and has made all the necessary provisions. The message and work of Jesus Christ has shown that God is willing to identify fully with our condition in order to accomplish this. This is the meaning of God as Trinity. God, from overflowing love rooted in the divine communion, reaches out to us. God changes us through Jesus Christ and invests us with the Spirit. Grace is the love of God that goes before us, seeks us out, calls us in. Not only is our true home in God, but God continually yearns and works to bring us back there. Grace surrounds us, and if we open ourselves to this offer and relationship, we come home. This is the good news.

WHAT IS THE GOOD NEWS?

However, for many today the good news is that they are "sick, not sinning." A reorientation has taken place in our culture. This change has been aided by the church's moralistic identification of salvation with the power to behave better. It also reflects "the displacement of theology by psychology" and its "naive identification of redemption with human potential development."[1] This perspective is pervasive, cutting across many boundaries, liberal and conservative, religious and secular, rich and poor. One writer for an evangelical Christian publication put it this way: "The good news is that my addictions—sex, sugar, others as yet undiscovered!— and my co-dependence are diseases, not moral ills."[2] Many find a kind of release in this redefinition, and sometimes it remains a lifelong self-identification.

For many, this new definition can relieve overwhelming guilt, reduce perfectionism, promote hope, motivate realistic action. These are significant achievements. Yet through this reframing, one is understood more like a machine that is "out of order" than like someone essentially out of relationship. This redefinition falls short of the message and promise of grace. Sin itself is not good news, it is an accurate diagnosis of our problem. Only a frank acknowledgment of one's separation from God—and one's own part in the break—makes possible a fully restored communion with God. With such an acknowledgment, we know immediately where to turn for the solution. The solution, God's grace in Jesus Christ, restores communion.

Actually, the situation has become more problematic. For some the quest of self-realization instead of God-realization is still primary. But for many today even this reorientation has become too arduous. Over time the elusive pursuit of human potential has become increasingly difficult. This is a rapidly changing and disoriented world, with intense competition over resources and increasingly fragile social structures. Selves are impoverished, lost in bureaucracies, internally chaotic. For many people, the primary goal has become simply to quiet the chaos within. Self-absorption is then fueled more by hope of finding any kind of self at all than by a goal of fulfilling a known but hindered self. In this context, many people have reduced their sights significantly, seeking the stepped-down goal of inner calm.

> Plagued by anxiety, depression, vague discontents, a sense of inner emptiness, the "psychological man" of the twentieth century seeks neither individual self-aggrandizement nor spiritual transcendence but peace of mind, under conditions that increasingly militate against it. Therapists, not priests or popular preachers of self-help or models

of success like the captains of industry, become his principal allies in the struggle for composure; he turns to them in the hope of achieving the modern equivalent of salvation, "mental health."[3]

Many people today simply want to move from emotional turmoil to a sense of well-being. They want to achieve some form of internal stasis in a confusing age. Whether a stable state is sought through pharmacology, psychotherapy, group immersion, or spiritual practices, this goal is different from and far short of God's grace. There are others, however, who desire this psychic stabilization but seek it from an encounter with God, that is, through grace. This can be especially true for those who see addiction as a spiritual disease. People understand that through acknowledging God and being open to God's grace, they are given the power to step back from the destructive behavior of addiction. When recovery functions this way, it is a success. Many spiritual journeys start at this point. But this stabilization cannot be an end in itself, for it is too limiting a view. Grace should not be sought as just one more aid in the realization of self. If one turns toward God primarily to obtain divine energy and the ability to change behavior, one is seeking not communion but its benefits. This is far short of both divine intention and human longings. Grace is not the spiritual equivalent of "cosmetic psychopharmacology."[4] Nor is grace primarily an infusion of divine energy that brings mental health. Grace is the presence of God.

GRACE, THE PRESENCE OF GOD

The topic of grace is a complicated one in the history of theology. Many volumes have been written and many arguments conceived. Scripture and tradition present many sides of grace. It is God's loving-kindness, saving activity, gift, power of God through Jesus Christ. Through all this, one point stands out: Grace is the presence of God. Modern interpretation has been especially strong in this presentation.[5] Grace is not, fundamentally, a substance, process, energy, or something else at our disposal. Grace does propel our movement toward God—and through this action our behavior can and usually does change. But grace is not primarily like spiritual vitamins. It is not essentially a help toward reaching our human potential or an activation of human virtue. These may happen. But at base grace is nothing less than God reaching out toward us. Grace is God present for us in Jesus Christ through the Holy Spirit. Grace is God's self-giving. Grace as God's presence also implies relationship. Although it is accepting, it must also be accepted. This cannot be merely a passive or one-time acceptance on our part. The life of grace requires that we respond "and continue to respond to God's invitation by our receptive attitude of love and of (living) faith and hope."[6]

Two things stand in the way of this: our limitations as creatures and our sin. Our finitude makes it necessary that God take the initiative, and God does. That is the message of the incarnation of Jesus Christ. This invitation is repeatedly extended as the Holy Spirit woos and pursues us. But overcoming the obstacle of sin requires a cooperating action on our part. Fortunately, that action is impelled by God's grace (grace as prevenient, going before). Yet although the initiative rests with God, we are free to reject the offer of restored communion. "Sin is first and foremost not self-destruction, but a breaking of the Covenant." In sin, "the sinner *himself* throws off the life of grace by refusing it (or usurping it; that is, refusing to accept it precisely as a grace)."[7]

Ultimately, then, sin is not bad behavior. Neither is grace the power to do better. Both of these are results. Sin, instead, is a breaking of the relationship with God. Grace is a restoration of that covenant. Through grace, we understand the good news that, although sin is deadly, God has the power to overcome it. Any view of sin or grace that stops short of this is inadequate. We are not forever identified by our sin (or our sickness), but by our relationship to God. Acknowledging our sin is primarily acknowledging our separation from God, both willful and inadvertent. It is only when we accept God's grace that we gain a proper understanding of our sin. We see its essential nature, and we see that it is overcome in God. This is good news.

It is not such good news, then, that we are "sick, not sinners," for both the diagnosis and the expected outcome are essentially limited. In seeking to deflect moral approbation, we risk instead rejecting a fully restored communion with God. We are not merely "out of order," we have sinned. We have rejected God's offer of relationship. All is not lost, however. The most optimistic, holistic outcome ironically only follows the most radical diagnosis of the situation. "Though apparently the doctrine of human sinfulness is more pessimistic than the rival theories are, it is fundamentally more optimistic."[8] Given God's unending desire for us, love, and patience, God is always ready to resume the relationship. Thus, while sin may be like addiction, it is not a permanent condition that has no hope of complete recovery. It is not essential to our nature.

The good news is that grace works to fully restore our humanity. "The doctrine of creation . . . implies that man's fundamental nature, obscured and corrupted though it is, is perfect. His perfection as a creature, or his health, is not a far-off achievement . . . it is rather the underlying datum of life." We can legitimately expect more of life, even though we will battle sin continually. Those who seek spiritual health should have some expectation of enjoying it. "Well-being, joy, peace, effective activity are as near as health is to the sick man, not as remote as man is from the ape or the completed building from the blueprint."[9]

Grace, then, is more than divine energy and power to promote better behavior. It is more than a tool chest of coping devices. It is more than inner calm, emotional stasis, or serenity. Grace has content and meaning. It is God present for us, and it is an objective change in our status in relationship to God. Where once we lacked a center and were alienated from God, we now have an integration point, a home, a restored relationship.

Grace is also more than hope. It is more than simply a promise of healing at some future date. People are often drawn to addiction-recovery groups because they are offered a sense of hope. Sheer hope—even hope without an objective content—is often seen as redemptive, prompting forward movement and action. However, when hope itself is seen as the redemptive element, there is a serious problem. For in this dynamic, the past—along with many of its relationships and memories—is often written off as the stage of darkness, disease, hopelessness. This is not only tragic but damaging. There is a danger in "ascribing a redemptive power to hope itself [for] to save humankind by reducing them to their future is to destroy them." Grace is not simply about sheer hope or even primarily about some future transformation. Instead, "in the biblical eschatology the end is not the final stage that consigns all previous stages to an irrevocable, and irrelevant, past. It is not the abrogation of the past, it is the consummation of the whole."[10] Just as Jesus came not to destroy the law but to fulfill it, grace does not totally remake a person into someone different. Instead, it integrates, satisfies, and re-creates that person in a better way. They are a "new creation" because they are now in Christ. They are not a new creation because their original state was fundamentally flawed and had to be entirely replaced.

This is an important caveat for Americans. We are too much accustomed to pulling up stakes, turning our backs on the past, and starting again, whether geographically, with careers, or in relationships. Grace as restored communion with God redeems the whole of life, not just the future. Although God is timeless, God's grace reaches backward as well as forward. We do expect a completed restoration in the future, but we have more to live on now than hope. Restoration begins when communion is restored. Grace is not simply forward looking, forcing us to turn our backs on the past. Our history is not written off or relegated to a pre-graced state. We do not live in a hopeful twilight zone between diseased past and future health. Grace is more than hope and new future. All of our lives, past, present, and future, are touched by God's grace. All of life is consummated, gathered up, and given meaning through the divine-human encounter. As we enjoy ongoing communion, more of the past becomes "usable" and meaningful, restored and rectified. More of our present lives are reconstructed along the divine pattern. To my mind, God is more like the householder than the bulldozer operator. God gathers up the remnants and pieces, creatively making something beautiful and useful out of them, rather than leveling the site and starting again.

GRACE IS NOT ABOUT CONTROL OR DESTRUCTION

In the same way, grace is not about God winning the battle for control. An excessive focus on the problem of self-will often causes this mistaken impression. Similarly, a distortion happens when we try to correct that problem by focusing on our finitude, limitations, and powerlessness. Though many respond to this approach, there is probably an equal number who react against this message by digging in their heels, refusing to let grace in. Although this may seem, or even be, sheer perversity, the problem can lie as much with the presentation as with the hearers. Given the increasing sense of powerlessness in a globalized and bureaucratized environment,[11] fighting the control battle may be almost like a survival issue to some people. A depiction of grace—of allowing God into one's life—as a battle of wills is inherently problematic. Though this emphasis has a long history, it is not necessarily the most appropriate way today to understand the divine-human encounter.

Grace instead is a reordering of things. Through opening ourselves to the presence of God, we realize we have been wrong about our selves and about God. The real problem has not been that God rapaciously wants to control us and we have not let that happen. The portrayal of God as the divine despot who demands submission gives a dissonant tenor to conversion. Part of our resisting God's grace actually springs from this erroneous image, "our willful perception of God as the arch-rival of our ego."[12] When we focus inordinately on self-will, we can add to our wrong, fear-ridden perceptions of God. Even if this approach "works" and a person acknowledges God, this method can easily produce passivity and manipulability instead of intelligence and maturity. God wants to reorder our lives, not diminish them. There is room for authentic personhood and true freedom in relationship with God. It can only be found there.

There also is room for our past to be evaluated fairly, in all its variety, and for it to be accommodated as we reorient to God. Not everything about our past was addictive or diseased. I do not agree that "to be alive is to be addicted." It is not essential that we experience grace as a "stripping away" or the creation of a profound "emptiness."[13] This process may happen in the healing from addictions, but it is not essential to a theology of grace. It is true that images of sacrifice and annihilation have been valid aspects of Christian spirituality.[14] However, when they are coupled with American antitraditionalism, transiency, individualism, and proneness to violence, the results can be counterproductive and destabilizing for the seeker. They are frequently also profoundly hurtful to others, as past relationships and experiences are repudiated, categorized, or devalued. This denies the pervasiveness, endurance, and prevenience of God's grace that has always surrounded us.

God's work is a redeeming of all things. It puts all things back in order (apocatastasis). The very glory of God is that God *can* make something new with these broken pieces we leave lying around. God, like the frugal and creative housekeeper, keeps the home functioning. God can work with even the meagerest of human resources, to create or re-create something beautiful. Fairly young persons may be able to start over and over again. But there comes a point when there just simply is not enough time left in a life to keep beginning anew without the "baggage of the past." Additionally, a divesting of the past is too often ultimately fruitless and destructive. Instead we can model God, work to redeem the past, or at least make something better with the fragments.

Grace, then, is not destructive. To my mind, it is rather like the force of gravity. It is as though life without grace were a poorly constructed space capsule, launched into outer space beyond the reach of gravity. Very little has been secured, and the equipment and furniture fly around dangerously. When the ship reenters the earth's atmosphere and gravity is restored, all the objects fall back into place. They may need to be arranged again, some things do need repair, and a few things are now unnecessary or unusable. But it is not a total destruction.

Of course, there is a distinct and crucial element of obedience in Christian discipleship. Scripture presents God as righteousness and truth, a standard to which there is only one appropriate response. Biblical images make clear that God abhors evil and will triumph over it. God, by definition, is not tame, manageable, or ever fully known. However, it is a broad and frightening leap to be asked to submit to a God about whom one knows very little. If God is presented as an insatiable controller, destroyer, stripper away of addictions—even a "loving, accepting" one—some people will be loath to make the jump, and sometimes for understandably self-preserving reasons. Yet the solution is not to domesticate God into a God "of one's own understanding." This picture of God lacks a consistent content and is as inherently untrustworthy as one's own changing mental scenery. Instead, the fundamental mystery and immensity of God is balanced by what we do know of God, the image we see in Jesus Christ. This is the place where the grace of God reaches a climax. The God we see there, although laying a rightful claim on us, is self-giving, trustworthy, and approachable.

Even so, we are not forced to submit to this God. It is not as though God were a rapist, or even an abusive husband who insists he is doing it "for our own good." God does not despise our finitude and vulnerability (we were made that way). God does not resent every little thing we love like a jealous, petty, or violent human lover. God does, however, want our attention, even our full attention—a difficult task for human beings. But God then returns the favor by giving us as much of the divine self as we can receive. Therefore, we are repeatedly invited to redirect our attention, turn from our sin, take a step. This is hard enough. Fortunately, we need not drum up our own grace or supply our own energy to power a reorientation to God. Grace is a gift; we can only accept or reject it.

Unlike many human gifts, this one has no strings attached. "The gift begets gratitude, not an infinite debt which people can never pay off, and which keeps them indentured for life. . . . Real grace begets graciousness and not repayment on the installment plan." As God comes to us in Jesus Christ, it is not a substitution nor a displacement. Instead, it makes us free persons, freely freeing others. "The grace of Christ does not lord it over its recipients but empowers them to be themselves and to be free enough to serve others joyfully and spontaneously in turn. . . . to present themselves in compassionate service to others, in turn not displacing but enabling those others."[15] Therefore, grace frees us and turns us outward, making us graciously social. Grace also functions socially. It is not a private arrangement between the seeker and God.

Grace Is Social

We are each embedded in a web of relationships. If anything, this web could be more firmly spun than it often is for most of us in America today. While some may find the web too constricting, many others are only dangling by a thread. Yet grace comes to us through this network. Grace is God's presence to us. While that seems to imply an individual God-human encounter, the divine presence is most often mediated through our family, groups, friendships, business contacts, institutions, and other social forms. It is mediated through history itself, as we inherit these forms along with interpretive frames, styles of living, and even adaptive physiological characteristics that have evolved over time. Just as our surrounding social forms can help habituate us to sin, they can also condition us to proper ways to love and care for self and others. They are salutary precisely as they urge us to see beyond our personal horizons, identify with larger causes, and acknowledge that our lot is cast inexorably with many others.

Sin is a social reality, the moral and personal aspect of evil with systemic repercussions. Likewise, grace is a social reality. One cannot cure a social malady solely on individual terms. Working on a large problem "one person at a time" is risky. It ignores the exponential quality of sin and evil, as it combines and grows in ways new and larger than the sum of its parts. A cooperative systemic approach to such evils as addiction must be taken, even as we continue to attend to individuals. This has to be done carefully, for social forms cannot be either universally distrusted or trusted indiscriminately. No social form mediates grace consistently, and, on the other side, few are thoroughly sin-filled. This makes discernment a chief duty for mature persons.

Small groups are social forms. They can mediate God's grace, but they can just as easily promote their own interests and survival. They can be too inward looking, resistant to criticism, and unwilling to question their deepest presuppositions and structures. They can encourage dependence, accommodation, a dulling of the ear to the quiet voice of God. They can thus contribute to sin—especially sin as alienation from God—by making it easier to listen to the group's voice than to the quieter voice of God. All this is even more likely when the groups are disconnected from a larger history of discernment, from the checks and balances of self-conscious institutional connections, and when they have no agreed-upon standard by which to measure their "group conscience." God accommodates to our condition by mediating grace even through the prosaic human social structures we so often malign—church, school, government, family. A small group, therefore, does not necessarily need complete autonomy, fluidity, and independence to experience God's grace. This autonomy may sometimes be a salutary counteractive to a church (and other embedded social forms), which easily grow cold, rigid, and authoritarian. Yet there is a protective factor in religious institution that—at its best—understands its identity in attending deliberately to God's voice, looking specifically for the Holy Spirit's guidance, and willing to be ruthlessly self-critical when necessary. Understanding that grace is social should prod us to join readily with others, rather than automatically to separate. Grace calls us to look not only beyond our lone self but also beyond our group's self-interest.

Unfortunately, the revivalist impulse in American religion has fostered an individualist understanding of conversion and sanctification, as if these processes can happen divorced from context and community. Though small groups are social forms, they do not automatically correct this. The problems of individualism are easily replicated in contemporary therapeutic or self-help groups, both secular and religious. This can happen even when addiction recovery is understood to be a mutual journey, with group survival as a key. For the thrust is more often mutual aid of individual journeys than a communal mission, identity, and health. It can be a tacit permission to listen tolerantly to a million monologues, rather than fostering true interdependence and accountability. Small groups are helpful when they get persons to look beyond themselves, at times even forming rudimentary or partial communities. But this, too, can be a limited function. The key is: What serves as the common bond and focus for the group? Unless the members self-consciously understand their focus to be God's message and mission, the danger is that a collective self-centeredness will simply take the place of individual self-focus. It is not enough to base group cohesion on members' individual vulnerability apart from each other, or even their joint strength together. Unless the group aims for God's grace to hold them together, they are placing their trust in weak and ephemeral hands.

Grace and Addiction

God's grace addresses that slightly sour, out-of-sorts, or downright dirty, desperate feeling that people generally carry around with them. God's grace is greater than that feeling, and greater even than its reality. This feeling, whether vague or all-consuming, is what I think people are describing when they feel inexplicably drawn to a disease metaphor. This may especially be the case when the person has no clear and primary biological involvement in addiction. This feeling may have prompted the addictive inclination or sprung from it. Whether we always feel slightly "off" and disgruntled or downright dirty and ruined, we cannot ignore that we have cooperated with or contributed to our negative state. However, that is not the end of the message. The good and often surprising news is that grace is the larger reality. Once we allow our sin to be placed in the light of grace, it loses some of its power. Sin is still horrible, and it still can eventually kill if left unchecked. But the reality of grace dwarfs the reality of sin, putting it back into perspective.

This sounds good in theory. But the final question here is: What can we expect from God's grace in relationship to addiction? What possibilities are offered? Can we expect a positively good life, or only an arresting of the problem, at best? It may be realistic to teach that we must learn to live with our particular vulnerabilities, especially if we believe no power can actually transform them. It is hard reality that once sins are committed—no matter what their source—we cannot redeem ourselves from them. We cannot even take away their effects. No program or therapy or discipline can win an ultimate victory over vulnerability or sin. However, the Christian hope goes further than that. Grace, God's presence, can and does transform. This can happen slowly or literally overnight. It is generally different and more painful than we think it will be. It is also much more freeing and joyful than we have any reason to hope. We can have setbacks and we can stop the process, for it requires continual cooperation. But grace will work realistically, at a pace we can manage. The depth and extent of the psychological and physical consequences will affect the rate of change.

Grace is not primarily the energy to improve behavior. It is not primarily an infusion of willpower, or a control battle that God wins. Nevertheless it "works" to turn a person away from the destructive behaviors we label addiction. God's presence gives us glimpses of the joy, beauty, health, and integrity that is our birthright as divine creations. This joy helps us turn away from the lure of evil. It helps us stop ignoring our better judgment and gives us the hope to walk in another direction. This sounds simplistic, and it is mysterious. But it is not a secret. This is not hidden knowledge, reserved for the learned, the initiated, or the old-timers. Nor is grace dependent upon the number of meetings or services one attends. Grace is God self-revealing. God *wants* to communicate this to us. It does not, therefore, begin primarily in our feelings, in our will, or in our minds. It can only be known through faith, which is a response, a trust, and a risk. One needs only a bit of faith at the outset. It begins as we turn toward the love that is being offered us in relationship with God.

Grace can be like a delightful tune, playing from somewhere in the background, and we are captivated enough to walk toward it, trying to find the source. It can be like a sharp jolt in the middle of a long lecture, waking us from our drowsiness and drifting. It can be like a painful stumble, making us aware that the path is more dangerous than we thought. It can be like the comic grin of a friend, trying to make us laugh. Grace comes in as many varied ways as we do, but it wants to turn each of us in the same direction. It is easy to ignore, it is not coercive, and we can easily dismiss it. It may well come again, although ignoring it can get habitual. But in every case, grace promises more than we think is possible. And it promises something it can deliver. It promises freedom, life, health, relationship, and love. In other words, grace is the heart of God, welcoming us back home.

NOTES

Chapter 1: Theology and Addiction

1. The Twelve Steps is a condensed version of the Alcoholics Anonymous (AA) method for dealing with alcohol problems. See *Alcoholics Anonymous: The Story of How Many Thousands of Men and Women Have Recovered from Alcoholism*, 3d ed. (New York: AA World Services, 1976), 59–60; this is the so-called Big Book and will be referred to by that name in the notes that follow.
2. An extensive discussion of these and other small groups is given by Robert Wuthnow, *Sharing the Journey: Support Groups and America's New Quest for Community* (New York: Free Press, 1994).
3. *1995–1996 United States Alcoholics Anonymous Directory* (New York: AA World Services, 1995).
4. Robert Wuthnow conducted a social study surveying many small groups and cites numerous statistics. See especially the Introduction, as well as "The Quest for Community," in *Sharing the Journey*.
5. For data on and critique of the small group movement, see Robert Wuthnow, *Sharing the Journey,* passim.
6. Arthur L. Greil and David R. Rudy, "Conversion to the World View of Alcoholics Anonymous: A Refinement of Conversion Theory," *Qualitative Sociology* 6:1 (Spring 1983): 5, 6.
7. From the cover of 1994 meeting list for Alcoholics Anonymous, Center Jersey Intergroup, 21 Samdin Boulevard, P.O. Box 4096, Trenton, NJ 08610.
8. See Stanton Peele's numerous works, especially *The Diseasing of America: Addiction Treatment Out of Control* (Lexington, Mass.: Lexington Books, 1989). See also Harry Gene Levine's pivotal historical study, "The Discovery of Addiction: Changing Conceptions of Habitual Drunkenness in America," *Journal of Studies on Alcohol* 39:1 (1978): 143–74; and the works of Robin Room, for example, "Drinking and Disease," *Quarterly Journal of Studies on Alcohol* 33:4 (1972): 1049–59.
9. See Wuthnow, Introduction, and "The Quest for Community," in *Sharing the Journey*.
10. The 44 percent statistic comes from a study of more than 3,000 self-help groups by the New Jersey Self-Help Clearinghouse. It appears to be representative of a nationwide trend. See Edward J. Madara and Barrie Alan

Peterson, "Clergy and Self-Help Groups: Practical and Promising Relationships," *Journal of Pastoral Care* 41 (1987): 213–20; as cited in Wuthnow, *Sharing the Journey*, 113–14, 433.

11. Richard Reid-King, "Twelve Steps to the Church?" *The Christian Century* (Jun. 12–19, 1991): 613–14.

12. The intensity of this claim ranges from analogy to identity. For examples of very close identification, see Patrick McCormick, *Sin as Addiction* (Mahwah, N.J.: Paulist Press, 1989); Gerald May, *Addiction and Grace: Love and Spirituality in the Healing of Addictions* (San Francisco: HarperSanFrancisco, 1988); William Lenters, *The Freedom We Crave—Addiction: The Human Condition* (Grand Rapids: Wm. B. Eerdmans Publishing Co., 1985); and Dennis Morreim, "A Theological/Biblical Perspective of the Twelve Steps of Alcoholics Anonymous for Implementation in Ministry" (D. Min. diss., Luther Northwestern Theological Seminary, St. Paul, Minnesota, 1984). Cornelius Plantinga in *Not the Way It's Supposed to Be: A Breviary of Sin* (Grand Rapids: Wm. B. Eerdmans Publishing Co., 1995) also deals with the issue but indicates that sin and addiction are not identical. Nevertheless, he accepts much of the addiction paradigm in his section on sin and addiction.

13. Some have gone all the way toward seeing sin as addiction. A group known as Sinners Anonymous has been adopted by some churches. See Ray Thornton, "Sinners Anonymous," *Faith at Work* (Sept./Oct. 1988): 10–11.

14. Gerald May, *Addiction and Grace*, viii. See also John Martin, *Blessed Are the Addicts: The Spiritual Side of Alcoholism, Addiction, and Recovery* (New York: Villard Books, 1990).

15. Richard Reid-King, "Twelve Steps to the Church?" 613–14.

16. For an interesting comparison, see Oliver R. Whitley "Life with Alcoholics Anonymous: The Methodist Class Meeting as a Paradigm," *Journal of Studies on Alcohol* 38:5 (1977): 831–48.

17. See Donald A. Luidens, Dean R. Hoge, and Benton Johnson, *Vanishing Boundaries: The Religion of Mainline Protestant Baby Boomers* (Louisville, Ky.: Westminister/John Knox Press, 1993); and Nancy T. Ammerman, "Golden Rule Christianity: Lived Religion in the American Mainstream," unpublished paper, delivered at the Lay Liberalism Consultation and sponsored by the Louisville Institute for the Study of Protestantism and American Culture, Louisville Theological Seminary, May 23–24, 1995.

18. Overeaters Anonymous, "About OA," information card (OA, P.O. Box 92870, Los Angeles, CA 90009).

19. This is broached, for example, in Andrew Delbanco and Thomas Delbanco, "A.A. at the Crossroads," *The New Yorker* (March 20, 1995): 50–63. A good survey of sometimes conflicting views of addiction that may be held simultaneously in the public mind is William R. Miller and Ernest Kurtz, "Models of Alcoholism Used in Treatment: Contrasting AA and Other Perspectives with Which It Is Often Confused," *Journal of Studies on Alcohol* 55: (March 1994): 159–66.

20. Nevertheless, this focus does not necessitate distinguishing "true AA" from diluted or mixed imitations, even though that is an important point.

21. There are various accounts of the Big Book's initial creation, its status as primarily the work of Bill Wilson, the debate among members over its final content, and its publishing history. See Ernest Kurtz, *Not God: A History of Al-*

coholics Anonymous (Center City, Minn.: Hazelden Foundation, 1979), especially pp. 67–78.

22. Later, *Twelve Steps and Twelve Traditions* (New York: AA World Services, 1981) joined the Big Book as a standard reference. First published in 1952 (with later editions in 1953 and 1981), it has also become important for members in understanding the AA perception of the alcoholic predicament. This text is a clear presentation by Wilson of the "AA way of life." Since it was first published thirteen years after the Big Book, and although I was informed by this text, I chose to focus my close analysis on the Big Book.

23. Because of the conversion-like quality of AA or recovery group experiences, some liken the recovery phenomenon to cultlike, or at least sectarian, behavior. Others note this element with guarded approval, cautious lest Alcoholics Anonymous be identified with religion. See Arthur L. Greil and David R. Rudy, "Conversion to the World View of Alcoholics Anonymous; Francesca Alexander and Michele Rollins, "Alcoholics Anonymous: The Unseen Cult," *California Sociologist* 7 (Winter 1984): 33–48; and Robert Kenneth Jones, "Sectarian Characteristics of Alcoholics Anonymous," *Sociology* 4 (1970): 181–95. Kurtz more positively recognizes the phenomenon, see *Not God,* 183; and AA psychiatrist Dr. Harry M. Tiebout understood it as a beneficial psychological process, see "Conversion as a Psychological Phenomenon," National Council on Alcoholism, Washington, D.C., from 1944 paper read to New York Psychiatric Society. See also James O. Prochaska and Carlo C. DiClemente, "In Search of How People Change: Applications to Addictive Behaviors," *American Psychologist* 47:9 (Sept. 1992): 1102–14; and Carlo C. DiClemente, "Alcoholics Anonymous and the Structure of Change," in *Research on Alcoholics Anonymous: Opportunities and Alternatives,* ed. Barbara S. McCrady and William R. Miller (New Brunswick, N.J.: Rutgers Center of Alcohol Studies, 1993), 79–97.

24. See Klaus Makela, "Implications for Research of the Cultural Variability of Alcoholics Anonymous" (particularly pp. 200–202), and Robin Room, "Alcoholics Anonymous as a Social Movement" (170–76), in *Research on Alcoholics Anonymous,* ed. Barbara S. McCrady and William R. Miller; and Kathleen Anne Flynn, "Performing Sobriety: Story and Celebration in Alcoholics Anonymous," Ph.D. diss., Northwestern University, Evanston, Illinois, 1994.

25. Today a common initial recommendation is "90 in 90": that is, 90 meetings in 90 consecutive days.

26. Regular Friday AA meeting in Princeton, New Jersey, Fall 1994.

27. Bill Pittman, *AA: The Way It Began* (Seattle: Glen Abbey Books, 1988), 189.

28. The Big Book, xiv.

29. Correspondence from Ernest Kurtz to author on January 9, 1995.

30. Tradition No. 10 says, "No A.A. group or member should ever, in such a way as to implicate A.A., express any opinion on outside controversial issues—particularly those of politics, alcohol reform, or sectarian religion. The Alcoholics Anonymous groups oppose no one. Concerning such matters they can express no views whatsoever," (*Twelve Steps and Twelve Traditions,* 192).

31. The Big Book, 93–95.

32. See the review of Wilfred Sheed's *In Love with Daylight: A Memoir of Recovery* (New York: Simon & Schuster, 1995) by Robert Stone, "Looking the Worst in the Eye," *New York Review of Books* (Apr. 6, 1995): 4–6. Reviewer Stone says Sheed, who went through alcoholism treatment and continued on

in Alcoholics Anonymous, had eventually to leave it. "It's in his Catholicism that Sheed collides head-on with the AA people. In spite of its agnostic brand of religiosity, the Program is, at its core, deeply Protestant, even Calvinist. It involves a denial of the doctrine of free will, a surrender to and utter reliance upon grace, which he was unlikely, by instinct, to accept."

Chapter 2: The Changing Discourse

1. Male member, AA meeting, Asbury Park, New Jersey, August 1994.
2. Alcoholics Anonymous General Service Conference, "A Letter to a Woman Alcoholic" (n.d.), 4.
3. Alcoholics Anonymous, "So You Love an Alcoholic: Take Courage; There Is Hope" (New York: World Service Conference, n.d.), Al-Anon Family Groups.
4. The 1994 meeting list for Alcoholics Anonymous, Central Jersey region.
5. Kenneth Blum and Michael Tractenberg, "New Insights into the Causes of Alcoholism, *Professional Counselor* (March/April 1987), 33.
6. Barbara Yoder, *The Recovery Resource Book* (New York: Simon & Schuster, 1990), 32.
7. Conrad Bergendorff, *Pastoral Care for Alcoholism: An Introduction* (Center City, Minn.: Hazelden Foundation, 1981), 2.
8. National Public Radio, *Morning Edition*, "Alcohol Abuse and Treatment," five-part series, October 4–8, 1993.
9. Bette S. Tallen, "Co-dependency: A Feminist Critique," *Sojourner: The Women's Forum* (January 1990): 20–21. A most biting critique is leveled by Wendy Kaminer. She says (using codependency as the prime example), "Sickness . . . is more marketable than sin [but] what looks at first like a therapeutic view of evil turns out to be religious instead. . . . Addiction and recovery look a lot like sin and redemption." She decries this as "probably millennium fever . . . everybody wants to be reborn." *I'm Dysfunctional, You're Dysfunctional: The Recovery Movement and Other Self-Help Fashions* (New York: Vintage Press, 1993), 18–20. A similar critique undergirds such groups as Rational Recovery, Secular Organizations for Sobriety, and Women for Sobriety. On these groups see "Clean and Sober—and Agnostic," *Newsweek* (Jul. 8, 1991). It would be a mistake, however, to conclude that members of these groups are always atheist or agnostic. Robert Muscala, for instance, who founded the Muscala Chemical Health Clinic in Minneapolis, connected with Rational Recovery, is a Roman Catholic and uses as a slogan, "Even religious people need a rational recovery."
10. Space only permits a few examples. See Patrick McCormick, *Sin as Addiction* (Mahwah, N.J.: Paulist Press, 1989); Gerald May makes the connection in a positive way but focuses on a more generic spirituality in *Addiction and Grace: Love and Spirituality in the Healing of Addictions* (San Francisco: HarperSanFrancisco, 1988). See also Tim Stafford, "The Hidden Gospel of the Twelve Steps," in the evangelical publication *Christianity Today* 35:8 (Jul. 22, 1991); *The Journal of Ministry in Addiction and Recovery,* formed in the 1990s, adopts this perspective. Minister Vernon Bittner has consciously made a Christian adaptation of the Twelve Steps; he is executive director of the Institute for Christian Living in Golden Valley, Minnesota, and

author of several books on this topic, such as *Breaking Free* (Burnsville, Minn.: Prince of Peace, 1986).

11. Karl Menninger's *Whatever Happened to Sin?* (1973; reprint, New York: Bantam Books, 1988) is perhaps the best-known book to note this disappearance. Examples of a small contemporary resurgence of interest are Cornelius Plantinga's *Not the Way It's Supposed to Be: A Breviary of Sin* (Grand Rapids: Wm. B. Eerdmans Publishing Co., 1995), and Ted Peters, *Sin: Radical Evil in Soul and Society* (Grand Rapids: Wm. B. Eerdmans Publishing Co., 1994).

12. Jonathan Edwards, the New England pastor noted for his work in the great eighteenth-century American religious revival, is often identified by a sermon about "sinners in the hands of an angry God." Rather than being harsh and judgmental, however, this sermon speaks about a merciful God.

13. Overgeneralization is very common. One pastor, for example, insisted in a newspaper article, "*Most* alcoholics look at the church as the enemy . . . as a place that condemned them and did not offer the comfort and care that they needed" (emphasis mine). And yet this man, a recovering alcoholic himself, describes how his pastor "hauled [me] to every AA meeting [in town] and showed me he loved me and cared for me despite my addiction." See "Pastor/counselor Turns Own Addiction into Positive Force to Assist Others" (*Warren [Ohio] Times Observer,* Mar. 2, 1994, A-3).

14. For a succinct treatment, see Edward Farley, "Sin/Sins," in *Dictionary of Pastoral Care and Counseling,* ed. Rodney J. Hunter (Nashville: Abingdon Press, 1990), 1173–76.

15. See Michael J. Bader, "Looking for Addictions in All the Wrong Places," *Tikkun* (Nov./Dec. 1988); "Are You Addicted to Addiction?" *Utne Reader* (Nov./Dec. 1988); and such works as Stanton Peele, *The Diseasing of America: Addiction Treatment Out of Control* (Lexington, Mass.: Lexington Books, 1989); Wendy Simonds, *Women and Self-Help Culture: Reading Between the Lines* (New Brunswick, N.J.: Rutgers University Press, 1992); and Wendy Kaminer, *I'm Dysfunctional, You're Dysfunctional.*

16. Gerald May, *Addiction and Grace,* 11.

17. Richard K. Fenn, *The Secularization of Sin: An Investigation of the Daedalus Complex* (Louisville, Ky.: Westminister/John Knox Press, 1991), 61–62. Søren Kierkegaard understood the concept of dread not to be a secularization of the sin concept but the experience of sin itself. See Søren Kierkegaard, *The Concept of Dread,* trans. Walter Lowrie (Princeton, N.J.: Princeton University Press, 1972).

18. See Peter Conrad and Joseph W. Schneider, *Deviance and Medicalization: From Badness to Sickness* (St. Louis: C.V. Mosby Co., 1980); Michel Foucault, *Birth of the Clinic: An Archeology of Medical Perception* (New York: Vintage Books, 1975); and the classic work about the increasing influence of the therapeutic paradigm, Phillip Rieff, *The Triumph of the Therapeutic:Uses of Faith After Freud* (New York: Harper & Row, 1966).

19. Kathleen Anne Flynn argues, for example, that "the storytelling (and accounting) practices inherent in the 'therapeutic language' of professional treatment, and those inherent in the 'language of the heart' found in traditional AA culture, present recovering alcoholics with a major clash of paradigms which must be negotiated successfully if they are to maintain sobriety" ("Performing Sobriety: Story and Celebration in Alcoholics

Anonymous," Ph.D. diss., Northwestern University, Evanston, Illinois, 1994).

Chapter 3: The Relationship of Sin and Addiction

1. H. Richard Niebuhr, "Man the Sinner," *Journal of Religion* 15 (1935): 272–73.
2. This point was made to me by Edward Dowey, Emeritus Professor of History of Doctrine at Princeton Theological Seminary. Richard Fenn goes further, saying, "What societies take to be sin is, to put it simply, a social product." Richard K. Fenn, *The Secularization of Sin: An Investigation of the Daedalus Complex* (Louisville, Ky.: Westminster/John Knox Press, 1991), 62.
3. H. Richard Niebuhr, "Man the Sinner," 273–74.
4. Reinhold Niebuhr, for example, says, "To believe that there is a devil is to believe that there is a principle or force of evil antecedent to any evil human action" (Reinhold Niebuhr, *The Nature and Destiny of Man,* vol. 1 [New York: Charles Scribner's Sons, 1964], 180).
5. "Hamartano—Sin in the Old Testament," in *Theological Dictionary of the New Testament*, ed. Gerhard Kittel (Grand Rapids: Wm. B. Eerdmans Publishing Co., 1979), 267–86.
6. This can be found in such works as Søren Kierkegaard, *The Sickness Unto Death,* ed. and trans. Howard V. and Edna H. Hong (Princeton, N.J.: Princeton University Press, 1980), and Reinhold Niebuhr, *Nature and Destiny of Man.*
7. Illustrated in the work of Søren Kierkegaard, *Sickness,* and in Jurgen Moltmann, *The Theology of Hope: On the Ground and Implications of a Christian Eschatology,* trans. James W. Leitch (London: SCM Press, 1967).
8. Reinhold Niebuhr, *The Nature and Destiny of Man,* vol. 1, 183–84.
9. Edward Farley, *Good and Evil: Interpreting a Human Condition* (Minneapolis: Fortress Press, 1990), 137.
10. Edward Farley, "Psychopathology and Human Evil: Toward a Theory of Differentiation," *Crosscurrents in Phenomenology,* ed. R. Bruzina and B. Wilshire (The Hague: Martinus Nijhoff, 1978).
11. See Andrew Sung Park, *The Wounded Heart of God: The Asian Concept of Han and the Christian Doctrine of Sin* (Nashville: Abingdon Press, 1993).
12. For an excellent example, see Mary Potter Engel, "Evil, Sin, and Violation of the Vulnerable," in *Lift Every Voice: Constructing Christian Theologies from the Underside,* ed. Susan Brooks Thistlethwaite and Mary Potter Engel (New York: Harper & Row, 1990).
13. Park, *The Wounded Heart of God,* 70.
14. Farley, "Psychopathology and Human Evil," 229.
15. Farley, *Good and Evil,* 136–37.
16. Niebuhr, *The Nature and Destiny of Man,* 185.
17. Ibid., 194.
18. Edward Farley disagrees with Niebuhr's interpretation of sin as pride, seeing it as a premature identification. "In our view, refusal of finitude is the negative side of the *eros* toward the eternal, toward meaning and permanence, and evil arises out of the *mundanizing* of the proper object of that *eros*" (Farley, "Psychopathology and Human Evil," 220).

19. Kierkegaard, *The Sickness Unto Death,* 44–49, 107–17.

20. Niebuhr, *The Nature and Destiny of Man,* 208.

21. This is well represented in Niebuhr, *The Nature and Destiny of Man,* 228–33.

22. Karl Barth, *Church Dogmatics,* IV/2 (Edinburgh: T. & T. Clark, 1958), 403–5.

23. Kierkegaard, *Sickness,* 49–53.

24. Ibid., 78–96.

25. Ibid., 78–80.

26. Niebuhr, *The Nature and Destiny of Man,* 233.

27. For additional reflections on this, Judith Plaskow, *Sex, Sin, and Grace: Women's Experience and the Theologies of Reinhold Niebuhr and Paul Tillich* (New York: University Press of America, 1980); Daphne Hampson, "Reinhold Niebuhr on Sin: A Critique," in *Reinhold Niebuhr and the Issues of Our Time,* ed. Richard Harries (Grand Rapids: Wm. B. Eerdmans Publishing Co., 1986), 46–60; Susan Dunfee Nelson, "The Sin of Hiding: A Feminist Critique of Reinhold Niebuhr's Account of the Sin of Pride," *Soundings* 65:1 (Spring 1982): 316–27.

28. Many secular and feminist writers have noted this about the self-help culture. Wendy Simonds, for example, says, "Many psychologically oriented self-help authors want to deemphasize women's connections with others" (*Women and Self-Help Culture: Reading Between the Lines* [New Brunswick, N.J.: Rutgers University Press, 1992], 56). One extreme result can be therapists urging troubled persons to physically "detach" from family members for a lengthy period, even mothers from children, ostensibly to help the patient "find herself." This was ably presented in the four-hour two-part PBS Frontline shows #1312–1313, "Divided Memories," aired April 4 and 11, 1995; transcripts available from Journal Graphics, Inc., 1535 Grant Street, Denver, CO 80203.

29. Phillip Rieff, *The Triumph of the Therapeutic: Uses of Faith After Freud* (New York: Harper & Row, 1966).

30. Farley, "Psychopathology and Human Evil," 211.

31. Engel, "Evil, Sin, and Violation of the Vulnerable," 156.

32. Reinhold Niebuhr, *The Nature and Destiny of Man,* 219–27.

33. Dennis Donovan says, "This paradox—the apparent lack of self-control over a behavior that is used by the addicted person to exert control over and cope with other aspects of life—appears to cut across the objects of addiction" (Dennis Donovan, "Assessment of Addictive Behaviors: Implications of an Emerging Biopsychosocial Model," in *Assessment of Addictive Behaviors,* ed. Dennis Donovan and Alan Marlatt [New York: Guilford Press, 1988]). See also G. Alan Marlatt and Judith R. Gordon, eds., *Relapse Prevention: Maintenance Strategies in the Treatment of Addictive Behaviors* (New York: Guilford Press, 1985).

34. Reinhold Niebuhr, *The Nature and Destiny of Man,* 233.

35. Ibid., 250.

36. Richard C. Erickson, "Reconsidering Three Dichotomies," *Journal of Religion and Health* 21:2 (Summer 1982): 120.

37. Erickson, "Reconsidering Three Dichotomies," 121.

38. Ibid., 117.

39. See Michael Bavidge, *Mad or Bad?* (New York: St. Martin's Press, 1989).

40. A succinct treatment of this can be found in Ted Honderich, *How Free Are*

You?: The Determinism Problem (New York: Oxford University Press, 1993), 53–54. He summarizes the theory of determinism as: "Each mental event, including each choosing or deciding, is tied to a simultaneous neural event in that the two things are nomic correlates. Since the neural event happened, whatever else had been happening, the mental event happened, and the neural one would not have happened without the mental one. Each such psychoneural pair is the effect of a causal sequence, whose initial causal circumstance had in it early neural and bodily events and also certain environmental events. Each action, in a general sense of the word, is the effect of a causal sequence whose initial circumstance included a psychoneural pair which itself included an active intention." He summarizes the theory of free will as: "Choices and decisions are different from other mental events in that they are originated by the self. That is to say that they are owed to it in such a way, of which no more can be said, that the person is in a way responsible for them. He or she could have decided otherwise, given things exactly as they were and the past exactly as it was."

41. Although the free-will-versus-determinism argument continues in secular discussion, the church has increasingly ignored the related free-will-versus-predestination issue. After hundreds of years and considerable acrimony, many persons have agreed with the World Conference on Faith and Order declaration of 1937 that settling the paradox of human free will and divine grace is not essential for vital faith. This is not to say, however, that debate about the paradox of human freedom and divine action has been abandoned. See Thomas F. Tracy, ed., *The God Who Acts: Philosophical and Theological Explorations* (University Park, Pa.: Pennsylvania State University Press, 1994), which contains several articles on this topic.

42. Farley, *Good and Evil*, 136.

Chapter 4: The Theological Roots of Alcoholics Anonymous in the Oxford Group

1. Regarding the genesis of the name, see John F. Woolverton, "Evangelical Protestantism and Alcoholism 1933–1962: Episcopalian Samuel Shoemaker, the Oxford Group, and Alcoholics Anonymous," *Historical Magazine of the Protestant Episcopal Church* 52 (March 1983): 53–65.

2. This strategy is evident in a few contemporary writers, who find the Oxford Group/Alcoholics Anonymous connection compelling because it seems to connect Alcoholics Anonymous with traditional Christianity. Although very much a minority voice in the recovery movement, this ethos does give justification to those who would like to combine an AA type of spirituality and message with church ministry. Examples of this impulse include Dick Burns, who has written a number of books stressing Christian/Alcoholics Anonymous connections: *The Oxford Group and Alcoholics Anonymous: The AA–Good Book Connection* (Seattle: Glen Abbey Books, 1992); *Dr. Bob's Library: An AA–Good Book Connection* (Wheeling, W.Va.: The Bishop of Books, 1992); and *New Light on Alcoholism: The A.A. Legacy from Sam Shoemaker* (Corte Madera, Calif.: Good Book Publishing Co., 1994). There are also a number of doctoral and doctor of ministry theses with this emphasis, such as Dennis Morreim, "A Theological/Biblical Perspective of the Twelve Steps of Alcoholics Anonymous for Implementation in Ministry," D.Min. diss.,

Luther Northwestern Theological Seminary, St. Paul, Minnesota, 1984; and Charles Taylor Knippel, "Samuel M. Shoemaker's Theological Influence on William G. Wilson's Twelve-Step Spiritual Program of Recovery," Ph.D. diss., St. Louis University, St. Louis, Missouri, 1987.

3. Even when writers note the Oxford Group connection, they usually do not stress the conceptual elements. When, occasionally, they consider a few common themes, the emphasis is usually on the elements rejected. Even Ernest Kurtz, *Not God: A History of Alcoholics Anonymous,* (Center City, Minn.: Hazelden Foundation, 1979), who otherwise gives excellent coverage of the Oxford Group connection, does not dwell on the conceptual similarities. See also John H. Peterson, "The International Origins of Alcoholics Anonymous," *Contemporary Drug Problems* 19:1 (Spring 1992): 53–74. The few exceptions include Woolverton, "Evangelical Protestantism and Alcoholism." Somewhat more problematic exceptions are the partisan approach of Knippel, "Shoemaker's Theological Influence" and the even more partisan treatment by Dick Burns, *The Oxford Group and Alcoholics Anonymous.* For a more common and accessible case in point where the Oxford Group connection is totally absent, see Andrew Delbanco and Thomas Delbanco, "A.A. at the Crossroads," *The New Yorker* (Mar. 20, 1995): 50–63.

4. The writer, James Houck, was responding to the Delbancos' article on AA's history. The letter writer is exceptional in his acceptance of the close identification of AA with the Oxford Group; James W. Houck, Timonium, Md., "In the Mail," *The New Yorker* (May 1, 1995): 10.

5. The middle and late nineteenth century had been a time of focus on personal sin, as witnessed in the waves of revivalism. However, when the Oxford Group emerged in the early twentieth century, the American Protestant revivalistic focus on individual sin and conversion was being edged out by an emphasis on social reform. While this included an awareness of human weakness and need, there was a new confidence in dealing with it. This perspective enjoyed increasing acceptance in the intense early part of the century. Yet reformers sustained many threats to their perspective during the period between 1913 and 1933; see Otis L. Graham, Jr., *An Encore for Reform: The Old Progressives and the New Deal* (New York: Oxford University Press, 1967), 172. The repeal of Prohibition in December 1933 was a major blow to American Protestantism. It would never regain its old confidence. For this and other reasons, the climate of mainline Protestantism at the time of AA's emergence was chastened and anxious, not triumphant. In their theological orientation, the mainline churches were generally not focused on sin. Therefore, it would have been possible to adopt a religious approach in continuing the fight against alcoholism without a strong doctrine of sin.

6. Laurence William Grensted, *What Is the Oxford Group?* (London: Oxford University Press, 1933), 19.

7. See Walter H. Clark, "The Contribution of the Groups," in Correspondence section, *The Christian Century* (Jan. 24, 1934): 125–26; Samuel Shoemaker, "Houseparties Across the Continent," *The Christian Century* (Aug. 23, 1933): 1056ff; A. C. McGiffert, Jr., "A Theologian Appraises Buchmanism," Correspondence, *The Christian Century* (Sept. 5, 1934): 118–19; and editorial, "A God-Guided Dictator," *The Christian Century* (Sept. 9, 1936): 1182–83; see Reinhold Niebuhr's critique, especially the last paragraph in "Hitler and Buchman," *The Christian Century* (Oct. 7, 1936): 1315–16.

Niebuhr vehemently criticized the Oxford Group saying Buchman's praise of Hitler reveals its "social philosophy" in all its "childishness and viciousness" (1315).

A lively debate waged in Britain as well. One area of controversy in Britain revolved around the Group's practice of public confession, witness, and guidance. Some saw "sharing" as akin to the confessional, others as egotistic and potentially scandalizing. Guidance was considered too limited a method and nonrational. Some saw the movement as theologically sterile, lacking essential elements of Christian theology. Some saw it as parallel and helpful to the churches, others as a poor substitute. The movement was considered by many to be elitist, with no place for social concern. Finally, many feared the movement was highly authoritarian, even to the point of tolerating Fascist and Nazi sympathies. Later on, its fervent anticommunism promoted similar worries among observers. See D. W. Bebbington, "The Oxford Group Movement Between the Wars," in *Voluntary Religion,* ed. W. J. Sheils and Diana Wood (Oxford: Basil Blackwell, 1986). A generally positive attitude toward it was maintained, however, by Emil Brunner, *The Church and the Oxford Group* (London: Hodder & Stoughton, 1937), who had some group experience.

8. One play, *Susan and God,* performed in 1937 at the Plymouth Theater in New York, as well as other popular literature, ridiculed the group without directly mentioning it; Rachel Crothers, *Susan and God* (New York: Random House, 1938). See Ruth McKenney, *Industrial Valley* (New York: Harcourt, Brace & Co., 1939); see also *Brensham Village,* part two of *Brensham Trilogy,* by John Moore (Oxford: Oxford University Press, 1984, first published in 1946).

9. "I thank heaven for a man like Adolf Hitler, who built a front line of defense against the anti-Christ of communism. . . . Of course I don't condone everything the Nazis do. Anti-Semitism? Bad, naturally. . . . But think what it would mean to the world if Hitler surrendered to the control of God. Or Mussolini. Or any dictator. Through such a man God could control a nation overnight and solve every last bewildering problem" (Quoted in Reinhold Niebuhr, "Hitler and Buchman," *The Christian Century* [Oct. 7, 1936]: 1315–16, reprinted in *Christianity and Power Politics,* [Charles Scribner's Sons, 1940], 159–65).

10. This also appears to have been a breaking point for Samuel Shoemaker's cooperation with them; see Woolverton, "Evangelical Protestantism and Alcoholism," 57.

11. Edward Luttwak, "Franco-German Reconciliation: The Overlooked Role of the Moral Re-Armanent Movement," in *Religion: The Missing Dimension of Statecraft,* ed. Douglas Johnston and Cynthia Sampson (New York: Oxford University Press, 1994).

12. Bill W., "When A.A. Came of Age," in *Alcoholics Anonymous Comes of Age* (New York: Harper & Brothers, 1957), 39.

13. Personal correspondence with Ernest Kurtz, August 31, 1994. Also see his *Not God,* 234–36.

14. Carl Jung and William James are often mentioned. A guest sermon in a Unitarian church in Columbus, Ohio, suggested that because the Twelve Steps refer to God as Higher Power, recovery meetings are really little Unitarian gatherings. (Barry Keenan, First Unitarian Universalist Church, Columbus, Ohio, October 29, 1995.)

15. A Roman Catholic priest, Fr. Ed Dowling, aided Wilson. Occasionally and informally—especially in Roman Catholic circles—the Twelve Steps is compared favorably with the spiritual program of Ignatius of Loyola.
16. Quoted from 155–56 of Reginald Pound, *A. P. Herbert* (London: Michael Joseph, 1976), in Garth Lean's *Frank Buchman: A Life* (London: Constable & Co., 1985), 281. For a description, see Samuel Shoemaker, who gives a first-hand account of the team efforts and group practices in "Houseparties Across the Continent," *The Christian Century* (Aug. 23, 1933): 1056ff; but see also in the same issue, Douglas J. Wilson, "A Critique of Buchmanism." These and other sources show that while Buchman desired a measure of social reconciliation between classes, in practice this desire functioned more as tokenism.
17. Allan W. Eisler, *Drawing-Room Conversion: A Sociological Account of the Oxford Group Movement* (Durham, N.C.: Duke University Press, 1950), 161.
18. Grensted, *What Is the Oxford Group?*, 5; compare the Big Book's claim that the goal is to "restore us to sanity (59)."
19. An insider's highly favorable description of Oxford Group methods is given by an early core book of the movement, A. J. Russell, *For Sinners Only* (London: Hodder & Stoughton, 1932). See also his *One Thing I Know* (London: Hodder & Stoughton, 1933). An interesting outsider's description of Oxford Group methods as they evolved later is given by Geoffrey Williamson, *Inside Buchmanism: An Independent Inquiry into the Oxford Group Movement and Moral Re-Armament* (London: Watts & Co., 1954). See also Oxford Group leader Garth Lean's biography, *Frank Buchman*.
20. Russell, *For Sinners Only*, 189–204.
21. One can see this even in the description of a more objective observer, Henry P. Van Dusen, in "The Oxford Group Movement: An Appraisal," *Atlantic Monthly* (August 1934): 242. A satire on the Oxford Group, showing their pride in reforming a drunkard who was actually simply playing along with them, only highlights this sort of work as typical of them; see *Brensham Village* by John Moore.
22. See Kurtz, *Not God*, p. 24, who says Groupers believed that "the continuing small percentage of alcoholics to attain sobriety . . . proved the correctness of their own view. 'Alcoholics just weren't worth all that trouble,' and each week a few additional Groupers received guidance that Bill Wilson should abandon his efforts with drunks and turn instead more directly to the aims of the Group as a whole." Kurtz refers readers to the foundational history of Alcoholics Anonymous, Bill W., *Alcoholics Anonymous Comes of Age*, especially pp. 74–75, and Robert Thomsen's *Bill W.* (New York: Harper & Row, 1975), 256. Although I agree with Kurtz, p. 9, that alcoholics were certainly not the primary focus of the Oxford Group, my reading suggests that they dealt with this problem frequently and prided themselves on some success with it. It was part of the image they presented of themselves.
23. Grensted, *What Is the Oxford Group?*, 5.
24. The Big Book, 161.
25. *Remaking the World: The Speeches of Frank N.D. Buchman* (London: Blandford, 1947), x.
26. Russell, *For Sinners Only*, 7.
27. See Eisler, *Drawing-Room Conversion*, 211–12, who also believes they have a cultlike character.

28. Williamson, *Inside Buchmanism,* 165.
29. Audience member's public comment at author's seminar at Concordia College, Moorhead, Minnesota, Fall 1994.
30. He had planned to work with the author of a book much read and quoted in Oxford Group circles, H. A. Walter, *Soul-Surgery: Some Thoughts on Incisive Personal Work* (Calcutta: Association Press, 1919), but the author died unexpectedly early in his mission career. See Theophil Spoerri, *Dynamic Out of Silence: Frank Buchman's Relevance Today* (London: Grosvenor Books, 1976), 56.
31. Eisler, *Drawing-Room Conversion,* 162–63; Clark, "The Contribution of the Groups," 108–10.
32. Walter Houston Clark, *The Oxford Group: Its History and Significance* (New York: Bookman Associates, 1951), 119ff.
33. B. E. Gwyer, "Comments of an Educationalist," in *Oxford and the Groups,* ed. Richard Crossman (Oxford: Basil Blackwell, 1934).
34. Eisler, *Drawing-Room Conversion,* 173.
35. See Walter, *Soul-Surgery,* a work much used by the Oxford Group.
36. Grensted, *What Is the Oxford Group?,* 23.
37. Eisler, *Drawing-Room Conversion,* 161–80, 192.
38. The Big Book, 7.
39. Grensted, *What Is the Oxford Group?,* 24.
40. "A Revolution to Cure a Revolution," in *Remaking the World: The Speeches of Frank N.D. Buchman.*
41. Eisler, *Drawing-Room Conversion,* 210.
42. Luttwak, "Franco-German Reconciliation," 47.
43. Al-Anon meeting, Stratford St. Paul's United Methodist Church, Delaware, Ohio, Fall 1990.
44. Woolverton, "Evangelical Protestantism and Alcoholism," 59. Kurtz, however, does not find sufficient evidence to claim this; personal correspondence with the author, January 9, 1995.
45. Conversational comment of Hazelden treatment counselor to the author, Hazelden Foundation, Center City, Minnesota, winter 1992.
46. A number of these anecdotes can be found in Garth Lean, *Frank Buchman.*
47. See "That Knotty Marriage Problem" in Russell, *For Sinners Only,* 268–80.
48. See Janice Haaken, "From Al-Anon to ACOA: Codependence and the Reconstruction of Caregiving," *Signs* 18:2 (Winter 1993): 321–45; Charlotte Davis Kasl, "The Twelve-Step Controversy," *Ms.* (Nov./Dec. 1990): 30–31, and *Women, Sex, and Addiction: A Search for Love and Power* (HarperCollins, 1992); Gail Unterberger, "Twelve Steps for Women Alcoholics," *The Christian Century* 106:37 (Dec. 6, 1989): 1150–52.
49. See Virginia Perrot, "Many Women Struggle with the Issue of Powerlessness," *Hazelden News and Professional Update* (Sept. 1991): 6–7; also, Cynthia Downing, "A Double-Dose of Powerlessness: Sex-Role Socialization and Alcoholism in Women," *Addiction and Recovery* (July/Aug. 1991): 20–23; and Nan Van Den Bergh, "A Feminist Perspective on Addictions," ibid., 30–33.
50. Pia Rosenqvist notes that, for instance, the young attractive woman "newcomer" garners immediate interest from male members, while the long-time female member might function as mother. For this and other reasons, people are advised to choose a sponsor of the same sex. The research she notes

has found far fewer women than men in leadership positions on any level, local or national; see Pia Rosenqvist, "AA, Al-Anon, and Gender," *Contemporary Drug Problems* (Winter 1991): 687–705. Although much of Rosenqvist's research was conducted in Nordic countries, it points to similar problems on the American scene. When I noted that Hazelden separates men and women in treatment, it was explained to me that women alcoholics invariably try to help the male alcoholics rather than attending to their own problems (Hazelden visit, winter 1992). Some of my own experience comes from regular Saturday night AA and Al-Anon meetings in Delaware, Ohio, 1990–92, as well as other meetings and comments from members.

51. See Russell, *One Thing I Know,* ix–xii, and C. Irving Benson, *The Eight Points of the Oxford Group: An Exposition for Christians and Pagans* (London: Oxford University Press, 1936).

52. See Knippel, "Shoemaker's Theological Influence," 52. For a Groupist-inspired but more traditional Christology, see L. W. Grensted, *The Person of Christ* (New York: Harper & Brothers, 1933).

53. D. W. Bebbington, "The Oxford Group Movement Between the Wars," in *Voluntary Religion,* ed. W. J. Sheils and Diana Wood (Oxford: Basil Blackwell, 1986), 504.

54. Samuel Shoemaker, "The Decision of 1941," 3, Shoemaker Papers, Record Group 101-6-6, Episcopal Church Archives, Austin, Texas, quoted in Knippel, "Shoemaker's Theological Influence," 61–62.

55. Frank Child, "A Vicar's Welcome," in *The Meaning of the Groups* (London: Methuen, 1934).

56. W. H. Clark, *The Oxford Group: Its History and Significance* (New York: Bookman Associates, 1951), 113–14.

57. Garth Lean defends Buchman's loose hold on Christian doctrine as he related to non-Christians, saying he just wanted to help persons "take the next step" to God, in *Frank Buchman,* 513.

58. Grensted, *What Is the Oxford Group?,* 16.

59. *As Bill Sees It: The A.A. Way of Life* (New York: Alcoholics Anonymous World Services, 1967), 95, quoted from a 1954 letter.

60. See Clark, *The Oxford Group,* chap. 16, and Child, "A Vicar's Welcome," 4, 6–7.

61. Emil Brunner, *The Church and the Oxford Group* (London: Hodder & Stoughton, 1937), 95.

62. Kurtz speaks of Wilson's "lifelong friendship" with Shoemaker; *Not God,* 24. *New Yorker* letter writer James Houck remembers Wilson always referred to Shoemaker as his "chief source"; "In the Mail," 10. Although he takes a clearly apologetic approach, retired lawyer Dick Burns is convinced that Wilson knew Shoemaker very early in his Oxford Group experience and had many private sessions with him; see Dick B., *New Light on Alcoholism,* especially chap. 6.

63. See Samuel Shoemaker, "Houseparties Across the Continent," describing a 1932 tour through Canada and the United States.

64. Woolverton, "Evangelical Protestantism and Alcoholism," 54, says "Shoemaker at the invitation of . . . Wilson . . . was able in the 1950s to cast a religious aura about that organization. [This] led many members of AA to look upon the Episcopal church as a place of acceptance and even refuge for those suffering from alcoholism.

65. Bill W., *Alcoholics Anonymous Comes of Age*, 261. See also the official biography of Wilson, *Pass It On: The Story of Bill Wilson and How the A.A. Message Reached the World* (New York: AA World Services, 1984), 174.
66. Samuel Shoemaker, *The Conversion of the Church* (New York: Fleming H. Revell, 1932), 20.
67. Helen Smith Shoemaker, *I Stand by the Door: The Life of Sam Shoemaker* (New York: Harper & Row, 1967), 58. Although it would be stretching a point to make close comparisons with addiction treatment centers, it is true that many residential centers (especially those deeply influenced by Alcoholics Anonymous, such as Hazelden) focus on day-to-day life issues, stress reeducation rather than specifically medical interventions, and use AA-style small groups and personal counseling as key methods.
68. A detailed study of Shoemaker's thought can be read in Knippel, "Shoemaker's Theological Influence"; I am following in part his detailed work here. See especially chap. 3.
69. Helen Shoemaker, *I Stand by the Door*, 82. According to her, the fellowship experienced at a mission house party was exceptional. She describes how churchmen spent a weekend with men at the mission.
70. Samuel Shoemaker, "The Types of Sin," untitled manuscript [ca. 1930], Shoemaker Papers, Record Group 101–40-32, Episcopal Church Archives, Austin, Texas, as cited in Knippel, 125.
71. Shoemaker indicates that sin is an offense against God's holiness, and God is not merely exasperated by sin but hates it. Knippel presents a good selection of quotes from Shoemaker's private papers regarding these points; see "Shoemaker's Theological Influence," chap. 3.
72. This might have provided a useful theological avenue to pursue. For if he had made this connection from a Reformed perspective, stressing the bondage of sin, he could have played with popular understandings of diseased powerlessness to claim that there was no recourse but the work of Christ.
73. Knippel, "Shoemaker's Theological Influence," 126–27.
74. Woolverton, "Evangelical Protestantism and Alcoholism," 52, 64.
75. See Samuel Shoemaker, *The Conversion of the Church*, 17–18; also Woolverton, "Evangelical Protestantism and Alcoholism," 56.
76. Helen Shoemaker, *I Stand by the Door*, 42.
77. Samuel Shoemaker, *The Conversion of the Church*, 17–18.
78. After a "quiet time," Shoemaker reported that he understood Christ to be the head, not Buchman. Shoemaker thought many of Buchman's criticisms of the church were valid. However, he said, "I happen to love the organized church in spite of its timidity and ineffectiveness, and I wish that she would lead instead of following." Eventually, he put his total energies toward that goal. See Helen Shoemaker, *I Stand by the Door*, chap. 11.

Chapter 5: The Break with the Oxford Group

1. For example, see Norman Clark, *Deliver Us from Evil: An Interpretation of American Prohibition* (New York: W. W. Norton & Co., 1976), and Joseph Gusfield, *Symbolic Crusade: Status Politics and the American Temperance Movement* (Urbana, Ill.: University of Illinois Press, 1963).
2. See "Bill's Story," the Big Book, esp. pp.10–12. John F. Woolverton, "Evangelical Protestantism and Alcoholism 1933–1962: Episcopalian Samuel

Shoemaker, the Oxford Group, and Alcoholics Anonymous," *Historical Magazine of the Protestant Episcopal Church* 52 (March 1983): 53–65, cites a letter, p. 60.

3. One of the most comprehensive histories is Ernest Kurtz, *Not God: The History of Alcoholics Anonymous* (Center City, Minn.: Hazelden Foundation, 1979). Woolverton contends that over time Wilson increasingly encouraged the religious aura that Alcoholics Anonymous was to acquire. See "Evangelical Protestantism and Alcoholism," 54.

4. I am using the term "early AA members" to indicate the distinctive group of alcoholics within the Oxford Group who went on to form Alcoholics Anonymous. At first, some identified themselves as the "alcoholic squadron" of the Oxford Group. Some had begun to use the name Alcoholics Anonymous informally by 1938. See Kurtz, *Not God*, 74.

5. On those who drank more through Prohibition, see, in the Big Book "The Keys of the Kingdom," 304–5f; "Alcoholic Anonymous Number Three," 183–84; and "He Thought He Could Drink like a Gentleman," 213. Ernest Kurtz (*Not God*, 30) summarizes Dr. Bob Smith's attitude: "Passage of the Eighteenth Amendment had brought hope. He couldn't drink if he couldn't get it."

6. Wilson was the only one of the four original AAs who had almost no religious training. Of the four, Wilson and one other had generally aversive reactions to the church, but not tied specifically to their alcohol use. The other two indicated they had tried the resources of their faith to help with the problem. See the Big Book, pp. 157–58. Of the numerous narratives in Alcoholics Anonymous, it is striking that only some report a childhood religious background, although research by Kurtz has discovered that "at least seven or eight others did have a conventional religious upbringing." Ernest Kurtz, correspondence with author, January 9, 1995; *Not God*, 73.

7. Woolverton, "Evangelical Protestantism and Alcoholism," 56.

8. Bill W., *Alcoholics Anonymous Comes of Age* (New York: Harper & Brothers, 1957), 74–75. This is also indicated by *Twelve Steps and Twelve Traditions* (New York: Alcoholics Anonymous World Services, 1981), 142.

9. See "Bill's Story" in the Big Book, 13: "I ruthlessly faced my sins." See also his comment that the Big Book "reeks of sin, sickness, and death," Letter, 1950, quoted in *As Bill Sees It* (New York: AA World Services, 1991), 116.

10. Woolverton, for instance, insists that "the 'initial spiritual answer' to Wilson's problem of alcoholism did not stick": "Evangelical Protestantism and Alcoholism," 60. One of the most insistent examples on the other side is Dick Burns, who worked to prove that Alcoholics Anonymous is based on solid Christian principles Wilson learned from Shoemaker and the Oxford Group. See Dick B., *New Light on Alcoholism: The A.A. Legacy from Sam Shoemaker* (Corte Madera, Calif.: Good Book Publishing Co., 1994), and *The Oxford Group and Alcoholics Anonymous: An AA–Good Book Connection* (Seattle: Glen Abbey Books, 1992). Tim Stafford, very sympathetic to the ethos and work of Alcoholics Anonymous, examines the Oxford Group roots and considers the Twelve Steps amenable to Christianity, but in the end he claims Wilson was "unredeemed"; see "The Hidden Gospel of the 12 Steps," *Christianity Today* 35:8 (July 22, 1991).

11. Bill W., "When AA Came of Age," in *Alcoholics Anonymous Comes of Age*, 37–39. Regarding Dowling, see also Kurtz, *Not God*, 47.

12. Bill W., "When AA Came of Age," 11. This move is similar to that made by Ernest Kurtz, who sees Alcoholics Anonymous as presenting insights that predate and implicitly judge those of modernity. However, he also sees affinities with neo-orthodox thought and especially with existentialism. See "Why A.A. Works: The Intellectual Significance of Alcoholics Anonymous," *Journal of Studies on Alcohol* 43:1 (1982): 38–80.

13. See John H. Peterson, "The International Origins of Alcoholics Anonymous," *Contemporary Drug Problems* 19:1 (Spring 1992): 68–70.

14. According to a memo from Irving Harris, once assistant pastor with Shoemaker, Wilson from the start wanted to confine his efforts to alcoholics. Shoemaker supported him in that, against the objections of other Groupers. Irving Harris, Memorandum Regarding Bill and Sam: "At that time in New York the usual result of a full-blown experience like Bill's consisted of full-time participation in the activities of one of the several Oxford Group traveling teams. And Bill's new friends in the Group frequently urged him to get going in the customary team activity. Having shaken off the deadly grip of alcohol, he was consumed with a desire to spend his time not in general evangelism, or 'life-changing,' but in helping other alcoholics. . . . Sam was never personally persuaded that Bill should participate in the general team travel that was going on. He was impressed by the sincerity of Bill's own convictions about what he should do and advised him to follow his own deepest convictions even to the extent of incurring the disapproval of other leaders in the Group" (Dick B., *New Light on Alcoholism*, 325–27).

15. "Naturally enough, they did not think too highly of our objective, limited as it was to alcoholics. From our point of view, we felt very sure we couldn't do much about helping the Oxford Group to save the whole world. But we were becoming more certain every day that we might be able to sober up many alcoholics" (Bill W., *Alcoholics Anonymous Comes of Age*, 65, 74).

16. See the Big Book, 25, 29, 56, but also see the other side on p. 30.

17. Regular Friday AA meeting, Princeton, New Jersey, October 1994.

18. Stanton Peele disagrees with the inordinate extension of this categorization. But he feels he may have been somewhat responsible when he extended addiction theory to cover love. See Stanton Peele and Archie Brodsky, *Love and Addiction* (New York: Taplinger Publishing Co., 1975). For his critique, see *The Diseasing of America: Addiction Treatment Out of Control* (Lexington, Mass.: Lexington Books, 1989).

19. Bill W., *Alcoholics Anonymous Comes of Age*, 269–70.

20. Ibid., 270. Others from Shoemaker's time and our own have suggested the church model itself on AA. See Robert K. Nace, "Alcoholics Anonymous Speaks to the Church," *Journal of Clinical Pastoral Work* 2 (1949): 124–32.

21. The Big Book, 58.

22. Ernest Kurtz calls this "the spirituality of imperfection." He strongly suggests that this is an antidote to modern narcissism and self-focus, not the promulgation of it. Ernest Kurtz and Katherine Ketcham, *The Spirituality of Imperfection: Modern Wisdom from Classic Stories* (New York: Bantam Books, 1992).

23. Woolverton, "Evangelical Protestantism and Alcoholism," 62.

24. Gerald May, *Addiction and Grace: Love and Spirituality in the Healing of Addictions* (San Francisco: HarperSanFrancisco, 1988), 11.

25. Ernest Kurtz, "Why A.A. Works," 38–80, 52.

Chapter 6: How the Big Book Sees the Alcoholic Predicament

1. *Alcoholics Anonymous: The Story of How Many Thousands of Men and Women Have Recovered from Alcoholism*, 3d ed. (New York: AA World Services, 1976), hereafter referred to as the Big Book, xxiv, xxvi, xxviii.
2. Ibid., 18.
3. Ibid., 157.
4. Ibid., 33. One Hazelden worker, a recovering alcoholic herself, insisted to me that if she were to begin drinking tomorrow, although she has been sober many years, she would be as far along in "the disease process" as though she had never stopped drinking. Hazelden visit, winter 1992.
5. The Big Book, 39.
6. Ibid., 73.
7. Ibid., 88.
8. Ibid., 125.
9. Ibid., 46.
10. Ibid., 62.
11. Ibid., 39.
12. Ibid., 30.
13. Ibid., 94.
14. Ibid., 66, xxviii; see also 24, 33, 92.
15. Ibid., 85.
16. Ibid., 30.
17. Ibid., 18.
18. Ibid., 17; see also 89.
19. Ibid., 89; see chapter 7, "Working with Others."
20. Ibid., 22; see also 20.
21. Ibid., 92.
22. Ibid., 24.
23. Ibid., 34; see also 23–25.
24. Ibid., 21.
25. Ibid.
26. Ibid.
27. Ibid., 108.
28. Ibid., 85.
29. Ibid., 58–59.
30. Ibid., 32–35, 41.
31. Ibid., 37–48.
32. Counselor's conversation with author, Rocky Hill, New Jersey, August 1994.
33. The Big Book, 127.
34. Ibid., 103.
35. Ibid., 133.
36. Ibid., 53.
37. Ibid., 60.
38. Ibid., 62, 67–68.
39. For a criticism, see David Rieff, "Victims All?: Recovery, Co-dependency, and the Art of Blaming Somebody Else," *Harper's Magazine* (Oct. 1991): 49–56.
40. The Big Book, 62.
41. Ibid., 62–64.

42. Ibid., 58. Today there is more focus on "dual diagnosis"—those who suffer from alcoholism and a mental/emotional problem—as well as concern that many people are multiply addicted.
43. Ibid., xxvii.
44. Ibid., 25.
45. Ibid., 72–75.
46. Ibid., 76–77.
47. Ibid., 44–48.
48. Ibid., 46, 49, 55, 131–32, 87; see also 50, 74. This is similar to Shoemaker's understandings.
49. Ibid., 46.
50. Ibid., 62–68, 71.
51. For speculation on its individualism and potential as a social movement, see Robin Room, "Alcoholics as a Social Movement," in *Research on Alcoholics Anonymous: Opportunities and Alternatives,* ed. Barbara S. McCrady and William R. Miller (New Brunswick, N.J.: Rutgers Center of Alcohol Studies, 1993), 167–87.
52. The Big Book, chap. 8, "To Wives," 104–21.
53. Ibid., 50.
54. Ibid., 84–85.
55. Ibid., 63.
56. Ibid., 132–33.
57. Ibid., 153.
58. Ibid., 63.
59. Ibid., 85.
60. Ibid., 60.
61. Ibid., 116: "We wives found that, like everybody else, we were afflicted with pride, self-pity, vanity and all the things which go to make up the self-centered person; and we were not above selfishness or dishonesty."
62. For instance, Walter Clark says they have "a more humble state of mind"; Walter Houston Clark, *The Oxford Group: Its History and Significance* (New York: Bookman Associates, 1951). Kurtz says AA "steadfastly and consistently rejected absolutes" (Ernest Kurtz, *Not God: A History of Alcoholics Anonymous* [Center City, Minn.: Hazelden Foundation, 1979], 50).
63. Dennis Morreim, "A Theological/Biblical Perspective of the Twelve Steps of Alcoholics Anonymous for Implementation in Ministry," D.Min. diss., Luther Northwestern Theological Seminary, St. Paul, Minnesota, 1984, 285. Ernest Kurtz has disagreed with me on this, insisting that, after a few years in AA, persons do return to church. As I indicate, my experience does not confirm this on any widespread basis. Ernest Kurtz, conversation with author, June 6, 1995.

Chapter 7: The Expansion of the Addiction–Recovery Model

1. Ernest Kurtz stresses that the "'physical illness' aspect was borrowed from the times." Personal correspondence from Ernest Kurtz to author, January 9, 1995. See also his *Not God: A History of Alcoholics Anonymous* (Center City, Minn.: Hazelden Foundation, 1979), 158.
2. Mark Keller, "The Disease Concept of Alcoholism Revisited," *Journal of Studies on Alcohol* 37:11 (1976): 1711.

NOTES TO PAGES 98–101

3. See David Berenson, "Powerlessness—Liberating or Enslaving? Responding to the Feminist Critique of the Twelve Steps," in *Feminism and Addiction,* ed. Claudia Bepko (New York: Haworth Press, 1991), 80.

4. Mark Keller goes back to early civilizations to ground the disease theory of alcoholism; see his "A Historical Overview of Alcohol and Alcoholism," *Cancer Research* 39 (July 1979): 2822–29, and "The Disease Concept of Alcoholism Revisited." A less partisan presentation is given by Albert Wilkerson, "A History of the Concept of Alcoholism as a Disease," Ph.D. diss., University of Pennsylvania, Philadelphia, Pennsylvania, 1966. He sees the first clear declaration to have come from Benjamin Rush. Harry Gene Levine explains that the disease concept is no more than two hundred years old. See "The Discovery of Addiction:Changing Conceptions of Habitual Drunkenness in America," *Journal of Studies on Alcohol* 39:1 (1978): 143–74.

5. See Michel Foucault, *The Birth of the Clinic: An Archeology of Medical Perception* (New York: Vintage Books, 1975), and *Madness and Civilization: A History of Insanity in the Age of Reason* (New York: Vintage Books, 1975).

6. Levine's article, "The Discovery of Addiction," is helpful. See also Joseph R. Gusfield, *Symbolic Crusade: Status Politics and the American Temperance Movement,* (Urbana, Ill.: University of Illinois, 1963). Wilkerson's dissertation too, deals with this subject.

7. Wilkerson, "Alcoholism as a Disease," 3; Robin Room, "Sociological Aspects of the Disease Concept of Alcoholism," *Research Advances in Alcohol and Drug Problems* 7 (1983): 74. Room also quotes a *New York Times* article that points to the "growing recognition that alcoholism is a medical and not a moral problem," 47.

8. Levine, "The Discovery of Addiction."

9. E. M. Jellinek, "Phases in the Drinking History of Alcoholics: Analysis of a Survey Conducted by the Official Organ of Alcoholics Anonymous," *Quarterly Journal of Studies on Alcohol* 7:1 (1946): 1–88; "Phases of Alcohol Addiction," *Quarterly Journal of Studies on Alcohol* 13:4 (1952): 673–84; and *The Disease Concept of Alcoholism* (New Haven, Conn.: College and University Press, 1960).

10. Herbert Fingarette, a professor and consultant on alcoholism and addiction to the World Health Organization, explains: "In sum, Jellinek's highly influential articles were based on questionnaires completed by 98 male members of A.A. Of the 158 questionnaires returned, Jellinek had eliminated 60. . . . Jellinek also excluded all questionnaires filled out by women because their answers differed greatly from the men's. No wonder Jellinek spoke of the limitations of the data," (*Heavy Drinking: The Myth of Alcoholism as a Disease* [Berkeley, Calif.: University of California Press, 1988], 21). See also Robin Room, "Sociological Aspects of the Disease Concept of Alcoholism," especially 56–57.

11. Clive Graymore, *Alcoholism: Insight into the Addictive Mind* (London: David & Charles, 1987). See also "Reports of Officers, Hospitalization of Patients with Alcoholism," *Journal of the American Medical Association* 162 (1956): 750.

12. Ernest Kurtz, "Spirituality and the Secular Quest: Twelve-Step Programs," in *Spiritual and the Secular Quest.* World Spirituality Encyclopedic History of the Religious Quest, vol. 22, ed. Peter Van Ness (New York: Crossroad, 1996).

13. Robin Room, "Drinking and Disease," *Quarterly Journal of Studies on Alcohol* 33:4 (1972): 1049.

14. William R. Miller, "Alcoholism: Toward a Better Disease Model," *Psychology of Addictive Behaviors* 7:2 (1993): 129; and Mark Keller, "The Disease Concept of Alcoholism Revisited," 1695–96.

15. J. R. Milam and Katherine Ketcham, *Under the Influence: A Guide to the Myths and Realities of Alcoholism* (New York: Bantam Books, 1983). Summations, some with refutations, are in William R. Miller, "Alcoholism: Toward a Better Disease Model," 129–36; William R. Miller and Ernest Kurtz, "Models of Alcoholism Used in Treatment: Contrasting AA and Other Perspectives with Which It Is Often Confused," *Journal of Studies on Alcohol* 55 (March 1994): 159–66; Robin Room, "Sociological Aspects," 47–49.

16. Robin Room is significant here; see his "Sociological Aspects," 49, 52; and "Drinking and Disease," 1050. See also Herbert Fingarette, *Heavy Drinking*; Stanton Peele, *The Meaning of Addiction: Compulsive Experience and Its Interpretation* (Lexington, Mass.: Lexington Books, 1985), and *The Diseasing of America: Addiction Treatment Out of Control* (Lexington, Mass.: Lexington Books, 1989). A refiner is William R. Miller, "Alcoholism: Toward a Better Disease Model," 129–36. Although defending the concept, Mark Keller refers to the challenges in "The Disease Concept of Alcoholism Revisited," passim. See also David E. Smith, Harvey B. Milkman, and Stanley G. Sunderwirth, "Addictive Disease: Concept and Controversy," in *The Addictions: Multidisciplinary Perspectives and Treatments,* ed. Harvey Milkman and Howard Shaffer (Lexington, Mass.: Lexington Books, 1985), 145–59; and John Wallace, "The New Disease Model of Alcoholism," *Western Journal of Medicine* 152:5 (May 1990): 502–5.

17. See Dennis M. Donovan, "Assessment of Addictive Behaviors: Implications of an Emerging Biopsychosocial Model," in *Assessment of Addictive Behaviors,* ed. Dennis Donovan and Alan Marlatt (New York: Guilford Press, 1988), 3–48.

18. Room, "Sociological Aspects," 50.

19. Room, "Drinking and Disease," 1056.

20. Room, "Sociological Aspects," 51.

21. William R. Miller, "Alcoholism: Toward a Better Disease Model," 131. See also Robin Room, "Sociological Aspects."

22. Susan Sontag, *Illness as Metaphor* (New York: Vintage Books, 1979), 55.

23. William R. Miller and Ernest Kurtz, "Models of Alcoholism Used in Treatment," 159–66.

24. Troy Duster, *Backdoor to Eugenics* (New York: Routledge & Kegan Paul, 1990), vii, as quoted in Ted Peters, *Sin: Radical Evil in Soul and Society* (Grand Rapids: Wm. B. Eerdmans Publishing Co., 1994), 310.

25. For a contrasting use of genetic results, compare social liberal Steve Jones, *The Language of the Genes: Solving the Mysteries of Our Genetic Past, Present, and Future* (New York: Doubleday, 1994), with the pessimistic work on racial intelligence by Richard Herrnstein and Charles Murray, *The Bell Curve: Intelligence and Class Structure in American Life* (New York: Free Press, 1994).

26. Room contends that it may have; see Robin Room, " 'Healing Ourselves and Our Planet': The Emergence and Nature of a Generalized Twelve-Step Consciousness," *Contemporary Drug Problems* (Winter 1992): 737. But Wuth-

now believes these groups are part of a small-group phenomenon that will only increase in importance and influence. See Robert Wuthnow, *Sharing the Journey: Support Groups and America's New Quest for Community* (New York: Free Press, 1994).

27. Philip Rieff, *The Triumph of the Therapeutic: Uses of Faith After Freud* (New York: Harper & Row, 1966).

28. An excellent article dealing with gender issues in the development and progression of Al-Anon and related groups is Janice Haaken's, "From Al-Anon to ACOA: Codependence and the Reconstruction of Caregiving," *Signs* 18:2 (Winter 1993): 321–45.

29. One analysis is Janice Haaken, "Beyond Addiction: Recovery Groups and 'Women Who Love Too Much,'" *Free Associations* 3(1):25 (1992): 85–109.

30. On a given Thursday in 1994, for example, the *Columbus Dispatch* would publish a full-page listing of the times and meeting places of local mutual-help groups. A significant percentage would be "anonymous" groups or in some way use the Twelve Step method.

31. Class discussions with students and informal conversations with members, 1991–1994.

32. Robin Room, " 'Healing Ourselves and Our Planet,' " 717–40. See also Bette S. Tallen, "Twelve Step Programs: A Lesbian Feminist Critique," *NWSA Journal* 2:3 (Summer 1990): 402–3. The AA situation is noted in Andrew Delbanco and Thomas Delbanco, "A.A. at the Crossroads," *The New Yorker* (Mar. 20, 1995), 50–63. See also Mark Gauvreau Judge, "Recovery's Next Step," *Common Boundary* (Jan./Feb. 1994): 16–24.

33. Lily Collett, from a *Mother Jones* (July/Aug. 1988) article reprinted in *The Utne Reader* (Nov./Dec. 1988): 69–76. Robin Room offers evidence that this may be a movement of the "drugged generation," losing old habits but still using the ethos of the 1960s and 1970s: " 'Healing Ourselves and Our Planet,' " 724.

34. Ernest Kurtz, "Why A.A. Works: The Intellectual Significance of Alcoholics Anonymous," *Journal of Studies on Alcohol* 43:1 (1982): 38–80.

35. This can range from seeing "addiction as a type or category of sin"—Denise McLain Massey, "Addiction and Spirituality," *Review and Expositor* 91 (1994): 9–18—to saying that "all of us suffer from addiction"—Gerald May, *Addiction and Grace: Love and Spirituality in the Healing of Addictions* (San Francisco: HarperSanFrancisco, 1988), 3–4. May, although not writing in an explicitly church context, is read by many church persons and directs an institute of spirituality, Shalem, in Washington, D.C.

36. Directed to Presbyterian seminarians, for instance, is David Prince, "A Church and the Twelve-Step Movement," *Testament* (Princeton Theological Seminary, 1994): 30–32; to Baptists, Thomas H. Cairns, "Addiction and the Role of the Church," *Review and Expositor* 91 (1994): 43–51. Matthew Fox has addressed the Roman Catholic Church in "Is the Catholic Church Today a Dysfunctional Family?" *Creation* (Nov./Dec. 1988): 23–37; and all of volume 8 of *Studies in Formative Spirituality* was devoted to "Spiritual Formation and Problems of Addiction" (May 1987). A standard liberal publication read by many ran Anne Wilson Schaef's "Is the Church an Addictive Organization?" *The Christian Century* (Jan. 3–10, 1990): 18–21. Directed to more conservative audiences was William O'Brien, "The Disciple and the Leper," *The Other Side* (Jan./Feb. 1993): 16–21; and Tim Stafford, "The

Hidden Gospel of the Twelve Steps," *Christianity Today* 35:8 (Jul. 22, 1991): 14–21. This is only a small sample of a large body of articles.

37. An example of a hard-line dispositional disease approach directed to the church is an article by Stephen Apthorp, which claims that congregations consist "mostly of people who have been or are drastically harmed by alcoholism or drug abuse" and most preachers "will have come from a dysfunctional family. . . . usually through compulsive substance abuse" (Stephen Apthorp, "Drug Abuse and the Church: Are the Blind Leading the Blind?" *The Christian Century* [Nov. 9, 1988]).

38. See Thomas H. Cairns, "Addiction and the Role of the Church." This is representative of scores of articles appearing in the late 1980s and 1990s. Howard Clinebell, one of the first in this area, wrote on the topic in the 1960s, *Understanding and Counseling the Alcoholic* (Nashville: Abingdon Press, 1968).

39. See John A. Martin, *Blessed Are the Addicts: The Spiritual Side of Alcoholism, Addiction, and Recovery* (New York: Villard Books, 1990), and Michele S. Matto, *The Twelve Steps in the Bible: A Path to Wholeness for Adult Children* (Mahwah, N.J.: Paulist Press, 1991).

40. Epworth United Methodist Church in Columbus, Ohio, for example, was conceived around a recovery model. The United Methodist Church of Kingston, New Jersey, has experienced growth through explicit attention to recovery themes. The pastor of Liberty Presbyterian Church in Delaware, Ohio, runs a weekly adaptation, "Sinners Anonymous." He commissioned Twelve Step banners, which were then hung all around the sanctuary. Robin Room says that "sometimes a generalized 12-step consciousness takes over the host organization itself." He tells of a Baptist church in San Francisco that "reorganized itself as a community center" because hundreds more attended evening twelve-step meetings than Sunday worship. The pastor became the center's executive director. Robin Room, " 'Healing Ourselves and Our Planet,' " 717–40.

41. John F. Woolverton, "Evangelical Protestantism and Alcoholism 1933–1962: Episcopalian Samuel Shoemaker, the Oxford Group, and Alcoholics Anonymous," *Historical Magazine of the Protestant Episcopal Church* 52 (March 1983): 64–65.

42. Therefore I don't agree when Kurtz states, with a positive note, that the Oxford Group "embraced no specific theological positions." Ernest Kurtz, *Not God*, 48.

43. John Peterson contends it was just that; see "The International Origins of Alcoholics Anonymous," *Contemporary Drug Problems* 19:1 (Spring 1992): 53–74.

44. Peterson says that "the basic methodology of the 'old' Oxford Group movement, as continued and developed by A.A., is not derived solely from the cultural patterns of middle-class American Protestants, but may be adapted to different cultural patterns as movements spread across cultural and linguistic boundaries" ("International Origins," 71). See also Klaus Makela, "Implications for Research of the Cultural Variability of Alcoholics Anonymous," in *Research on Alcoholics Anonymous: Opportunities and Alternatives,* ed. Barbara S. McCrady and William Miller (New Brunswick, N.J.: Rutgers Center of Alcohol Studies, 1993).

45. See Rachel V., "The Formless Form: Buddhism and the Twelve-Step Pro-

grams," *Tricycle: The Buddhist Review* (September 1992): 33–36. However, she is a former Roman Catholic.

Chapter 8: The Nature of the Problem

1. *Alcoholics Anonymous Comes of Age* (New York: Alcoholics Anonymous Publishing, 1957), 67–68.
2. This turned up as a dissertation topic in the 1980s. For example, William R. Lenters, says, "The addiction experience is the human experience. . . . We all pass through the crucible of addiction" (See "A Strategy for Liberation from Addiction as a Human Condition," D.Min. diss., Fuller Theological Seminary, Pasadena, California, 1983, 4). Gerald May, M.D., says that "to be alive is to be addicted" (*Addiction and Grace: Love and Spirituality in the Healing of Addictions* [San Francisco: HarperSanFrancisco, 1988]).
3. See Edward Farley "Sin/Sins," in *Dictionary of Pastoral Care and Counseling*, ed. Rodney J. Hunter (Nashville: Abingdon Press, 1990), 1174.
4. An intriguing reference in popular fiction regarding this was brought to my attention by my editor, Timothy Staveteig. Lawyer and cop Mack Malloy reflects on his previous AA experience: "Somehow over the long haul I found AA sadder than being a drunk, listening to these folks, 'My name is Sheila and I'm an alcoholic.' . . . It was a little too much of a cult for me, the Church of Self-denunciation, I used to call it [but] I welcomed the support and got all warm and runny about a number of the people who showed up each week and held my hand" (Scott Turow, *Pleading Guilty* [New York: Warner Books, 1993], 162).
5. Reinhold Niebuhr, *The Nature and Destiny of Man*, vol. 1 (New York: Charles Scribner's Sons, 1964) especially chapter 9.
6. Edward Farley, *Good and Evil: Interpreting a Human Condition* (Minneapolis: Fortress Press, 1990), 124–26. See also Paul Ricoeur, *The Symbolism of Evil* (New York: Harper & Row, 1967), part 2.
7. There was some debate whether Niebuhr had unconsciously adapted it from a prayer of Theodor Wilhelm (Oetinger). Niebuhr published the following version in 1951: "God, give us the serenity to accept what cannot be changed; Give us the courage to change what should be changed; Give us the wisdom to distinquish one from the other." Niebuhr was dismayed at its subsequent commercialization. See Richard Wightman Fox, *Reinhold Niebuhr: A Biography* (New York: Pantheon Books, 1985), 290–91.
8. Reinhold Niebuhr, *Nature and Destiny of Man*, vol. 1, 250.
9. Compare the best-selling and genetically deterministic work of Richard Herrnstein and Charles Murray, *The Bell Curve: Intelligence and Class Structure in American Life* (New York: Free Press, 1994), with that of geneticist Steve Jones, *The Language of the Genes: Solving the Mysteries of Our Genetic Past, Present, and Future* (New York: Doubleday, 1994), who sees genetics as only one factor among many. Jones notes, however, the unfortunate popularity of deterministic arguments and the way they can be used to justify the social oppression of minorities, saying that "confusion arises when inheritance and genetics are assumed to be the same" (Steve Jones, "Our Favorite Genes," *Newsweek* [Jan. 2, 1995]: 111). Another writer cites the funding concerns of scientists, leading to "overblown rhetoric and misleading metaphors to convey the importance of their work. . . . The media have appropriated genetic

images in ways that serve their goals. . . . The power of genetic images for the public derives less from people's interest in science than its relationship to social concerns." She speaks of the pervasive language of biological determinism, such that "The gene in popular culture is an anthropomorphized entity—given a wide range of behavioral attributes." In the end, scientists need to exercise more responsibility. "Much of the popular rhetoric about genes draws support from the promises generated by scientists and the language they use to describe their research. In the interest of public understanding, then, scientists should restrain their tendencies to oversell their work and consider the biases and beliefs that will ultimately shape the uses of a powerful science—one that offers prospects for promising applications, but that also opens the possibilities for pernicious abuse" (Dorothy Nelkin, "The Grandiose Claims of Geneticists," *Chronicle of Higher Education* [March 3, 1993]: B1–2).

10. Francesca Alexander and Michele Rollins, "Alcoholics Anonymous: The Unseen Cult," *California Sociologist* (Winter 1984): 33–49.

11. I noted this, for instance, among the Shakers. See Linda Mercadante, *Gender, Doctrine, and God: The Shakers and Contemporary Theology* (Nashville: Abingdon Press, 1990).

12. For a good concise description, see Farley's introduction to *Good and Evil*.

13. Interview, summer 1993.

14. For a review of this theory, among others, see Dennis M. Donovan, "Assessment of Addictive Behaviors: Implications of an Emerging Biopsychosocial Model," in *Assessment of Addictive Behaviors,* ed. Dennis Donovan and Alan Marlatt (New York: Guilford Press, 1988), 3–48.

15. Wilson once wrote that alcoholics were "trying to grope their way toward God in alcohol" (Letter, 1960, quoted in *As Bill Sees It* [New York: AA World Services, 1991], 323).

16. The Calix Society, for example (7601 Wayzata Boulevard, Minneapolis, MN 55426), is an officially approved Roman Catholic group that aids AA members to further their spirituality in the Catholic tradition. Treatment centers specifically for priests also exist. The founders of Alcoholics Anonymous feared Roman Catholic rejection of their program because of its Protestant roots, yet it has proved acceptable to many Roman Catholics.

17. James F. Keenan,"The Problem with Thomas Aquinas's Concept of Sin," *Heythrop Journal* 35 (1994): 412–14. The Protestant Reformers rejected the older but related idea that mortal sins (like formal sin) are those with consent and reflection. They understood sin to be opposed to faith, not virtue. Sin here is not wrongful action—the opposite of virtue—but lack of trust and belief in God. There is a danger, then, in appropriating the addiction thematic as an analogy to sin. Contrary to the Reformers' corrective, sin may tend again to be placed opposite virtue rather than opposite faith. The stress on abstinence and other behavioral objectives pushes the movement in this direction, in spite of the early step of acknowledging God. For a brief discussion, see *The Westminster Dictionary of Christian Ethics* (Louisville, Ky.: Westminster/John Knox Press, 1986), 585.

18. On Pelagianism, see Reinhold Niebuhr, *Nature and Destiny of Man*, vol. 1, 245ff.

19. Wilfred Sheed wryly noted something similar, saying, "At the first several AA meetings they marched us into at Happy Valley I'd noted that the speaker

seemed invariably to have divorced his wife early on in recovery, almost as if it were part of the program" (Wilfred Sheed, *In Love with Daylight: A Memoir of Recovery* [New York: Simon & Schuster, 1995], 156).

Chapter 9: Who Is Responsible?

1. Paul Ricoeur also explains this givenness or "mysterious aspect" of evil being "already there"; see *The Conflict of Interpretation: Essays in Hermeneutics* (Evanston, Ill.: Northwestern University Press, 1974), 284. See also *The Symbolism of Evil* (New York: Harper & Row, 1967).
2. An example is the theory of "kindling," presented in an accessible way in Peter D. Kramer, *Listening to Prozac* (New York: Penguin Books, 1993).
3. See Stanley Rosenman, "Pacts, Possessions, and the Alcoholic," *American Image* 12:3 (Fall 1955): 241–74.
4. See Ted Honderich, *How Free Are You? The Determinism Problem* (New York: Oxford University Press, 1993), 241–74.
5. Reinhold Niebuhr, *The Nature and Destiny of Man,* vol. 1 (New York: Charles Scribner's Sons, 1964), 251–64.
6. For a psychoanalytic interpretation of this see Rosenman, "Pacts, Possessions, and the Alcoholic."
7. Robin Room, "Sociological Aspects of the Disease Concept of Alcoholism," *Research Advances in Alcohol and Drug Problems* 7 (1983): 65–66.
8. The Big Book, 129.
9. Donald Capps gives some reasons for modern narcissism in *The Depleted Self: Sin in a Narcissistic Age* (Minneapolis: Fortress Press, 1993).
10. The Big Book, 122, 127.
11. Some popular books include Sharon Wegscheider-Cruse, *Choicemaking: For Co-Dependents, Adult Children, and Spirituality Seekers* (Pompano Beach, Fla.: Health Communications, 1985); Anne Wilson Shaef, *Co-Dependence: Misunderstood and Mistreated* (San Francisco: Harper & Row, 1986); and Melody Beattie, *Codependent No More* (New York: Harper & Row, 1987).
12. On the battle over "self-defeating personality disorder" as a mental illness, see John Lea, "Battling Over Masochism," *Time* (Dec. 2, 1985): 76; also Deborah Franklin, "The Politics of Masochism," *Psychology Today* (January 1987): 52–57.
13. Critiques include Sandra C. Anderson, "A Critical Analysis of the Concept of Codependency," *Social Work* 39:6 (November 1994): 677–85; Frank P. Troise, "An Examination of Cermak's Conceptualization of Codependency as Personality Disorder," *Alcoholism Treatment Quarterly* 12:1 (1995): 1–16; Janice Haaken, "From Al-Anon to ACOA: Codependence and the Reconstruction of Caregiving," *Signs* 18:2 (Winter 1993): 321–45; Jo-Ann Krestan and Claudia Bepko, "Co-dependency: The Social Reconstruction of Female Experience," in *Feminism and Addiction,* ed. Claudia Bepko (New York: Haworth Press, 1991); Katherine van Wormer, "Codependency: Implications for Women and Therapy," *Women and Therapy* 8:4 (1989): 51–63; Wendy Kaminer, "Chances Are You're Co-dependent Too," *New York Times Book Review* (Feb. 11, 1990); Bette S. Tallen, "Co-dependency: A Feminist Critique," *Sojourner: The Women's Forum* (January 1990): 20–21; and Christine Flynn Saulnier, "Twelve Steps for Everyone? Lesbians in Al-Anon," in *Understanding the Self-Help Organization: Frameworks and*

Findings, ed. Thomas J. Powell (Thousands Oaks, Calif.: Sage Publications Inc., 1994), 247–71.

14. The Big Book, 7. Wilson learned from a doctor that "in alcoholics the will is amazingly weakened when it comes to combating liquor, though it often remains strong in other respects."

15. Comments, Big Book meeting, October 21, 1994, Princeton, New Jersey.

16. Student, class, winter quarter, 1994.

17. Piet Schoonenberg, *Man and Sin: A Theological View* (Notre Dame, Ind.: University of Notre Dame Press, 1965), 83–84.

18. Edward Farley, *Good and Evil: Interpreting a Human Condition* (Minneapolis: Fortress Press, 1990), 136ff. Farley also says, "It should be clear that in Paul, Augustine, Martin Luther, and John Calvin, the freedom that sin removes and salvation restores is not the formal capacity of free choice."

Chapter 10: The Humbling of Pride

1. Ernest Kurtz, *Not God: A History of Alcoholics Anonymous* (Center City, Minn.: Hazelden Foundation, 1979), 70–71, 236–40.

2. See Marjorie Hewitt Suchocki, who has a succinct summary and contemporary treatment of this theme in *The Fall to Violence: Original Sin in Relational Theology* (New York: Continuum, 1994), especially chapter 5.

3. Niebuhr traces this theme, starting with the apostle Paul. Reinhold Niebuhr, *The Nature and Destiny of Man,* vol. 1 (New York: Charles Scribner's Sons, 1964), 186–87, n.1.

4. The Big Book, 60.

5. Al-Anon, *The Dilemma of the Alcoholic Marriage* (New York: Al-Anon Family Headquarters, 1971), 3. Haaken has noted how this precept began to be used to resist masculine domination only after the influence of feminism became felt in America (Janice Haaken, "From Al-Anon to ACOA: Codependence and the Reconstruction of Caregiving," *Signs* 18:2 [Winter 1983]).

6. An intervention is a planned and staged surprise confrontation of a presumed addict by a group of significant people (spouse, employer, therapist, family members, friends) in his or her life. It is meant to influence the person to enter treatment; sometimes the planners have a car waiting outside to transport the person to a preselected center. On intervention see Vernon Johnson, *I'll Quit Tomorrow* (New York: Harper & Row, 1980). On coercion, see Archie Brodsky and Stanton Peele, "AA Abuse," *Reason* (1991): 34–39.

7. Groups such as Secular Organizations for Sobriety, Rational Recovery, Women for Sobriety, and American Atheists Addiction Recovery Groups make this point. See David Wilson, "Secular Organizations for Sobriety, Recovery Without Religion," M.A. thesis, Sonoma State University, Rohnert Park, California, 1991; and David Gelman, "Clean and Sober—and Agnostic," *Newsweek* (July 8, 1991): 62–63. See also Albert Ellis, "Why Alcoholics Anonymous Is Probably Doing Itself and Alcoholics More Harm than Good by Its Insistence on a Higher Power," *Employee Assistance Quarterly* 1:1 (Fall 1985): 95–96; and Archie Brodsky and Stanton Peele, "AA Abuse."

8. See Gail Unterberger, "Twelve Steps for Women Alcoholics," *The Christian Century* 106:37 (Dec. 6, 1989): 1150–52; Charlotte Davis Kasl, *Women, Sex, and Addiction: A Search for Love and Power* (New York: HarperCollins, 1992), and "The Twelve-Step Controversy," *Ms.* Magazine (Nov./Dec.

1990): 30–31; Bonita L. Swan, *Thirteen Steps: An Empowerment Process for Women* (San Francisco: Spinsters/Aunt Luke Book Co., 1989); see for example, Jean Kirkpatrick's *Turnabout: Help for a New Life* (Dubuque, Iowa: Kendall Hunt, 1978), passim.

9. Cecil Williams, "No Hiding Place," *The Other Side* (Jan./Feb. 1993): 24. The most scathing critique from a gender perspective is Wendy Kaminer's *I'm Dysfunctional, You're Dysfunctional: The Recovery Movement and Other Self-Help Fashions* (New York: Vintage Press, 1993). See also Bette S. Tallen, "Twelve-Step Programs: A Lesbian Feminist Critique," *NWSA Journal* 2:3 (Summer 1990): 402. See also Wendy Simonds, *Women and Self-Help Culture: Reading Between the Lines* (New Brunswick, N.J.: Rutgers University Press, 1992), and bell hooks, *Sisters of the Yam: Black Women and Self-Recovery* (Boston: South End Press, 1993).

10. David Berenson, "Powerlessness—Liberating or Enslaving? Responding to the Feminist Critique of the Twelve Steps," in *Feminism and Addiction,* ed. Claudia Bepko (New York: Haworth Press, 1991): 80; see also Virginia Perrot, "Many Women Struggle with the Issue of Powerlessness," *Hazelden News and Professional Update* (September 1991): 6–7.

11. See Søren Kierkegaard, *The Sickness Unto Death,* ed. and trans., Howard V. and Edna H. Hong (Princeton, N.J.: Princeton University Press, 1980); and Reinhold Niebuhr, *Nature and Destiny of Man.* Here, however—unfortunately—the sin of inordinate self-loss is subsumed under what is considered the more consequential sin: inordinate self-will or defiance. On "sloth" see Karl Barth, *Church Dogmatics* (Edinburgh: T. & T. Clark, 1956), IV/2, 403–83.

12. This is a now-classic passage by Valerie Saiving, "The Human Situation: A Feminine View," in *Womanspirit Rising: A Feminist Reader in Religion,* ed. Carol P. Christ and Judith Plaskow (New York: Harper & Row, 1979), 37, 39. See also Judith Plaskow, *Sex, Sin, and Grace: Women's Experience and the Theologies of Reinhold Niebuhr and Paul Tillich* (Lanham, Md.: University Press of America, 1980); Susan Nelson Dunfee, "The Sin of Hiding: A Feminist Critique of Reinhold Niebuhr's Account of the Sin of Pride," *Soundings* 65:1 (Spring 1982): 316–27; Daphne Hampson, "Reinhold Niebuhr on Sin: A Critique," in *Reinhold Niebuhr and the Issues of Our Time,* ed. Richard Harries (Grand Rapids: Wm. B. Eerdmans Publishing Co., 1986), 46–60; Susan L. Lichtman, "The Concept of Sin in the Theology of Paul Tillich: A Break from Patriarchy?" *Journal of Women and Religion* 8 (Winter 1989): 49–55.

13. Kierkegaard notes, "No despair is entirely free of defiance; indeed, the very phrase 'not to will to be' implies defiance. On the other hand, even despair's most extreme defiance is never really free of some weakness" (Søren Kierkegaard, *Sickness Unto Death,* 49).

14. It is interesting that the church-based recovery group Sinners Anonymous defines the problem disease as "control." A member says that through this group "I have discovered that a number of my unhealthy traits are the result of an underlying problem of codependence stemming from equally unhealthy behavior patterns developed in my childhood, and that codependence is in turn a form of the Sin disease inherited from my parents' lives" (Ray Thornton, "Sinners Anonymous," *Faith at Work* [Sept./Oct. 1988]: 10–11).

15. Wilfred Sheed, *In Love with Daylight: A Memoir of Recovery* (New York: Simon & Schuster, 1995), 115, 117–18.
16. Jurgen Moltmann, *The Theology of Hope: On the Ground and Implications of a Christian Eschatology*, trans. James W. Leitch (London: SCM Press, 1967), 22.
17. Andrew Sung Park brings a Korean minjung theological perspective. Although he does not deal with addiction recovery, his critique confirms the argument for the societally disempowered. Andrew Sung Park, *The Wounded Heart of God: The Asian Concept of Han and the Christian Doctrine of Sin* (Nashville: Abingdon Press, 1993), 10. See also Mary Louise Bringle, *Despair: Sin or Sickness* (Nashville: Abingdon Press, 1990).
18. Park, *The Wounded Heart of God*, 12 (*author's italics*). The second quote continues (pp. 17–18): "Han is a negative letting go which is desolate, barren, bitter, and meaningless. In a sense, han is not a true letting go, since it is forced upon self and impinged upon it by oppression, which destroys the self's organizing center."
19. That Kierkegaard predicted the modern prevalence of the problem of self-loss was called to my attention by William Cahoy of St. John's University, Collegeville, Minnesota. See Kierkegaard on "the crowd," especially in *Two Ages, Kierkegaard's Writings*, vol. 14, trans. Howard V. and Edna H. Hong (Princeton, N.J.: Princeton University Press, 1978), 62–68, 78–96, and in *The Point of View for My Work as an Author*, trans. Walter Lowrie (New York: Harper & Row, 1962), 107–20. Recent attention has been drawn by Heinz Kohut, *The Analysis of the Self: A Systematic Approach to the Psychoanalytic Treatment of Narcissistic Personality Disorders* (New York: International Universities Press, 1971), and by Christopher Lasch, *The Culture of Narcissism: American Life in an Age of Diminishing Expectations* (New York: Warner Books, 1979). Donald Capps makes the theological connection in *The Depleted Self: Sin in a Narcissistic Age* (Minneapolis: Fortress Press, 1993).
20. Park, *The Wounded Heart of God*, 73.
21. Park, *The Wounded Heart of God*, says (pp. 76–77) that "while women's basic problem is han, they nonetheless can commit sin. . . . They often do so by perpetuating patriarchal structures and practices at the expense of other women, spinning the wheel of sin and han yet more."
22. Bill Wilson said, when splitting with the Oxford Group, "Naturally enough, they did not think too highly of our objective, limited as it was to alcoholics. From our point of view, we felt very sure we couldn't do much about helping the Oxford Group to save the whole world. But we were becoming more certain every day that we might be able to sober up many alcoholics" (*Alcoholics Anonymous Comes of Age* [New York: Harper & Brothers, 1957], 74).
23. It's unclear who first came up with the 96 percent figure or from where it was derived. Many use it. Sharon Wegscheider-Cruse, for example, claims that 96 percent of the entire population is codependent; see *Co-Dependency: An Emerging Issue* (Pompano Beach, Fla.: Health Communications, 1984). (I often wonder who and where the other 4 percent are and how they were discovered.) Anne Wilson Schaef says that everyone who has any contact with an alcoholic is a practicing codependent; *Women's Reality* (San Francisco: Harper & Row, 1985), 29. These are not scholarly works, but they have been very influential on cultural perceptions.
24. Some of the most widely read popular books on this topic include Melody

Beattie, *Codependent No More* (New York: Harper & Row, 1987); Robin Norwood, *Women Who Love Too Much* (New York: Simon & Schuster, 1986); Sharon Wegscheider-Cruse, *Co-Dependency;* and Anne Wilson Schaef, *Co-Dependence: Misunderstood and Mistreated* (New York: Harper & Row, 1986).

25. Two excellent articles by Janice Haaken that trace and analyze the growth of the movement in relation to gender issues are "Beyond Addiction: Recovery Groups and 'Women Who Love Too Much,' " *Free Associations* 3(1):25 (1992): 85–109, and "From Al-Anon to ACOA: Codependence and the Reconstruction of Caregiving," *Signs* 18:2 (Winter 1993): 321–45.

26. Haaken, "Beyond Addiction," 87.

27. Kurtz suggests that the term "enabling" did not start with Al-Anon but within the treatment world, particularly from Vernon Johnson at the Johnson Insitute. Letter to author, April 1, 1995.

28. Haaken, "Beyond Addiction," 92–93.

29. The Big Book says (p. 77) that ultimately "our real purpose is to fit ourselves to be of maximum service to God and the people about us." Some have noted it has become more difficult to get members to do "service work." The Delbancos quote one member: "It's getting harder all the time just to find a volunteer for setting up the coffeepot before the meeting, or scrubbing it out after. . . The idea of helping others in order to help yourself is in trouble" (Andrew Delbanco and Thomas Delbanco, "A.A. at the Crossroads," *The New Yorker* [Mar. 20, 1995]: 63).

30. Timmen Cermak, *Diagnosing and Treating Co-dependence* (Minneapolis: Johnson Institute, 1986), 20, and "The Myth of Narcissus and Echo: Codependence as the Complement of Narcissism," paper presented at the National Consensus Symposium on Children of Alcoholics and Co-dependence, Warrenton, Virginia, 1991, 11, as cited in Janice Haaken, "From Al-Anon to ACOA," 325–26.

31. An excellent article on this difference, especially helpful because it draws out the theological implications, is Mary Potter Engel, "Evil, Sin, and Violation of the Vulnerable," in *Lift Every Voice: Constructing Christian Theologies from the Underside,* ed. Susan Brooks Thistlethwaite and Mary Potter Engel (New York: Harper & Row, 1990).

32. This is similar to the prioritizing of the two sides of sin by Kierkegaard in *The Sickness Unto Death* and Reinhold Niebuhr in *Nature and Destiny of Man.*

Chapter 11: The Role of the Higher Power, the Group, and the Results

1. Ernest Kurtz called my attention to a response from Bill Wilson to an atheist. "Since I was once a non-believer myself, and so in the early days were others, we realized that AA membership could not be conditioned upon belief or non-belief. Our experience then, and since, has been that if the open mind is maintained, then some sort of faith follows in due course—if this only be faith in the 'higher power' of the group itself. This is sufficient to maintain sobriety in practically all cases. In fact the first admission for an atheistically inclined person is to admit that neither he nor his fellowman add up to the creative power of the universe—namely, God" (Letter, Bill Wilson to Jim C., Jan. 11, 1961).

2. The Big Book, 46.
3. Ibid., 55.
4. Jeanne E., "Women and Spirituality," pamphlet (Hazelden Foundation, 1987), 1, 5.
5. The Big Book, 46.
6. Sue and Bill O., conversation, Princeton, New Jersey, February 1994.
7. Sue O., telephone conversation, February 1995.
8. Anecdotal evidence comes, for example, from the personal experience of Wilfred Sheed. In his autobiography he says, about his own struggles: "To meet at least a minimal need for physical expression (post-polio syndrome had eliminated the maximum ones), I asked the congregation at one of my AA meetings if anyone knew of a pool table around here, but I'd picked the wrong group: these guys were much too ethereal for that kind of talk. It is a widely held superstition that all AA meetings are equally valuable: AA is not a religion, and meetings are not masses, though many members regard them as such and are not noticeably discouraged from doing so (if it helps . . .). But the helplessly discriminating should be warned that, for instance, some groups understand the value of things like pool tables to a drowning man while others would say that shooting pool is just a Band-Aid for your real problems, and a regular no-pain, no-gain placebo to boot" (Wilfred Sheed, *In Love with Daylight: A Memoir of Recovery* [New York: Simon & Schuster, 1995], 193).
9. The Big Book, 17. I was struck by this at one Saturday morning AA meeting I attended in Asbury Park, New Jersey, in August 1994. To celebrate a black member's first anniversary of sobriety, a wealthy white woman who raised horses shared her story of malaise, depression, and irresponsibility. She was followed by several black men who told stories of poverty and problems with the law. There were hugs all around at the end and a tangible feeling of solidarity and joy. In my experience, however, this was an exceptional meeting. Many are more homogeneous socially and racially. This has a long history. As much as early AA wanted to help all alcoholics, there was a definite impulse to keep it "respectable," which meant de facto segregation and a focus on the middle class. Kurtz explains that early AA "would never print 'whites only' or 'blacks only' in a listing of meetings, but if the community understood such from the listed meeting place, well, that was reality—part of 'the things I cannot change'" (Ernest Kurtz, *Not God: A History of Alcoholics Anonymous* [Center City, Minn.: Hazelden Foundation, 1979], 149).
10. Wuthnow suggests some of these things. See Robert Wuthnow, *Sharing the Journey: Support Groups and America's New Quest for Community* (New York: Free Press, 1994), 12–16.
11. See Cecil Williams, "No Hiding Place," *The Other Side* (Jan./Feb. 1993): 22–24.
12. The court obviously doesn't agree regarding murder, since Paul Cox was convicted for a 1988 double murder through a confession he made in a Twelve Step meeting. But these confessions may be more frequently made, and much less frequently dealt with, than is realized. See "Confess and Be Happy: Hi, I'm Scott and I Killed My Girlfriend in 1971," *The New York Times Magazine* (Feb. 26, 1995): 24.
13. For an interesting comparison of the Methodist class meeting as a model for AA, see Oliver R. Whitley, "Life with Alcoholics Anonymous: The Methodist

Class Meeting as a Paradigm," *Journal of Studies on Alcohol* 38:5 (1977): 831–48.

14. "Somehow over the long haul I found AA sadder than being a drunk," says lawyer and ex-cop Mack Malloy in Scott Turow's novel *Pleading Guilty* (New York: Warner Books, 1993), 162.

15. Bunyan's *Pilgrim's Progress* illustrates this perspective.

16. Haaken suggests a psychological explanation of the interaction, especially as it functions in ACOA groups. She notes that, "while seeming to offer a reparative experience for many of [their previous familial] injurious relationships, many key principles and processes . . . are a re-enactment of the very pathology which the groups purportedly overcome." As in the dysfunctional home, "meaningful interaction" is prevented within the group by the ban on "crosstalk" and "an indiscriminate openness is cultivated, in which members are encouraged to express very private experiences within a group where other people often come and go as strangers. This undermines any potential for learning, through experiences with others, what makes situations or other people emotionally safe or trustworthy." Also, a " 'pseudo-mutuality' is cultivated . . . whereby group members are assumed to share a common personality disorder . . . intended to explain the life difficulties of group members" (Janice Haaken, "Beyond Addiction: Recovery Groups and 'Women Who Love Too Much,' " *Free Associations* 3[1]:25 [1992]: 102–4).

17. The Big Book, 63, 84, 153.

18. Ibid., 60.

19. Ibid., 85.

20. "Moderation Management" is a new approach. See Michael Marriott, "Half Steps vs. 12 Steps," *Newsweek* (March 27, 1995). Although it is an undercurrent, some people have always questioned the goal of complete abstinence. A National Public Radio program mentions attitudes held among professionals in England, where moderate drinking is considered a reasonable goal: "Alcohol Abuse and Treatment," five-part series, segment 13, *Morning Edition*, Frank Browning, October 4–8, 1993.

21. Ernest Kurtz offers another interpretation of "daily reprieve." He believes "the idea here is rather the classic spiritual one that some realities cannot be 'stored up' . . . no more than what you claim is 'daily bread.' . . . In my experience, the 'can't store up' is heard and spoken much more than the 'slippery slope' idea by those I deem truly sober." He agrees, however, that "we are near the edge of the theological puzzle of total assurance." Personal correspondence with author, April 1, 1995.

22. Conversation with seminar participant, Charis Institute, Concordia College, Moorhead, Minnesota, October 1994.

23. Wilfred Sheed, *In Love with Daylight*, 126.

24. Haaken, "Beyond Addiction," 100–101.

25. Ibid., 101–5.

26. Patrick McCormick has managed to balance theological integrity with knowledge of addiction, although he gives much weight to the addiction discourse. See his *Sin as Addiction* (Mahwah, N.J.: Paulist Press, 1989).

27. Karl Barth, *Church Dogmatics* (Edinburgh: T. & T. Clark, 1956), IV/1, 501. Ted Peters finds this quote helpful as well and does a succinct job of treating this topic; see *Sin: Radical Evil in Soul and Society* (Grand Rapids: Wm. B. Eerdmans Publishing Co., 1994), 320–27.

28. Blaise Pascal, *Pascal's Pensees,* trans. with introduction by A. J. Krailsheimer (Harmondsworth, England: Penguin, 1966), #938 [658], p. 323.
29. Piet Schoonenberg, *Man and Sin: A Theological View* (Notre Dame, Ind.: University of Notre Dame Press, 1965), 87.

Chapter 12: Grace and Recovery

1. Edward Farley, "Sin/Sins," *Dictionary of Pastoral Care and Counseling,* ed. Rodney J. Hunter (Nashville: Abingdon Press, 1990), 1173–76.
2. Patricia Broughten, writing for the evangelical publication *Daughters of Sarah,* relates her own experience. "It's Not a Matter of Willpower," *Daughters of Sarah* 13:2 (Mar./Apr. 1987): 16.
3. Christopher Lasch, *The Culture of Narcissism: American Life in an Age of Diminshing Expectations* (New York: Warner Books, 1979), 13.
4. This term is used in Peter D. Kramer, *Listening to Prozac* (New York: Penguin Books, 1993).
5. A useful summary of the biblical and related material can be found in Hans Conzelmann, "Charis," in *The Theological Dictionary of the New Testament,* ed. Gerhard Kittel and Gerhard Friedrich (Grand Rapids: Wm. B. Eerdmans Publishing Co., 1974). Aspects of the theological intricacies can be found in "Grace," in *Sacramentum Mundi: An Encyclopedia of Theology,* ed. Karl Rahner, (New York: Herder & Herder, 1968), 409–27. See also Brian O. McDermott, *What Are They Saying About the Grace of Christ?* (Ramsey, N.J.: Paulist Press, 1984).
6. Piet Schoonenberg, *Man and Sin: A Theological View* (Notre Dame, Ind.: University of Notre Dame Press, 1965), 68.
7. Ibid., 67.
8. H. Richard Niebuhr, "Man the Sinner," *Journal of Religion* 15 (1935): 273.
9. Ibid.
10. George S. Hendry, "Is Sin Obsolescent?" *Princeton Seminary Bulletin* 7:3 (new series 1986): 256–67.
11. For some commentary on this theme, see Donald Capps, *The Depleted Self: Sin in a Narcissistic Age* (Minneapolis: Fortress Press, 1993).
12. McDermott, *What Are They Saying About the Grace of Christ?,* 37.
13. May says, in *Addiction and Grace,* "Many of the old understandings to which I had been addicted were stripped away, leaving a desertlike spaciousness where my customary props and securities no longer existed. Grace was able to flow into this emptiness, and something new was able to grow" (Gerald May, *Addiction and Grace: Love and Spirituality in the Healing of Addictions* [San Francisco: HarperSanFrancisco, 1988], vi).
14. A popular example of this type of spirituality can be found in Hannah Hurnard's *Hindsfeet on High Places* (Old Tappan, N.J.: Fleming H. Revell, 1973), where the seeker is required periodically to place herself on the altar for sacrifice. For women and others who have been trained in the sin of "inordinate self-loss" already, this can function counterproductively.
15. McDermott, *What Are They Saying About the Grace of Christ?,* 52.

INDEX OF NAMES AND SUBJECTS